W9-CHI-733

# Houston Symposium 3

# INFORMATION TECHNOLOGY AND PSYCHOLOGY

## Prospects for the Future

**Editors:**
**Richard A. Kasschau, Roy Lachman,**
**and Kenneth R. Laughery**

**Series Editor: Richard A. Kasschau**

PRAEGER SPECIAL STUDIES • PRAEGER SCIENTIFIC

QA
76.9
P75
H68
1982

Library of Congress Cataloging in Publication Data

Houston Symposium (3rd: 1982: University of Houston)
   Information technology and psychology, a view of the future.

   Bibliography: p.
   Includes index.
   1. Electronic data processing—Psychological aspects—
Congresses. 2. Computers and civilization—Congresses. I. Kasschau,
Richard A. II. Lachman, Roy. III. Laughery, Kenneth R. IV. Title.
QA76.9.P75H68   1982        303.4'834        82-7673
ISBN 0-03-061771-5                           AACR2

Published in 1982 by Praeger Publishers
CBS Educational and Professional Publishing
a Division of CBS Inc.

© 1982 by Praeger Publishers

23456789 052 987654321
Printed in the United States of America

# Contents

# Preface

The past 30 years have witnessed enormous advances in information technologies. These advances have had a profound and irreversible effect on every institution of modern society. The burden of implementing information-processing technology, until quite recently, fell to professional experts trained in computer science and a relatively small cadre of managerial personnel. Responsibility for the utilization of computer technology started shifting away from these professionals several years ago. This relocation of responsibility and control promises to accelerate during the present decade as a result of continued technological advances and significant reductions in the costs of information-processing devices. Prospects for the universal availability of digital computers is no longer visionary but is now considered likely by cautious and conservative scholars.

A symposium was convened in 1980 at the University of Houston to examine the recent antecedents and future consequences of these developments in information technology. Distinguished spokespersons were invited from academic science, government, and business. This book contains the papers delivered at the symposium and the concluding discussion. Concerning the symposium itself, the speakers appeared in the order in which their papers are presented here. Although each paper was discussed following its presentation, the technical nature of many of the presentations suggested our best strategy for this symposium would be to delete the specific discussions. However, we have included the final general discussion as a summary of the many issues raised in individual papers. We did edit, but as lightly as possible only to remove redundancies, broken thoughts where a nod of the head communicated a thought covertly, and even to remove occasional low-information and repetitive phrases with which we all seem to be burdened. Aside from these alterations, no other disruption of the flow of the symposium occurs.

In accord with tradition, our moderator Raymond Nickerson has written a "post hoc" analysis of the symposium. He offers a good cross section of the issues, currents, and countercurrents generated by the papers and ensuing discussions, especially when combined with the general discussion. A major goal of both the symposium and the publication of its proceedings is to bring psychological expertise to bear on the design and documentation of information-processing systems and on the training of people to use those systems effectively.

As is so often the case in large undertakings such as this symposium, there are a number of people who aided in creating Houston Symposium 3 whom we would like to recognize and thank. In addition to the editors of this volume, other members of the Houston Symposium Committee— Jim Campion, Dale Johnson, and Frank S. Kessel—joined and supported us in a plethora of tasks related to the symposium. The transcriptions and communications would not have been possible without the faithful, patient, persistant ears and style of Brian Mariscal and Nancy Sheridan, our typists. Mike Lum was helpful in setting up and monitoring the recording equipment. Finally, our department chairperson, Roger F. Maley, continues to display ingenuity in finding the funds with which to conduct the Houston Symposium series. For that we are continually grateful to him. A series such as this could not survive and prosper without the contributions of people such as these.

Houston Symposium 4 will address "The child and other cultural inventions." But now, let's turn to an examination of psychology's continuing impact on society as we look at Information Technology and Psychology: Prospects for the future."

Richard A. Kasschau,
Roy Lachman, and
Kenneth R. Laughery

# Foreword

## Raymond S. Nickerson

The title of this symposium, "Information Technology and Psychology: Prospects for the Future," obviously invites speculation. What is this technology that has moved so rapidly over the past few decades going to do during the next few years? The title suggests special interest in the psychological effects of those developments, including, the symposium announcement notes, possible undesirable effects. How is this technology going to affect our lives? Any technology may be a promise to some people, a threat to others, a tool to still others. People may be, among other things, beneficiaries, victims, or users. The same person may assume all of these roles on different occasions or with respect to different aspects of the technology. How, in the case of information technology, can we maximize the occasions on which people can accurately perceive themselves as beneficiaries and users and minimize those on which they justifiably feel like victims?

Information technology means computers and communication. It is the technology of processing information and of moving it from place to place. Communication technology has made many major advances with the invention of the telephone and the radio during the latter part of the last century and the development of television during the middle of the present one. The electronic digital computer arrived on the scene at about the same time as television. The arrival of television was much more apparent to people in general than was that of the computer because of its immediate and obvious impact on our daily lives. The computer's role as a shaping force in information technology has been increasing steadily, however, and it promises to be a major, if not *the* major, determinant of the way this technology develops in the immediate future.

In attempting to anticipate how information technology will develop during the next few years, it may be useful to bear in mind not only the phenomenal growth of the computer industry during the last few decades but also the fact that what actually has happened was not foreseen by many people, if by anyone at all. The first commercially available computer, the UNIVAC I, was introduced in 1950,[1] and IBM installed its first computer, the 701, in 1953. Within 20 years there were approximately 100,000 computer installations in the world. With the advent of the microprocessor and the personal computer, counting "installations" no longer makes much sense. At the present time the computer industry is the third largest industry in the world. Only the automobile and oil industries are larger, but the computer industry is growing at the fastest rate. By the late 1980s, the total electronics industry is expected to reach about $400 billion.

Apparently, when computers first appeared on the scene, few individuals, if any, foresaw how ubiquitous they would shortly become. Lord Vivian Bowden, Principal of the University of Manchester Institute of Science and Technology, tells the delightful story of being given the task in 1950 of determining whether it would be possible for a commercial firm to manufacture computing machines and sell them at a profit. The interested company was Ferranti, which Bowden had just joined and which had just completed the first digital computer to be built by a commercial firm in England.

> I went to see Professor Douglas Hartree, who had built the first differential analyzers in England and had more experience in using these very specialized computers than anyone else. He told me that, in his opinion, all the calculations that would ever be needed in this country could be done on the three digital computers which were then being built—one in Cambridge, one in Teddington, and one in Manchester. No one else, he said, would ever need machines of their own, or would be able to afford to buy them. He added that the machines were exceedingly difficult to use, and could not be trusted to anyone who was not a professional mathematician, and he advised Ferranti to get out of the business and abandon the idea of selling any more of them (Bowden, 1970, p. 43).

It is easy, with the acuity of hindsight that our 1980 vantage point provides, to judge harshly such a gross miscalculation. But Professor Hartree was in good company with his conservative projection of the potential market for computing machines. According to one authority, "Shortly after the computer was invented, a statement was given wide circulation that all the computation in the country [United States] could be accommodated on a dozen—and later fifty—large-scale machines" (Diebold, 1969, p. 48). One suspects that a poll of those of Professor

Hartree's contemporaries whose opinions on this matter would have carried some weight would have supported his view. Certainly few people would have believed in 1950 that within 20 years 70 different companies would be producing over 370 different models of these machines.

The astounding growth of the computer industry is due, of course, to the fact that computers have turned out to be immensely useful devices. The earliest machines had very limited applications; the need to calculate trajectories of projectiles was a primary reason for the effort to develop them during the Second World War. Today the uses of computers are too numerous to count. Examples include: business data processing, industrial process control, weather forecasting, computer-aided instruction, system simulation, income tax processing, traffic-signal regulation, industrial design, urban planning, census analysis, medical diagnosis, patient monitoring, crime detection and investigation, war gaming, word-processing, typesetting, air-traffic control, space-vehicle guidance and navigation, chemical analysis, language translation, and home entertainment. Every year the list of uses is extended, in many cases the most exciting additions being those that were least expected.

The proliferation of computers and computer uses is naturally being accompanied by a general awakening to the enormous potential for both good and evil in future applications of these machines. A major challenge of the next few decades is to insure that on balance the use of this technology enhances the quality of human life, increases the degrees of freedom of the individual in society, and expands the opportunities for personal fulfillment. But such objectives will not be realized just for the wishing. If they are to be realized, it will be because competent and concerned individuals have had the determination to wrestle with some very complex issues. The great danger of our age probably is not that unscrupulous and avaricious individuals will exploit information technology for their own ends—which is not to say that this is not a danger—but, as Jerome Wiesner (1971) has pointed out, that a "depersonalizing state of affairs could occur without specific overt decision, without high-level encouragement or support and totally independent of malicious intent" (p. 8).

The implications that information technology has for our lives are beyond doubt very great; moreover, the greatest effects are likely to come as a result of developments that we cannot anticipate. What life will be like in another century or two is anybody's guess. However, what some of the more immediate implications are is already becoming clear.

The increasing concentration of information and power is one implication of computers that is beginning to attract attention and stimulate discussion. Information and control are two sides of the same coin. With the continued development of information technology will come increasingly powerful and efficient means of control—control over the environment, over social institutions, over governmental organizations and processes, over methods of production, and over individuals. One of the questions that we will be forced to face in the years ahead is whether humankind is sufficiently mature, intellectually and morally, to cope with truly efficient control systems.

A second implication has to do with machine intelligence and what this means for our view of ourselves as human beings. Norbert Wiener (1964) considered the fact that a machine had been programmed to learn, and that it was able to learn enough to beat its creator at a parlor game, to be a profoundly significant development. As the number of intellectual capabilities that people have and computers do not have decreases steadily, the age-old question of whether there is any essential difference between people and machines is being debated with renewed interest and from some new perspectives. Quite apart from the philosophical implications of machine intelligence, it now appears that we may soon begin to see significant practical applications of the considerable research that has been done in this area over the last 20 years. How these applications will affect our lives is not clear; *that* they will do so is certain.

A third implication of information technology, and one that is likely to be of special interest to many of the participants in this symposium, relates to emergence of a host of new computer-based tools and resources that are intended to be used by people who have not had technical training. These tools and resources are being designed for job-related purposes, for educational purposes, and for recreational purposes. The rapidly decreasing cost of computing hardware ensures that computer-based facilities will become increasingly available to people of all ages and with widely varying degrees of ability and education. The challenge to engineering psychology is to help design these resources in such a way as to make their computing power accessible to their users psychologically as well as physically.

A fourth, and much discussed, implication that information technology has for the future is an anticipated change in the function and significance of work that could result from widespread automation. Whether automation will in fact decrease the need for human labor, intellectual as well as physical, or only redistribute that need is a controversial question, but one that deserves much thought. The already-decreasing demand for human physical labor has implications for the work ethic that is so deeply ingrained in Western culture. It seems likely that there will be an increasing need for new attitudes concerning the role of work and the meaning of productivity, new mechanisms for distributing the wealth that is generated by automated means, new demands on educational institutions to prepare people for new and rapidly changing job markets, a new ethic of leisure.

Whether or not automation represents a threat (or a promise, depending on one's point of view), it is quite clear that information technology will have continuing and increasing influence in defining job opportunities and shaping job requirements. Already computer related vocations—programming, systems analysis, circuit design, computer operation and maintenance—are among the largest and fastest growing in the world. Moreover, an increasingly large number of people who are not trained as computer specialists are making direct use of computers as tools in their daily work: ticket agents, sales clerks, secretaries, bank tellers, lab technicians, pilots, stock brokers, and so on. Some of the changes in job situations that have resulted from the emergence of this technology have undoubtedly had depersonalizing, if not demeaning, effects; however, many of them have opened up challenging new opportunities and some have helped to upgrade and expand what were, to begin with, some rather boring jobs. As the applications of information technology multiply in the future, there will be few job situations that will not be affected by it, directly or otherwise. There will be countless opportunities to personalize and enrich jobs in ways that were not possible before. Whether these opportunities are seized, only the future will reveal.

I mentioned at the outset that information technology involves both communication technology and computer technology. Perhaps of greater significance for the future than either of these technologies is the increasingly close coupling between the two of them. The line between communication and computation is fading to the degree that in many cases it can no longer be found. This is illustrated by such developments as packet-switching computer networks, satellite communication systems, electronic mail, computer-based telephone systems, and information utilities (Nickerson, 1980). The primary purpose of each of these systems is communication; however, each of them has within it a considerable amount of computing capability without which it could not function. The emergence of these systems represents both some new challenges and some new opportunities for engineering psychologists and other scientists interested in the problem of making technology not only useful but usable.

It would be easy to extend this short list of general ways in which information technology may affect our lives in the future. Getting down to specifics is of course another matter. It is ever so much easier to come up with questions than to suggest compelling answers. Many of the questions clearly do not have easy answers—except the glib cliches to which we sometimes resort when we lack the taste or the talent for facing up to difficult problems. Information is as basic a commodity as energy. Like the technology for generating and distributing energy, the potential of information technology for both beneficial and detrimental effects is enormous. We are only beginning to appreciate this fact. The development and expansion of this technology during the immediate future promises to be even more spectacular than it has been during the immediate past. Our lives will be changed drastically in many ways as a consequence. Whether, on balance, the changes will be positive is not something we can afford to leave to chance. It is imperative that we attempt to anticipate specific potential effects of information technology on our lives, and to assure its application for the common good. The question of how best to understand and influence the development and use of this technology is worthy of a great deal of careful thought and discussion. It is, I suspect, in the hope of stimulating such thought and discussion that this symposium was convened.

## NOTE

[1]Several, perhaps a dozen, other experimental machines, more or less appropriately called digital computers, were in existence by 1950.

## REFERENCES

Bowden, V. The language of computers. *American Scientist*, 1970, *58*(1), 43–53.

Diebold, J. *Man and the computer.* New York: Praeger, 1969.

Nickerson, R.S. *Some human factors implications of the blurring of the line between communication and computation.* BBN Report No. 4577. Cambridge, Mass.: Bolt, Beranek and Newman, Inc., 1980.

Wiener, N. *God & Golem, Inc.* Cambridge, Mass.: M.I.T. Press, 1964.

Wiesner, J. The information revolution—and the bill of rights. *Computers and Automation*, May 1971, *20*(5), 8–10.

# Science, Technology, and the Fourth Discontinuity

## Gerald Holton

The title I have chosen for this launching of your ambitious symposium on today's most revolutionary technology borrows, I should confess at once, from an article by my colleague Bruce Mazlish.[1] Mazlish reminded his readers that Sigmund Freud, in his lectures at the University of Vienna between 1915 and 1917, identified the elimination of three conceptual discontinuities that marked the development of modern Western thought and, in each case, caused turmoil and anguish. The first was Copernicus' view that the earth, and therefore man, was not the center of the universe, but only—as Freud put it—"a tiny speck in a world-system of a magnitude hardly conceivable." The next was Darwin's, who "robbed man of his peculiar privilege of having been specially created, and relegated him to a descent from the animal world." And the third shock, Freud explained, came from his own work, which showed each one of us that "he is not even master in his own house, but that he must remain content with the various scraps of information about what is going on unconsciously in his own mind."

Not everyone will agree with the identification and numbering of these major transitions. But it is true that the work of the charismatic scientists, from Copernicus to Einstein, has amounted to breaking down barriers that had previously been taken for granted: the comfort of fundamental differences thought to exist between terrestrial and celestial phenomena, between man and other life forms, the conscious and the unconscious, the child and the adult, or space and time, energy and matter. In each case, a culture shock resulted from the discovery that such barriers did not exist, that the discontinuity gave way to a continuum.

The adjustment to these recognitions was painful, and indeed is not complete to this day in any of these cases among the general public. It is

1

not merely that each of those barrier smashers offended man's innate "common sense" and narcissism; even more ominous and frightening was the prospect of new freedoms that came with the elimination of the discontinuities—and, for many, the fear of exercising these freedoms.

The fourth discontinuity Mazlish considers is that between man and machine. It is his thesis that man has begun to realize that he is continuous with the tools and machines he constructs, that he is not only learning how to explain the workings of one in terms of the other, but is in fact forming a closer and closer physical, symbiotic relationship with the machine. At the same time, however, "man's pride, and his refusal to acknowledge this continuity, is the substratum upon which the distrust of technology and industrial society has been reared."

To illustrate his point, Mazlish discusses the nightmare of the servant-machine rising against its master—the myth of Frankenstein, or more accurately, the myth of Dr. Frankenstein and his unnamed monster. If you have not recently looked into Mary Shelley's novel, you may not recall why the monster turned to murder. The living thing Dr. Frankenstein had assembled was in fact human and virtuous, but of such horrible appearance that its creator, and others whom it tried to befriend, fled in panic. The wrath of the monster, in the first instance, was thus caused by the abandonment of his creator's responsibility for his own work.

"I was benevolent and good; misery had made me a fiend. Make me happy, and I shall again be virtuous." With this plea the monster persuades his maker to go back into the laboratory and put together a second monster, a helpmeet with whom he would leave the world of men and retire happily into the wilderness of the Americas. But when Dr. Frankenstein is about to breathe life into the female creature, he begins to have scruples. He reasons that at best this horrible pair will settle down to have children, "and a race of devils would be propagated upon the earth which might make the very existence of this species of men a condition precarious and full of terror. Had I right, for my own benefit, to inflict this curse upon everlasting generations?" And with this, even while the male monster is secretly watching him, Dr. Frankenstein destroys her. Now, of course, vengeance knows no bounds.

To contemporary sensibilities, the story contains some high ironies. Today, eager biologists and their corporate sponsors argue before the Supreme Court that they should be allowed to patent new life forms that are the products of both nature and man, such as genetically engineered bacteria. The legal question, fascinating as it is, is only one ramification of current, spectacular research in bioengineering. Such research is now heavily circumscribed by requirements for ethical and environmental impact statements—precisely the type of consideration that the unfortunate Dr. Frankenstein entered into so belatedly.

# THE DRIVE TO OMNISCIENCE AND OMNIPOTENCE

Indeed, this brings me to the point where I differ with my friend Bruce Mazlish concerning the locations of the fourth discontinuity. I think we crossed the man-tool boundary he is concerned with at a much earlier stage of human development, and the rabbis of medieval legend even anticipated the construction of a golem. Instead, the discontinuity being eliminated now is the difference between three previously separate, fundamental imperatives, those that animate progress, respectively, in science, technology, and society. To translate it to modern terminology, the novelty of Dr. Frankenstein was not that he made a recombinant man-machine monster, but that he became aware of the necessity for timely environmental and ethical impact statements of R & D. (Not even the good Lord himself, while engineering the transformation of clay Adam, and eventually into the improved model, Mark II, or Eve, appears to have thought of doing that.)

No one would maintain, of course, that in the past science, technology, and social advance were completely separate from one another in every case. That first great invention of mankind, agriculture, serves as the oldest counter example. But by and large, the barriers between them were thought to be reasonably clear. Even in the period leading to the industrial age of today, they were considered at most semi-permeable, with science and technology acting unilaterally on the social process. Thus, when Francis Bacon announced that "knowledge and human power are synonymous," he had in mind that what we would now call research and development could be used together to subdue nature in the service of man. Voltaire expressed the hope of the Enlightenment period "that reason and industry will progress more and more, that the useful arts will be improved, that all of the evils which have afflicted man...will gradually disappear." The Magna Carta of contemporary science policy, Vannevar Bush's report to President Roosevelt, *Science: The Endless Frontier*, was a direct descendant of the same expectation that the effects of science and technology on the fate of society are essentially unidirectional and beneficent.

But more and more, since the end of World War II, the realization has been spreading that the fates of science, technology, and society are linked in a much more complex and multilateral way. As one indicator, it has been recently estimated that nearly half the bills before the U.S. Congress have a substantial science/technology component. It is now also obvious that the establishment of the continuum of interactions between science, technology, and society has begun to shape each of these three elements at least as much as it does its own dynamics. And it is surely not an accident that some of the best early writings on this subject came from the father of the electronics-communication revolution, Norbert Wiener himself.

Two years after the publication of his great work, *Cybernetics* (1948), Wiener brought out *The Human Uses of Human Beings: Cybernetics and Society* (1950, now being reissued), which was designed, he explained, to bring out the "ethical and sociological implications of my previous work." The main point of the second work was, Wiener stressed, "a protest against the inhuman use of human beings," by which he meant above all the failure to bring the person—the citizen, consumer, worker—into a cybernetic relationship with the social organizations on which he depends. With this he opposed all unidirectional mechanisms in social institutions, arguing that uncontrolled resonances, or even fascistic totalitarianism, could be avoided only by the conscious design of institutions in which feedback is a primary rather than merely a cosmetic or perfunctory function.

Chiefly in reaction to the weapons race in the early Cold War years, Wiener was perhaps one of the first to grasp fully the malignant possibilities to which science and technology can be diverted. It was, however, not merely the spectacle of war-minded executives, legislators, and others that brought him to this realization. In his third book, *God and Golem, Inc.: A Comment on Certain Points Where Cybernetics Impinges on Religion* (1964), he probed below the level of public policy to study the root motivations, which he identified as three drives: knowledge, to power, and to "worship." The old relationships between these three—or for that matter, the historic paucity of interactions—had become completely changed by the advances of science and technology. Deep ethical problems were now coming to the fore, such as the meaning of *purpose* in man and machine when we deal with machines that "learn," that "reproduce themselves," and that become part of and coordinated with living persons. Wiener warned that wise action for dealing with the problems of our time is doomed so long as different factions continue to give absolute primacy to only one of the three components—treating knowledge "in terms of omniscience," power "in terms of omnipotence," and worship "only in terms of one Godhead." Such sharp separation distorts reality.

Francis Bacon, often considered the godfather of modern Western industrial society, launched the enterprise precisely with such distortions. In his *New Atlantis* the narrator tries to find the secret of the utopia that beckoned so seductively. At long last he is received by the ruler of the House of Salomon—the chief, so to speak, of the research and development laboratory forming the very heart of the New Atlantis—and, in a confidential audience, he is told: "God bless thee, my son; I will give thee the greatest jewel I have. For I will impart unto thee, for the love of God and men, a relation of the true state of Salomon's house.... The end of our foundation is the knowledge of causes, and secret motions of things; and the enlarging of the bounds of human empire, to the affecting of all things possible."

All things possible! Marlowe's *Faustus* had exclaimed: "Lines, circles, signs, letters and characters—/Aye, these are those that Faustus most desires, O what a world of profit and delight/Of power, of honor, of omnipotence/Is promised to the studious artisan." To this day, we see all around us the Promethean drive to *omnipotence through technology* and to *omniscience through science*. The effecting of all things possible and the knowledge of all causes are the respective imperatives of technology and of science. With the motivating imperative of society continuing to be the very different one of its physical and spiritual survival, it is now far less obvious than it was in Francis Bacon's world how to bring the three imperatives into harmony, and how to bring all three together to bear on problems where they superpose.

In graphic terms, one can represent the relationship between them, and their changes, by drawing three circles, each representing one of the elements: science, technology, and society. Initially, the three circles encroached on each other rather little; the whole point of Galileo's tragic flight was to insist on the autonomy of science. In principle, the three elements could stand apart, like three clover leaves, and any bargaining between could be correspondingly simple. But in time, each of the three circles grew in size and also moved to increase the area of overlap with the other two. Unlike Galileo's telescope and Faraday's electromagnet, the microcomputer is located squarely in the direct overlap of all three circles—just where the inherent contradictions of the three old, incommensurable imperatives are most active and just where the new, mediating institutions are least mature.

To be sure one can argue (and historians love to do just that) to what degree either science or technology ever had been or could be "pure." There are classic debates between Marxians, idealists, and all the others caught in the middle, on that very point. But the reality of today is captured more appropriately by the remark of Sir Peter Medawar in his new book, *Advice to a Young Scientist:* "The direction of scientific endeavor is determined by political decisions as ... acts of judgement that lie outside science itself." And there is no doubt that the most advanced technologies of our day, those represented by large-scale integrated circuits and by genetic engineering, not only are the products of powerful scientific and technological as well as social forces, but are also the focus of deep concern as each imperative contends for supremacy over the two others, in the absence of the cybernetic relationship for which Norbert Wiener had called.

I believe one should read your call to this very symposium in this spirit. The brochure announcing this meeting speaks first of the enormous technological advances in the United States over the past four decades that revolutionized "space science, the military, the computer industry, and related institutions." Until recently "the burden of implementing information-processing technology fell to professional experts," but with "continued technological progress such as in microprocessors, the impact will be felt by everyone, including the individual citizen," as computer technology more and more directly "impacts consumer products." And here is where the logic of the unilateral, imperialistic drive of technology threatens to become impotent instead of omnipotent: precisely because the fast-track technology has overtaken the capabilities of "the consumer...to master and utilize this technology," it "seems likely the endline user will soon become the bottleneck in the implementation of that technology....How are we to deal with the bottleneck...?"

And I would suggest we now ask also, what if the consumer does not settle for this passive role?

## SOME QUERIES FOR POLICY MAKERS

One answer you expect an academic to give is better education of the consumer. This can be interpreted as the application of an appropriate funnel to the bottleneck, thereby allowing the goods prepared by industry—for example, the microcomputers that are expected to inhabit one household in four by the end of the decade—to go more readily down the narrow throat. I will not quarrel here with this, as long as such education is in the service of undoing the present state of national, even international, disgrace to which we have regressed since the mid-1960s, the disgrace of ever decreasing scientific and mathematical literacy of students in the United States, of ever decreasing aid to the training and retraining of our school teachers in scientific subjects, and of ever greater erosion of the nation's dedication to the cause of sound education itself.

But surely we do not meet here simply to persist in the ancient, unilateral fallacy, proposing to use the funnel of education merely to prepare the citizen to become a more skillful operator of the sophisticated hardware and software that is descending on him from above. Nor would we be satisfied even with swinging the direction of the educational mandate around to the education of engineers and speak only of how we can enable these future-makers to fashion a better match between the rightful claims of science, technology, and society. Rather, I am painfully aware that educators are still far from having the sound basis on which to erect their own platforms for either task. Here is a short list of areas of vast ignorance that must be remedied before we can claim to speak with authority when we address either the bottlenecked citizen or the bountiful engineer.

1.   What is a reasonable theory, up-to-date and tested, for scientific and technological progress? Indeed, we would have to have such a theory to understand which is fueling which and to what extent, whether science is striving toward a "final state," and whether at various stages in the development of science it is more or less amenable to guidance and policy intervention ("finalization").

2.   Where are our tested models for the interactions between science, technology, and society? We don't lack contenders—from Bernal and Polanyi to Alvin Weinberg and Stephen Toulmin, from Merton and Don Price to Harvey Brooks, not to speak of the Marxian school or the pragmatism of day-to-day decisions made by the staff of the Office of Management and Budget. But when the chips are down, even the most level-headed among these theoreticians and policy makers can only agree with Harvey Brooks' recent statement that the interaction between science, technology, and society now allows us at best to be only cautiously optimistic about avoiding "catastrophe."[2]

3.   Technology and the individual: is there a necessary systemic incompatibility? One remembers here the widely popular arguments of Ellul and Mumford, which raised the specter that technology necessarily produces a "megamachine" within which the varieties of type, purpose, and interests of individuals are dissolved or sacrificed. Be that as it may, the joining of individual microprocessors and information technology products to a central "grid" and the dependence of the hardware on software that is both centrally provided and designed for the big market (lowest common level) are almost irresistible temptations for the near future, with all the dangers of monopoly, commercialism, and banalization that all too quickly became the hallmark of television.

4.   The other side of the same coin is, of course, governmental intervention through regulatory functions. Can the advance of technology be made to incorporate the societal imperatives, alongside the technological imperative, and thereby counter or preempt the more ignorant and autonomous regulatory attempts?

5.   Technology and the quality of life. This is, of course, the fundamental question; but is it not patently true that the application of technology to increase, say, scientific literacy has been very spotty at best? Are we about to be sold a new generation of "teaching machines" before we have discovered what general scientific literacy can be, how to reach it, what the deep obstacles to it are? And what is true about scientific literacy is doubly true for the educational process as a whole.

If technological advance has been in the service of the quality of life, as industry spokesmen are apt to say, why has there been—in the words of Bruce Hannay, vice-president for research and patents at Bell Laboratories, speaking to the American Academy of Arts and Sciences— "a steady decline in the general acceptance of the desirability of technological change"? Undoubtedly, technological advance has decreased the costs and increased the availability of energy, food, information, and basic medicine to large masses of people. Therefore the quality of life should in principle be recognized to have been advanced substantially. Yet there has been a parallel development of *pathologies*, which have caused the gifts of high technology, such as the computer or the nuclear reactor, to become in many quarters the very symbol of technological changes undermining societal objectives, the gift that is a Trojan horse— not to speak of the effect of sophisticated technology on military budgets, now at a level of 500 billion dollars a year worldwide, with 50 thousand nuclear warheads deployed and waiting, and with open calls for an increase of the annual defense budget of the United States alone to the level of one trillion dollars.

Under such shadows, what meaning can one assign to the phrase "quality of life"? For an operational definition of the components of the phrase, I would be tempted to go back to Franklin D. Roosevelt's definition of the "four freedoms" (in his message to Congress, January 6, 1941): freedom of speech and expression, freedom of worship, freedom from want, and freedom from fear. It was a mark of Roosevelt's insight to couple the last two "freedoms from." To the extent that science and technology pursue their own imperatives, they may indeed give us—as by-products, so to speak—freedom from want (in the sense of freedom from basic material needs). But except for the removal of superstition through greater scientific literacy, science and technology by themselves cannot increase the freedom from fear. On the contrary, the very instincts for survival and self-preservation, which animate social action, will demand assurances that the imperatives of science and technology are made, if not subservient to, at least harmonized with, that of society—and the more urgently precisely as the powers of science and technology increase. I do not think that there is a widespread fear of scientists and engineers as such—but there is a widespread fear that they, like Dr. Frankenstein, are still apt to make their impact considerations as an afterthought, and perhaps too late.

## THE EMERGENCE OF "COMBINED MODE" RESEARCH

This list of five basic questions highlights the enormity of our ignorance of the fundamental interactions. Yet, there are some indications of a very hopeful sort that at this very time a new relationship is emerging between science, technology, and society that may go far to rearrange the forces in an era dominated by the recognition of the fourth discontinuity. Although each of the three cloverleaves will undoubtedly retain an area of its own relative autonomy—and, in the case of basic research science, can do no less if science is to thrive—a model of interaction is emerging in the area of overlap, where the discontinuities have been disappearing. To this, I shall now turn, in the hope that if I exhibit the general case, you will find it easier to draw corresponding consequences for the subject of your specific expertise and concerns.

To summarize my point before illustrating it: when, as a historian of science, one studies the "center of gravity" of the choice of basic research problems on the part of good scientists, one can discern a marked shift in emphasis. At the time of Kepler, Galileo, and Newton, the researcher seems to have asked himself chiefly what God may have had in mind when creating the physical world. By the time of Maxwell the burning question had become what Faraday might had had in mind with his obscure ponderings about the field and how one might improve on them. This is still, and to a degree will remain, the type of puzzle that excites the basic researcher. But alongside, an alternative and complementary motivation for certain research scientists is making its appearance. The stimulus comes now not only from considering one's Creator or one's peers but, more and more frequently, *from perceiving an area of basic scientific ignorance that seems to lie at the heart of a social problem.*

Work motivated in this manner positions itself squarely in the area of overlap between science, technology, and society, without giving up its claim to being indeed basic research. It is basic research of a specific kind, which I term "combined-mode research," since it can be considered a combination of the discipline-oriented and problem-oriented modes. Note that it is not to be confused with such programs as RANN (Research Applied to National Needs) and similar ones, which encourage the application of *existing* basic knowledge to the meeting of supposed national needs; that has its place, and I am not arguing here against it—nobody could do so who has digested such lessons as the decade-long delay in starting serious work on long-range radioactive waste management. But I am, instead, speaking of the opposite of RANN and similar programs of applied research, namely, of *basic* research, located intentionally in uncharted areas on the map of basic science but motivated by a credible perception that the findings will have a fair probability—perhaps in a decade or more—to be brought to bear upon a persistent national or international problem.

With this we have, of course, reached disputed territory. For the better part of three centuries the consensus among basic research scientists has been that "truth sets its own agenda." Any intrusion of the consideration of utility that might eventually accrue from basic research has been thought to be incompatible with the agenda of the true scientist. From that point of view, omniscience first, omnipotence later. Did not the seventeenth-century giants teach us that reductionism is the way to success in the natural sciences and that applications to the seamless and endless complexities of societal problems are best left to serendipity or to later generations?

And in any case, have scientists not been remarkably blind when it came to occasional attempts to forecast practical applications of their work? Thus it is said Kelvin could see no use for the new Herzian radio waves except possibly communication with lightships, and Rutherford stoutly refused to the end of see any significant practical applications of his exploration to the atom. And last but not least, have we not learned from the Lysenko episode, and the constant drumfire of attacks on basic science by legislators in the West, that our first job is to fight for the preservation of "pure" scientific research? The anguished assessment of the chemist Francis W. Clarke in 1891 still largely holds true today: "Every true investigator in the domain of pure science is met with monotonously recurrent questions as to the practical purport of his studies; and rarely can he find an answer expressible in terms of commerce. If utility is not immediately in sight, he is pitied as a dreamer, or blamed as a spendthrift."

Certainly, the science of plate tectonics did not arise out of an effort to predict earthquakes, or genetics out of a desire to create a better harvest in the vegetable garden. On the contrary, it happened the other way around. Indeed, the history of science and technology is full of case studies that could be collected under some heading such as "how basic research reaps unexpected rewards."[3] It follows that anyone inclined to mix considerations of utility with the choice of basic research problems may be risking both the granting agency's money and his career as a scientist.

But now there are signs that this has been too simplistic a dogma when applied across the board. While it still is, will be, and must be true for the majority of basic research scientists, at least a small fraction of the research programs can be and, in fact, are now centered in what I have called earlier combined-mode research, in research where the imperatives of science and of society overlap instead of claiming mutual exclusivity. And while, from the viewpoint of social utility, basic research in the "pure" mode could be called "Project Serendipity," research in the combined mode might be called "Project Foresight" (by asymmetry with the ill-fated "Project Hindsight" that attempted to sketch the influence of the past on the present; I am concerned here rather with the influence of the present on the future).

It is appropriate to interject that this recognition is not a *normative* proposal on my part. I am not speaking as a science planner or missionary but as a historian of science who is describing what he sees happening in science today. I am also not assessing the long-range future of these developments. It might well turn out that combined-mode research, which by its very definition is difficult, requires more patience than our society now has for waiting for the promised payoff in social benefits.[4]

But there simply is no doubt that, under our very eyes, a mutation has been taking place, and programs are growing up specifically designed to seek fundamental new knowledge and scientific principles, in the absence of which current national or international needs are difficult to ameliorate or even to understand properly. It is, after all, not too hard to imagine plausible research areas that can hold the key to well-known societal dysfunctions. Even the "purest" scientists are likely to agree that much remains to be done in the field of cognitive psychology, the biophysics and biochemistry involved in the process of conception, the neurophysiology of the senses such as hearing and sight, or molecular transport across cell membranes, to name a few. As a result of such basic work we could plausibly expect in time to have a better grasp on such complex societal tasks as childhood education, family planning, improving the quality of life for the handicapped, and the design of food plants that can use inexpensive (brackish) water. Other basic research examples that come readily to mind might include the physical chemistry of the stratosphere; that part of the theory of solid states that makes the efficient working of photovoltaic cells still a puzzle, bacterial nitrogen fixation and the search for symbionts that might work with plants other than legumes, the mathematics of risk calculation for complex structures, the physiological processes governing the aging cell, research on learning and on career decisions of young people, the sociology underlying the anxieties some segments of the population have about mathematics and, indeed, about computers ("What the Bottleneck Can Tell the Bottle"), and the sociobiology of ancient tribalism that seems to be at the base of genocide, racism, and war in our time.

Any specific list of examples of this sort is open to challenges. But it is not difficult to imagine a consultative mechanism designed to identify the research areas that could benefit from such cultivation. There is no doubt that institutional innovations in this direction are sorely needed; unless the fundamental decisions of siting such research is made with the full participation of a wide spectrum of experienced and trusted research scientists, the effort would degenerate quickly.[5] The last thing science, or society, needs is some political command center for the approval or disapproval of basic research.

## A FIRST LIST OF "COMBINED MODE" PLANS

I turn now to a roundup of specific evidences of the rise of support for research in the combined mode, for research driven by (or targeted as the result of) perceived national need. In citing quite recent examples I do not wish to imply that this movement has no history whatever.

Particularly in the biomedical area there have been clear instances, from Pasteur to the founding of the NIH institutes. But combined-mode research in the biomedical field has in a sense been "easier" to start and to support (partly because of the immediate self-interest of the patrons—an example of the process of science and technology affecting the setting of social priorities—and partly because much of what has passed for basic research in that field is really closer to mission-oriented applied research on systems whose fundamental complexities have hardly been charted). The real test is outside the biomedical field.

A suitable point of departure for our accounting is provided by an address delivered in early 1978 by Frank Press, director of the Office of Science and Technology Policy (OSTP), and the science and technology advisor to the president.[6] Dr. Press described the science-policy planning that went into the budget for the federal funding of basic research for the fiscal year of 1979. In addition to the Office of Management and Budget (OMB), the heads of NASA and NSF, leaders in science and engineering from universities, industry, and the government, the process also involved consultation with the members of the Cabinet:

> During the course of our interactions on research with the departments and agencies, the President queries the Cabinet members on what they thought some of the important research questions of national interest were. Here are a few examples cited by the Cabinet officers:
>> Can simple chemical reactions be discovered that will generate visible radiation? How does the material pervading the universe collect to form complex organic molecules, stars, and galaxies? What are the physical processes that govern climate?...What are the factors—social, economic, political, and cultural—which govern population growth?...How do cracks originate and propagate in materials? How do cells change during growth and development? What are the mechanisms responsible for sensory signal processing, neural membrane phenomena, and distinct chemical operations of nerve junctions?...What predisposing factors govern cellular differentiation and function in plant and animal? (pp. 740–41)

These are of course questions of basic research for the "purest" Ph.D. theses at the best academic departments, and yet they are also precisely targeted in areas of perceived national need.

The same intention surfaced also in the reorganization of the NSF's applied research programs in February 1978, when, as part of the new Directorate for Applied Science and Research Applications, a division of Integrated Basic Research (IBR) was formed. Unlike the older, applied-research activity, which aims to encourage and accelerate the application of exiting basic scientific knowledge to a wide range of potential users, the division of IBR was formed to provide "support for basic research that has a high relevance to major problems" in selected topic areas in the basic research directorates. The operational meaning of these intentions became clearer in the Tenth Annual Report of the National Science Board, entitled *Basic Research in the Mission Agencies: Agency Perspectives on the Conduct and Support of Basic Research,* released by the president on August 2, 1978. In his covering letter to the Congress, the president specified that he had "encouraged the agencies to identify current or potential problems facing the Federal Government, in which basic or long-term research could help these agencies.... [The report also should be helpful] with setting priorities for future federally-supported research and development, and in making our spending in this area more effective."

In its memorandum to science writers and editors, on the same day, the NSF itself started its description of the report with the straight-forward and familiar sentence, "Basic research is useful." But this is no longer the vague, old promise, as in Vannevar Bush's *Science: The Endless Frontier* of some two dozen years earlier, that disease, ignorance, and unemployment would somehow be conquered if basic science were supported on a large scale, without any conscious attempt to link the input and the output. Rather, the new linkage is proposed to come about in a way which Vannevar Bush never considered in pursuing his main purpose, which was to provide what he called "special protection and specially-assured support" for pure research, so as to avoid what he saw to be the "perverse law governing research," namely, that "applied research invariably drives out pure." The initiatives of 1978, instead of concentrating on either pure or applied research in relative isolation, start with the novel and rather daring attempt to gather the perceptions of the various science-related mission agencies concerning their "priorities and gaps in their research agendas" (NSB report, 1978, p. 303). A list was assembled of the "problem areas that appear to merit national attention and that require basic research (if for no other reason than to complete our understanding of the problem)." The authors of the report were evidently aware of the difficulty of deciding on the relative importance of research programs even within a delimited area of science and of the increasing difficulty of such priority setting as the time span for planning increases. But as a public attempt at the identification of priorities and gaps, the document is of considerable interest and undoubtedly will be long studied by historians of science and technology when they consider the development of science policy in this country.

Also, as one might expect, the 16 agencies, ranging from the Department of Agriculture to the NSF, and from Department of Housing and Urban Development to the Veteran's Administration, are by no means equally adept in responding to the National Science Board's questions such as: "What promising or vital areas of research, not now supported but involving basic research, warrant increased emphasis and support by your agency?" But there emerge entirely plausible proposals nevertheless. Thus the Department of Agriculture provides a lengthy list of priorities, from agricultural research (starting with nitrogen fixation, photosynthesis, and genetic engineering for plants) to social science research (ending with "impact assessment"), all of them "areas of science in which a basic research approach is required," not only for agricultural and forest technology, but also, thoughtfully, for "the quality of life in rural communities and homes." The Department of Commerce's list includes, typically, atomic and molecular science (chemical reaction rates, ozone layer dynamics, very high temperature plasmas) and ends with a call for "over-all resources for the broad spectrum of basic research, free from competition from short-term applied projects."

There are enough passages of this sort in the total report to make the "purest" basic scientist feel right at home. If is, of course, in the nature of the exercise that such a feeling would not be generated on every page. Thus the list of priorities of the NIH is unexceptional (genetics, immunology, virology, cell biology, neuroscience) and, for the main "gap" area, neurobiology ("the ultimate challenge to medical research, representing the very pinnacle of our understanding of the human organism"). On the other hand, the same understanding of "basic research" does not seem to bolster such entries as that of the Army ("improvement of helicopter performance") or of the Maritime Administration ("propeller design").[7]

These initiatives of early 1978 were by no means the last. They were indeed strengthened in the discussions, concerned with the preparation of the budget for fiscal year 1980,[8] one year later.

This tendency gathered further momentum very recently with the release by the National Science Foundation of the two-volume report, *Five-Year Outlook: Problems, Opportunities, and Constraints in Science and Technology.*[9] As the release of the NSF accompanying the publication records, the report "discusses national issues that we will face during the next five years from a scientific and technical perspective. This is the first time such a long-range outlook on science and technology has been prepared."

The study was mandated by the National Science and Technology Policy, Organization, and Priorities Act of 1976. It represents a major effort to identify and describe "in depth problems of national concern that are most likely to need special attention through the mid-1980s and later, and to which science and technology can contribute in the coming years." The heart of the report is a book-length monograph prepared by the National Academy of Sciences, to which are added statements from 21 U.S. agencies, papers by individual specialists, and a synthesis presenting selected problems of U.S. society and the opportunities for science and technology to solve them. These were prepared by the NSF staff, under such headings as energy, materials, transportation, demography, space, agriculture, health, electronic revolution, and the hazards of toxic substance in the environment.

While the Vannevar Bush report, 35 years earlier, had concentrated on the necessity to support basic research regardless of how it eventually might fulfill the distant promise of helping to "create a fuller and more fruitful employment and a fuller and more fruitful life," the new *Five-Year Outlook* incorporates rather explicitly both the "pure mode" and the combined mode of basic research. Thus, in the covering statement of the director of the National Science Foundation, Richard C. Atkinson refers to the many examples in the volumes illustrating "the contribution of long-term research to the solution of national problems," but of course also calls for the continuation of support for research where the primary goal is "a better understanding of nature" regardless of whether any link can be discerned with "specific societal problems." He was signaling a preservation of a necessary balance between the old and the new expectations from basic research, a signal made the more necessary as the Congressional act that required the periodic preparation of a *Five-Year Outlook*, by its very specification of a relatively short period of preview, stressed only one of the two modes.[10]

Reading these important volumes, it is clear that the invisible hand, which has long been thought to be sufficient for guiding the process from the basic research laboratory to the specific application, is gradually becoming more visible. The language is quite frank: "Research should focus on the following long-range opportunities" (biological processes that develop food plants with less fertilizer and less fresh water, environmentally safe methods for controlling animal and plant pests and diseases, better understanding of acid rain); "we must emphasize at once research that will provide the scientific knowledge" for the development and commercialization of advanced energy technologies, such as nuclear fusion and direct solar conversion; "we must expand" the science on which risk assessments are based (Vol. 1, pp. 1–4).

Elsewhere there are long and detailed lists of fundamental research that must be encouraged, lists that show considerable overlap with those prepared two years earlier for the Tenth Annual Report of the NSB. From the point of view of the particular audience of this presentation it is of interest to note that "the electronic revolution," including computer technology, has received more visibility in this new report. The two chief "problems" highlighted are "how to use the capabilities of computer and communication sciences and technology to serve a wide range of commercial, public, and personal needs; [and] how to resolve the social, ethical, and regulatory issues that are emerging as a result of the electronic revolution" (Vol. 1, p. 31).

Volume 2 includes two separately commissioned, thoughtful essays on the impact of new communication technologies, particularly on privacy. This seems to me precisely the kind of area that, in a conference on psychology and society concerned with information technology in the 1980s, could be subjected to most fruitful study. Here, too, we encounter the conflicting imperatives of technology and society in the area of overlap. One reason for the perception that the consumer is becoming a bottleneck may have to do with the public attitudes in the United States about the overall state of privacy and how it is affected by the increasing use of computers by governmental and commercial agencies with which the public has to deal. The findings gathered by the survey commissioned by Sentry Insurance, designed and carried out by Alan Westin and the Louis Harris organization in 1978, are certainly sobering. Over 80 percent of those surveyed disapproved of the wide access that police (and others) have to personal bank account information without a court order, and—surely not unrelated—nearly two-thirds agreed with the statement that "If privacy is to be preserved, the use of computers must be sharply restricted in the future."

Since 1974, there has been a striking shift in the response of the general population to the proposition that "Americans begin surrendering their personal privacy the day they open their first charge account, take out a loan, buy something on the installment plan, or apply for a credit card." In 1974 slightly less than half agreed. By 1978, the fraction had risen to slightly over three-quarters (Vol. 2, p. 530). If only for reasons of self-interest, the computer industry now, as we have entered the era of the fourth discontinuity, might be expected to concentrate some of its research and development talent on this area of abuse and fear. History will judge the prophets of the silicone chip by the degree to which they are able to provide intelligent machines that not only make life more interesting and fruitful but also enhance personal freedom.

I have concentrated on examples taken from recent public documents published in the United States. Analogous and in some ways even more telling examples could be drawn from the international literature. For example, in Sweden, where such groups as trade unions have begun to take an energetic interest in science policy issues, there has been a shift to nudge science planning in accordance with social goals defined along sectoral lines.[11]

A report rather similar to these discussions for the United States was published by the National Council of Science and Technology (CONACYT) of Mexico in 1978.[12] In laying out the rationale for assigning high priorities to some research areas and not to others, CONACYT canvassed scientific representatives from the public, private, and academic sectors, including its various ministries. On this basis, areas of encouragement for basic research were identified (in addition to fields demanding encouragement for applied research and the development of technology).

Even UNESCO, in its planning document (21C-5) for the coming biennium, is adopting as one of its "themes" the "contribution to determining research priorities linked with human needs and the goals of society." It is not a major concern, however, since apparently the budget assigned is 0.1 percent of the total budget of UNESCO.

The space available has not allowed me to triangulate to the same point from yet other directions. The fact that the era of the fourth discontinuity demands a new, additional mandate for the pursuit of basic research as a contribution to the fulfillment of human needs has produced a number of related developments: one is a widening of the purview of the professional societies and corporate activities, seen best in the large increase of discussion of social concerns in the annual reports of the presidents of professional scientific societies.[13] Another is the rise of educational programs on science, technology, and society.[14] These are generally carried on in the spirit of giving young people who will be scientists or managers a double competence that was perhaps best indicated in Einstein's words when he addressed the students of the California Institute of Technology in 1931: "It is not enough that you should understand about applied science in order that your work may increase man's blessings. Concern for man himself and his fate must always form the chief interest of all technical endeavors...in order that the creations of our minds shall be a blessing and not a curse to mankind. Never forget this in the midst of your diagrams and equations."

\*    \*    \*    \*

All the evidence seems to me to point to the fact that, in our time, a historic transition has occurred in the direction of basic research policy, a transition for better or worse that we are only beginning to understand. In time's own laboratory, a new amalgam is forming that will challenge the inherited notions of every scientist, engineer, and social planner. Undoubtedly, we shall witness battles to preserve those autonomies that are and always will be essential. Undoubtedly, there will also be over-enthusiastic projects that cannot deliver on their promises. But if the new movement develops within the bounds of its genuine possibilities and responsibilities, the spectrum of research in science may well be greatly extended, its links to technology and society become more fruitful and certain, and its mandate reinforced.

As scientists, engineers, industrialists, or educators, we should welcome this promise; for any professional activity has a just claim to moral authority when, and only when, it is widely seen to honor both truth and the public interest. As we now plunge into the marvelous whirlpool of the new information-processing technology, let us not lose sight of this fundamental fact.

## NOTES AND REFERENCES

[1]Mazlish, Bruce. The fourth discontinuity. *Technology and Culture*, 1967, *8*, 1–15.

[2]Brooks, Harvey. Technology: Hope or catastrophe? *Technology in Society*, 1979, *1*, 1–17. His conclusion is: "So I end with the proposition that science is more hope than catastrophe, though, admittedly, it is nip and tuck."

[3]"How Basic Research Reaps Unexpected Rewards" is, in fact, the title of a pamphlet released by NSF, February 1980.

[4]For some reasons why, in the past, "we have not found good ways of encouraging much-needed inquiry, especially in the areas of the environment, the control of population growth, and the conversion of energy," see R.S. Morison, "Introduction" to the book *Limits of Scientific Inquiry*, R.S. Morison and G. Holton, eds., New York: W.W. Norton and Co., 1979, p. xviii.

[5]As Bruce L.R. Smith and Joseph J. Karlesky (*The state of academic science: The universities in the nation's research effort*, New York: Change Magazine Press, 1977) have noted, institutional deficiencies, including short cycles of funding by government and industrial sponsors, have also adversely affected the pursuit of "pure" research and resulted in a certain lack of venturesomeness. They identified in academic institutions a "notable shift away from basic research to applied and mission-oriented research"—precisely in the opposite direction from the combined mode—"and from risk-taking to relatively safe and predictable lines of inquiry." In industry, the same problem has appeared, as documented in *Science Indicators 1976* and *1978*, with a decade-long decrease in basic research expenditure and a change to short-term goals, often to "defensive research" that aims chiefly at the protection of old products against regulations.

[6]Press, Frank. Science and technology: the road ahead. *Science* 1978, *200*, 737–41.

[7]Elsewhere in the NSF report (p. 286) there is a frank discussion about the practical differences of drawing the line between basic and applied science in the mission agencies: "Every agency science administrator is plagued by the mission relevance question, especially in relation to basic research. For example, the Office of Naval Research (ONR) identifies support of pure mathematics as highly relevant to the Navy's mission, but perhaps this would not be so regarded in other sectors. Similarly, "NSF has been plagued since its inception by persons who ask how many of the supported projects can be justified and to what extent they relate to any conceivable national purpose. Scientists within the agencies feel that skepticism is due to a lack of understanding of what basic science is about and how it relates to the national purpose. The science administrator is caught between the scientist, who believes any scientific enquiry is justified, and skeptical citizens or Congressmen, who wonder how esoteric enquiries can warrant public fund support. As the pressure mounts, the research administrator finds applied research easier to justify than basic" (ibid.).

A more thorough analysis would demand that one faces a number of other practical problems: for example, how to deal with differences existing between basic and applied science in different fields, such as mathematics and cultural anthropology, or even physics and biology; how to prevent such political problems as either seeming to promise too much or incurring backlash when a problem turns out to be even more long-range and complex than originally foreseen on the most cautious model; or, for that matter, how to institutionalize the support of research in the combined mode in order to immunize it, at least during the early, vulnerable phase, from the axe of practical-minded budget cutters during a period of general retrenchment. As a top official of the OMB recently said, "Frankly, basic research is necessary in the long run, vulnerable in the short run." A good test case of this sort is the tortuous progress towards the fusion reactor, an effort in which a large component of fundamental research has been involved over a period of two decades without clearly reaching the promised goal of a limitless supply of energy with relatively low risk. The frustration that has been building up was captured in a recent comment by a Congressional aide: "There is a feeling that if you leave it to the scientists all the time, you won't get any energy out of it. It's becoming unacceptable to have an energy problem that costs half a billion dollars a year and doesn't produce anything."

[8]See, for example, *Science and Government Report, 9* (2) for February 1, 1979, and *Hearings Before the Subcommittee on Science, Technology, and Space, on Oversight on the Office of Science and Technology Policy,* March 7 and 21, 1979.

[9]Two Volumes; Government Printing Office, Superintendent of Documents, Washington, DC 20402, Stock Numbers 038-000-00442-5 and 038-000-00441-7.

[10]The legislative language requiring the NSF to prepare such volumes specifies that it "identify and describe situations and conditions which warrant special attention within the next five years, involving, (1) current and emerging problems of national significance that are identified through scientific research, or in which scientific or technical considerations are of major significance, and, (2) opportunities for, and constraints on, the use of new and existing scientific and technological capabilities which can make a significant contribution to the resolution of problems identified...or to the achievement or furthering of program objectives or national goals...."

[11]See Elzinga, Aant. The Swedish science discussion 1965—1975. *Social Indicators Research,* 1980, *7,* 379—99. The article is very interesting and, to many U.S. readers, will be disturbing. It also warns that "as pressure of sectorization increases, so does polarization of the scientific community into those who are receptive and those who resist this development." The opposition in fact contains not only the group "arguing from the idea of a free autonomous science based on liberal values," but also other groups, "often with a radical leftish social inclination, who oppose sectorization in its concrete form because the overall goals are determined by monopoly capitalist class interests" (p. 391).

[12]"The National Program for Science and Technology, 1978—1982." (CONACYT, Mexico, D.F., 1978) and Edmundo Flores, Mexico's program for science and technology, 1978—82. *Science,* 1979, *204,* 1279—82.

[13]For example, reports by George A. Pake and by Lewis M. Branscomb in *Physics Today,* April 1978 and April 1980, respectively.

[14]For representative brief descriptions, see the growth and development of STS education—three examples. *Science, Technology, and Human Values,* Spring 1980, *5,* 31—35. The programs described are those at Lehigh University, Stanford University, and M.I.T.

# Implementation of Computer Technology in the 1980s: A Semiconductor Perspective

## Charles H. Phipps

A recent survey article on microelectronics for the *Economist* magazine began with these comments:

> The following are among the unrealistic cliches being embedded in the public imagination:...commuting will become a distant memory; school children will learn their lessons electronically at home;...housewives will do their shopping at home...but will switch on their microwave ovens from their cars, etc....And all because of the ubiquitous electronic chip.

Now, if those opening remarks do not satisfy your desire for a balanced perspective, let me pass on to you the comments of George Heilmeier, our Vice-President of Corporate Research, Development and Engineering, regarding those who forecast the future. He quotes Lord Melbourne:

> What all the wise men promised has not happened, and what all the damned fools said would happen, has happened.

Now, I am not nearly as wise as George or those folks actually engaged in advancing technology, so I give you fair warning to beware of my remarks.

My perspective of technology changes is based on semiconductor technology. Semiconductor technology is among the major forces expanding and creating new applications for computers and the information revolution. In few previous periods of industrial history has any one technology created such extensive and rapid changes as semiconductor technology has over the past 20 years.

Now, this technology and its companions, computer and communication, are on the threshold of changing our personal lives: changing how we do our work, our shopping, and our learning; how we maintain our health and spend our leisure time. But there are major barriers to the realization of this potential. The barriers may substantially change both the form and the timing of this impact. However, all of these developments, if used properly, can be positive additions to the quality of our lives.

There are several questions that I will address in this presentation:

    1.   What is the nature of semiconductor technology that causes technologists to project so bold an impact?

    2.   How has this technology impacted computer technology?

    3.   What are some of the forces for changes in the 1980s, and how can these technologies respond to these challenges?

    4.   What are the barriers to realizing the full potential of these technologies?

    5.   What are some of the characteristics of technological change, particularly in the electronics field?

The physical form or appearance of electronic circuitry has changed substantially over the past 30 years (Figure 1). From the 1920s to 1950s, a span of some 40 years, an electronic circuit consisted of a vacuum tube and assemblage of some parts to go with it. Radio receivers generally used five to seven such circuits; television receivers, 20 to 30 circuits.

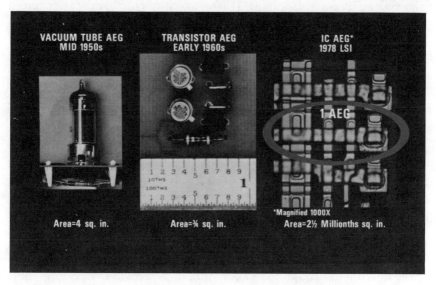

**Figure 1.** Advances in semiconductor technology

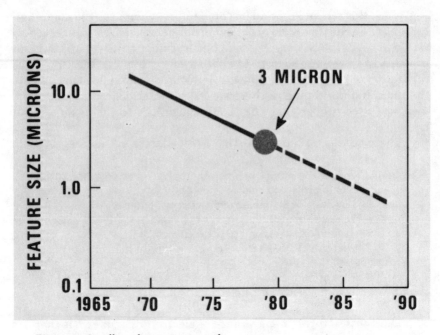

**Figure 2.** Smallest dimension trend

A transistor circuit is shown in the middle of Figure 1. Twenty-five years ago, the first transistorized radio was introduced. The transistor replaced only the vacuum tube, and electronic circuits still required an assemblage of parts around it. However, since the transistor required substantially less power, it was considerably smaller than the vacuum tube; it made possible the manufacture of computers containing thousands of logic circuits. In the 1960s, the integrated circuit was introduced, and now all portions of the electronic circuits were formed on the semiconductor material, as shown on the right of Figure 1.

One of the principal characteristics of semiconductor technology is the transfer of very complex patterns from photographic plates to the surface of a silicon slice. By various chemical processes, electronic circuits are formed within the semiconductor material precisely as defined by the photographic images. Over the years, there has been a steady trend decreasing the dimensions of the smallest feature of these images.

A decade ago, it was ten microns. Today, the smallest feature is about three microns, and by the mid-1980s to the latter part of the decade it will be one micron (Figure 2). A micron is one millionth of a meter, or about four 100,000ths of an inch. By comparison, the diameter of human hair is five to eight microns, and a pollen grain is in the range of one to three microns. Through the elimination of defects in the photographic plates, chemical processing, and the semiconductor material, the dimen-

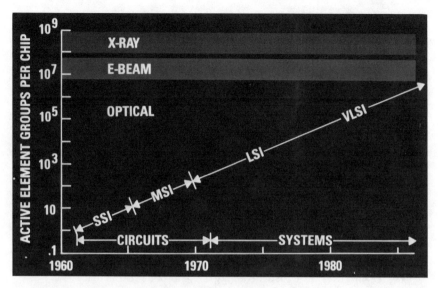

**Figure 3.** Semiconductor complexity trend

sions have decreased, as the useful area of the silicon has increased. These two factors have resulted in greater densities of electronic circuitry.

In Figure 3 we have an active element group (AE), which is essentially the same thing I called an electronic circuit. When integrated circuits were first placed in manufacture, almost 20 years ago now, their density was about one to ten circuits per device per package. By the early 1970s, they had progressed up to the range of 1,000 or so. Today, the state of the art is about 70,000 circuits per semiconductor device as contained in a package. As shown in Figure 3, we are approaching the practical limits of optically transferring the smallest features contained on these photographic plates, and during the 1980s we will have to switch to other means of imaging, such as electron beam and x-ray. This trend of increasing circuit complexity per device is expected to continue almost unabated at least through the next decade.

It is particularly significant that these processes are adaptable to very high volume manufacture. As a result, as circuit complexity has increased, the cost per circuit function has been dramatically reduced (Figure 4). This cost reduction, when applied to the logic and memory circuits of a computer, suggests that today a few thousand dollars of logic and memory circuitry functionally are equivalent to $50,000 of computer circuitry some ten years ago, and by the middle to late 1980s this same amount of logic and memory circuitry will probably be in the range of $100 or less (Figure 5).

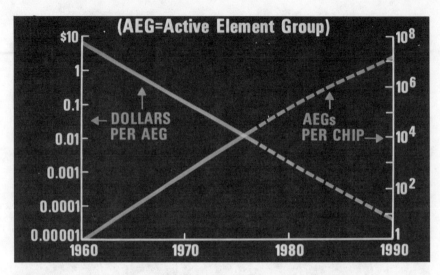

**Figure 4.** Lower user cost through greater product complexity

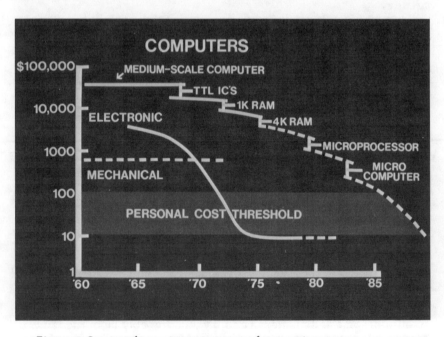

**Figure 5.** Semiconductor impact on cost of computing power

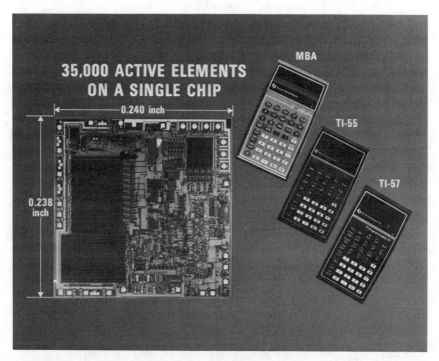

**Figure 6.** Scientific calculator—35,000 AEG's on a single chip

A photograph of a semiconductor integrated circuit used in a professional calculator is shown in Figure 6. It contains 35,000 logic and memory circuits within a silicon chip about a quarter on an inch square. That was used in professional calculators introduced in the 1976–77 time period.

A better understanding of the complexity of these logic and memory semiconductor devices can be obtained by comparing the circuitry and its interconnecting paths to a city block and the corresponding road network (Figure 7).

In the mid-1960s, the complexity of an integrated circuit was comparable to the street network of a small village, ten city blocks. By the early 1970s, its complexity was equivalent to that of a large suburban area. Today's LSI (large scale integrated circuits) circuits have logic and memory complexity comparable to the entire street network of Dallas and Fort Worth.

By the late 1980s, when one micron feature size is widely used, the circuit density will be comparable to a city street network covering all of Texas and its surrounding states. If you carry this analogy forward to the turn of the century, it may be possible to attain feature sizes on one-fourth micron, then silicon chips would have circuit complexities rivaling

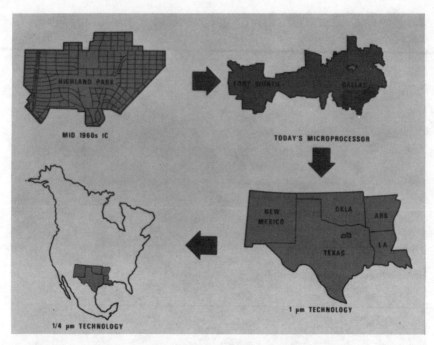

**Figure 7.** Complexity compared to high-density street network

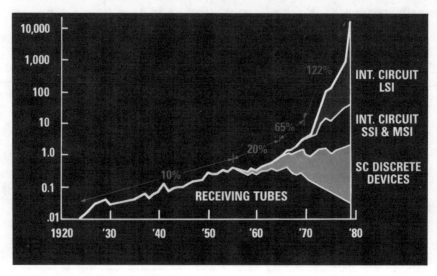

**Figure 8.** US small-signal AEGs

an urban network of streets that would cover much of the entire North American continent.

Now, another measure of the impact of semiconductor technology is the number of individual electronic circuits consumed each year in the United States. After 40 years of very modest 10 percent per year growth, which was largely the vacuum tube era, the number of electronic circuits in the 1970s increased at a rate of over 100 percent per year (Figure 8). The acceleration of electronic circuitry usage is linked to each technology advance.

Last year's consumption of over two trillion electronic circuits in the United States is not a comprehensible number, unless you compare it to the national debt. On a per capita basis, though, this is roughly 10,000 circuits for every person, or the equivalent of a fairly good scientific calculator for every person in the United States. Fifteen years ago, the per capita consumption of electronic circuits was about three circuits per person, or about one-half of a very simple radio receiver. By the year 1990, two million electronic circuits will be used in production of electronic equipment for every person in the United States. Two million electronic circuits are equivalent to a very good sized minicomputer system today. These comparisons provide a measure of the immense computing power that is going to be made economically available over the next decade. I'm not saying that we will produce a minicomputer system for every person in the United States, but it's that equivalency of computing power.

One reason for this very rapid growth of electronic circuitry is the development of semiconductor memories. Ten years ago it was too expensive to use semiconductor devices to perform memory circuit functions. This has changed, and today memory circuits represent 70 percent of all electronic circuits consumed. By 1990 that figure will increase to over 95 percent of all circuits consumed. The explosion in logic and consumption of electronic circuitry is really an insatiable appetite for memory.

The relationship of semiconductor technology to computer technology can be shown by relating its impact on the principal digital circuit functions used in the computers (Figure 9). In the late 1950s, transistors were used for the logic circuits of the early commercial computers.

By the mid-1960s, simple integrated circuits were being used for these logic circuits. In the early to mid-1970s, large scale integrated circuits (LSI) were being applied to memory functions, both those required for the permanent storage of instruction code, called read-only memories. In addition, they were also being used for temporary storage or random access memory. In addition, integrated circuits were also economical in regards to performance for many of the peripheral circuit functions found in the input and output equipments. These LSI devices

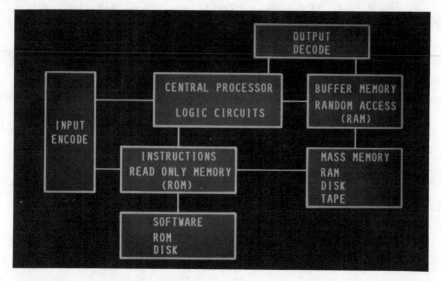

**Figure 9.** Digital circuit functions

of high complexity made it possible to offer very low-cost "computing" functions on a single semiconductor chip. This created the consumer calculator, the watch, the games, and a number of home appliance control applications throughout the past decade.

Semiconductor technology has also provided the coupling between these computer circuits and communications, which is the third leg of this information revolution. Its application may take the form of wired links, either fiber optics or coaxial cables, residences allowing two-way flow of pictures, graphics, data or messages. Or, it may involve low-cost earth satellite receivers, so that a large number of TV or communication channels may be received in the home. Semiconductor technology is providing light emitters and detectors for fiber optics links, high-frequency amplifiers and data acquisition circuits for coax links, and earth satellite receivers.

Before projecting the potential for the impact of semiconductor technology in the 1980s, it might be helpful to relate these developments to two consumer products introduced in the past decade. First, the simple digital watch gained widespread popularity in the mid-1970s. It accurately defines the passage of time in seconds, minutes, hours, days, and months (Figure 10). Further, it is programmed to recognize and identify the months of 28, 30, and 31 days; and when it has counted through 12 months of time, it identifies the passage of the year and restores its memory back to January first. This digital watch, right side of Figure 10, with its additional functions and its far greater accuracy is selling for

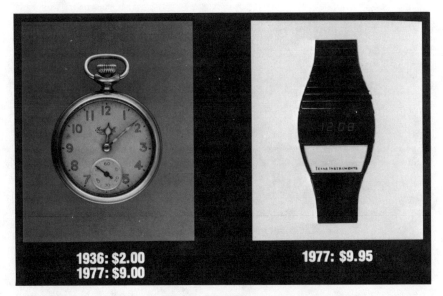

**Figure 10.** Digital watch versus popular mechanical watch

about the same real price as the $2.00 Ingersoll "Yankee" pocket watch of the middle 1930s, if the four and one-half times inflation of the past 40 years is taken into account.

Another example is the electronic slide rule calculator (Figure 11). It has approximately 5,000 circuit functions, it performs more functions with greater accuracy and ease than the K&E log-log duplex slide rule, which is so familiar to engineering students for the past 50 years. The slide rule in the late 1930s cost $12.50. If you relate those costs to current times, its cost would be about $60. This compares to the electronic slide rule calculator price of $25.

These examples illustrate an important attribute of electronics, particularly digital electronics, namely, the computer technology. Not only is the electronic product less costly than the prior art, but it has the potential to offer more functional capabilities, greater accuracy, and improved ease of use.

Now let's shift to the 1980s and look at four potential areas of impact: the office, the factory, the school, and the home. In each case, I will first describe some forces that may be the cause for change; then I'll talk about possible areas where electronic solutions will be technically and economically feasible. However, this is not a forecast. Instead, I am describing the potential for electronic solutions to respond to these challenges. What may actually take place is dependent upon overcoming nontechnical barriers that I will comment on a little later.

**Slide Rule**
**1933 : $12.50**
**1977 : $57.00**

**Electronic Slide Rule**
**Calculator**
**1977:  $24.95**

**Figure 11.** Calculator versus slide rule

Today the office worker is burdened by the impact of an information explosion, both in terms of paperwork and increasing communications. As a result, the picture in Figure 12 may be more typical than amusing.

In the face of these demands, office productivity increases have remained relatively low. The office is an unstructured environment, as compared to the manufacturing line, and the metrics for measurement of productivity are difficult to obtain. The investment per office worker is only about one-tenth that of the capital investment per manufacturing worker here in the United States. It remains at about $2,000 for the office employee, compared to $25,000 to $30,000 per factory worker. Solutions for the office will probably have to fit within this framework. It is unlikely that the tight capital base of the 1980s will allow any substantial shifts of capital from the factory to the office. Perhaps I am wrong, but that is one perception, even though office workers have become a large portion of the work force.

**Figure 12.** Information explosion impacts the office

Other forces for change include the limited availability of skilled clerical personnel and the increased costs for documentation preparation, storage, retrieval, and transmittal. It is estimated that office personnel spend over 60 percent of their time transforming data into information and 30 percent of their time communicating, copying, storing, and retrieving documents. Only the small remainder, some 5–10 percent, can be used for creative thought, for managing, or for planning of activities.

These major problems of the office worker require new solutions. Ways must be found to transform data into information more efficiently. The solution must be able to handle qualitative, as well as quantitative, information.

Now, what solutions might electronics offer? Electronic mail is rapidly approaching (Figure 13). Video display units with hard copy printers are replacing the typewriter. Inputs are edited, corrected, and reformatted without reducing them to paper; this information can also be transmitted and stored. The first phase of such a system is in place at Texas Instruments, sending over 100,000 messages per week via electronic network to plants throughout the world. Today, this is a message system. Future generations will allow pictorial information to be accessed, transmitted, and stored.

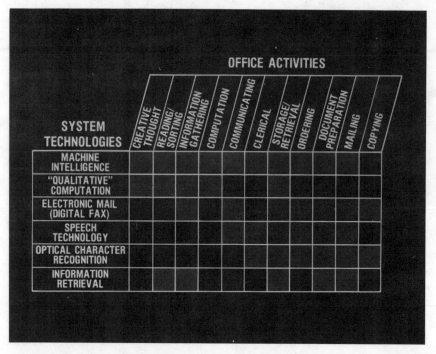

**Figure 13.** Potential electronic solutions in the office

There are other aspects of the office environment that restrict technical solutions. First, any restrictions on flexibility and individuality are likely to be resisted. Second, while technology may be fashionable on the factory floor, it is not respected in the office. In other words, people are not going to adapt their ways to those of the machine; instead, the machine must be capable of adapting to the people.

Speech technology, optical character recognition, and facsimile will aid in making office systems easier to use. However, these potential electronic solutions must allow the use of more natural interfaces between the office worker and the electronic equipment, such as free-form questions and simple query/response access to information. Most people will not make the effort to learn "computerese"; nor will the schools teach them. Sometime in the 1980s, greater logic and memory capacity will allow people to use a more natural language interaction with electronic data bases. When this solution is coupled to low-cost electronics to meet the capital investment per office worker threshold, then the "electronics" revolution will have its impact on the office.

Now, let's turn to the factory. Although electronics had been present on the factory floor for over a decade, its use has really been limited to test systems, control of individual operating stations for high-volume runs, and support systems for scheduling material and inventory control.

**Figure 14.** Electronic robot on calculator assembly line

The forces for change in the factory include:

- Decreasing productivity and loss of U.S. manufacturers' competitive position in world markets.
- Declining availability of workers who will perform the menial or dirty tasks.
- A demand for increased quality.
- Rapid shifts in the relative value of labor, material, capital, and energy.
- Major changes in the cost of distribution of goods and services versus the manufacturing economy of scale for many piece-part assembly operations.

Some statistics for manufacturing are helpful in assessing the opportunity:

- Over 70 percent of U.S. manufacturing operations are performed for production runs of less than 100 units. Dedicated automation equipment is not cost-effective under such circumstances.
- Conventional or general purpose machinery is actually performing or "doing" the job for only about 10 percent of the time; the

remainder is spent in loading, unloading, and setup times.
- Inspections and testing are manpower intensive.

Electronics technology has the potential to shift factory operations in a major way during the next ten years. Intelligent robots are in an early application phase at Texas Instruments (Figure 14). They offer versatility not permitted by dedicated automation equipment and can be cost-effective for operations when the product mix changes frequently.

By the mid-1980s, machine tools could have voice control for prompting, in addition to the senses of touch and sight. Such tools could diagnose themselves when they need repair or replacement.

Visual inspection, as well as placement of parts for work stations, will be performed more and more by electronic cameras. These intelligent camera inspection systems will work in concert with robots. They will check parts for orientation, recognize features and colors, and read numbers.

In education, which includes primary schools, high schools, and adult vocational training, there are several strong challenges to be met:

- The lack of discipline in the schools, which makes it difficult to teach in the traditional "one on many" approach.
- The dilution of teacher productivity and effectiveness due to assignment of many mundane tasks and paperwork.
- Students who must learn in what they perceive as a sterile and unimaginative environment, after growing up with excellent visual aids, such as color TV.
- A significant portion of the adult work force, perhaps as high as 20 percent, being essentially functionally illiterate.

There are potential electronic answers for these challenges. Instead of expensive mainframe-based, computer-aided instruction, products that are priced between the cost of a book and a typewriter have strong promise to impact the educational and adult training process. They will be purchased by the parents, as well as schools, and they will restimulate "drill" and self-paced instructions.

The first-generation learning aids for math and spelling are already on the market (Figure 15). The next generation of electronic learning aids will appear on the market within the next few years, and they cover a broader range of subjects: reading, grammar, foreign languages, writing, and music.

The home computer and its successive generations, including interactive communications, is another major opportunity (Figure 16). With their impressive color graphics, coupled with imaginative software and massive storage media, they could become indispensible tools in the schools, as well as the home, and be priced at no more than an electric typewriter.

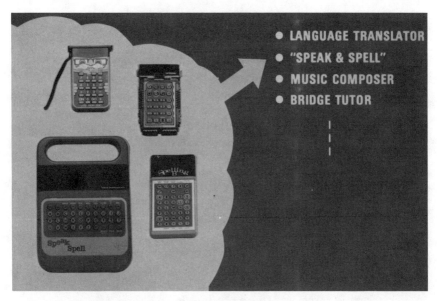

**Figure 15.** Electronic learning aids

**Figure 16.** Home computer

Such learning instruments will provide technology-driven answers to the problems of patient drill-and-practice tutoring and individually paced instruction.

Within the home, as well as in personal use, intelligent electronic products have the potential for a broad range of applications. Electronics will allow homeowners the capability of controlling their environment more directly than ever before: appliances will be operated according to the user's preprogrammed instructions and security may be provided by sensors and speech-controlled alarm systems that can be polled from remote locations.

The introduction of wideband communications into the home has a significant potential when coupled with low-cost, high-storage media. The use of such media, together with interactive home terminals to replace mail order catalogues, is a distinct possibility in the 1980s.

Wideband communications into the home will also provide low-cost access to common data bases for instructions, electronic mail, transaction processing, diagnostics for appliances, or information regarding personal health, legal matters, travel arrangements, and so forth.

The driving forces for these changes in the home are:

1.   The increased cost of shelter and energy, affecting the size of the home, its location, and travel to and from work. More people will be staying near their homes, which will probably be smaller and have less privacy.

2.   Two family incomes: allowing less time for household chores, requiring more specialization within the family, and creating the need for improved security since the premises will be unoccupied for longer periods of time.

3.   Rapid increases in the cost of services: maintenance, health, legal, travel, or whatever myriad of personal services that a highly specialized society may develop.

In the long run, by the end of this century, electronics in the home may provide a more "personalized" home environment, rather than a mechanical, impersonal one. Conceptually, it is possible that electronics could offer programs to reinforce creativity flairs in the arts, provide timely risk assessment for potential actions, and evaluate the individual's strengths and weaknesses in selected areas and then program course material accordingly.

As the homeowner adapts to these electronic applications, the average number of electronic circuits in the home will increase from about one thousand today to almost one-half million by 1990 (Figure 17). When these potentials are added to the potential applications in offices, school, and factory, the projection of two million electronic circuits per capita in 1990 may not only be a reasonable estimate, but perhaps even a conservative one.

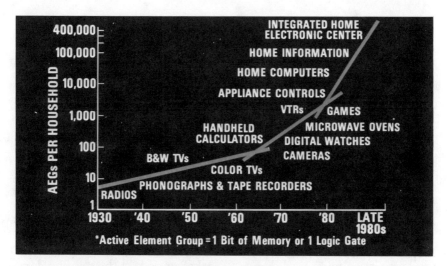

**Figure 17.** Buildup of AEGs in average home

These applications for the office, factory, school, and home are, again, cited only as *potential* applications. There is no assurance that they, indeed, will take place.

There are a number of barriers, principally nontechnical in nature, that must be overcome. Some of these barriers are: inertia (cultural and institutional), economic environment, regulations, and practitioners.

Inertia. This includes the personal patterns of selecting home locations, leisure activities, transportation modes, and communications networks for work and shopping. Some of these patterns may be a very strong part of society's underlying culture, and individuals may wish to pay a much greater price to continue them for longer than we anticipate.

Similarly, institutional practices and organization structures often strongly resist change. Here, the competitive forces generated by leading firms in each industry segment are a counterforce to the more resistant areas to adapt within a limited period of time.

The economic wherewithal must be available for both the user and the supplier to make these changes. Of particular concern for the United States in the 1980s is the availability of capital stock required both for production of electronics, as well as capital for replenishing the current manufacturing, office, and, perhaps, school base. The 1980s could be one of those critical junctures in the history of economic development that will determine our country's competitive position in the world markets for the next 30 to 50 years.

Regulatory barriers are imposed by federal and state agencies in order to prevent abuses of the general public by individuals and institutions. However, their practice has often had damaging long-term consequences. Some of these are:

- They are apt to preselect solutions, rather than to set goals or objectives.
- Some of the older agencies perpetuate the status quo of an industry, essentially representing the practitioners, rather than the public.
- There is a tendency to pursue a "zero-risk" course due to either the pressures of single-issue activist groups, or more often, fear of rebuke from congressional committees at some future date, who have the advantage of hindsight.

And, particularly, regulatory agencies are not institutions of executive responsibility and action; rather, they are organizations that are based upon divided responsibility, usually of equal political parity, and they are prone to adversarial debate and inaction.

The principal barrier, though, is neither with the individual user nor government regulatory bodies. It is the practitioners of technology. This challenge is to understand the user's real need, so that the solution does indeed provide real value, rather than just another product reflecting technology for technology's sake. The existence of electronics in the future products must be apparent to the user. The "input" and "output" interfaces must be in friendly and familiar language to the nontechnical person, so that the user's principal thought is on examining the information he needs, rather than on the method of extracting and developing that information.

In closing, there are several observations from the history of technical changes that are worth noting, and they may be helpful to ensuing discussions. The changes can be categorized as developments in electronics markets: (1) an extension of the electronics art, (2) the displacement of prior technology, and (3) the fulfillment of new needs.

First, these changes occur as rather rapid events, rather than slowly evolving as measured, not from the time of the basic inventions, but some time thereafter when the producers of products using the technology have crossed an economic threshold, and where the users have recognized needs and the means for implementing them. As examples:

- The initial impact of electrical power generation and distribution took place within the 30 years prior to World War I.
- The automobile attained widespread impact within 20 years after Henry Ford's first assembly line.
- Television gained major coverage of households within then years in the mid-1950s. The conversion of commercial air transport from prop-driven planes of 500–1,000 mile flights to large jets covering distances of 5,000 to 10,000 miles also occurred essentially within a ten-year span of time.

Second, although the initial applications of new technical solutions are often adaptations to stand-alone requirements, their real impact is realized only when existing systems or structures are reordered, or when new systems are created to fully take advantage of the new technology's potential. It is this "system's interdependency," both foreseen and unforeseen, that brings the issue of technology change into the arena of public debate.

Finally, it is the nature of electronics, more specifically computer technology, that a critical level of complexity is necessary before the initial application can be made. But once this threshold is crossed, there is an explosion of functional capabilities that can take place and can be added at very small incremental costs.

I have discussed with you the nature of semiconductor technology, the forces of change, the potential for electronic solutions in four major market areas, and the barriers to technology change, as well as the characteristics of technology developments.

I would like to summarize the issues and challenges of the 1980s for industry, education, and government.

For industry the first challenge is the leadership for timely investment in both computer technology and its applications, so that United States' industry will remain competitive in world markets. Second, electronics must be made easy to use and not have the "computerese" interface of today's products. And, third, personnel must be trained and educated throughout their careers, not only for design and manufacture of the product, but, particularly, for application and servicing.

In education, the future will require, first, the effective use of low-cost learning instruments, as well as computer-aided instruction in the classroom and in the home, so there will be a larger base of educable adults in the work force. Second, more basic R&D in the physical sciences must be pursued either through industry or government sponsorship. And, third, university education, particularly in science and technology, faces a difficult challenge to advance the excellence of training during a period of severe financial pressure. A semiconductor processing laboratory of any consequence today is a multimillion dollar investment, probably $10 to $20 million for an educational institution, and requires updating every three years or so. Computer facilities, particularly in new areas of applications such as speech, optical recognition, machine intelligence or artificial intelligence, and development of natural languages, are also multimillion dollar investments that must be renewed every three to five years.

In the government area, the first challenge is to make the economic environment conducive to longer range investments; both inflation and many of our tax regulations pull the horizon into the near term. There must be greater motivation for capital formation and for more R&D to be performed by industry and universities. Second, the trade and regulatory barriers for computer technology cannot be viewed within the isolation of U.S. markets. Computer technology is really information skills; it is not based on a natural resource or labor availability, and with today's dispatch of communications and commerce, these skills are rapidly being transferred throughout the industrialized world.

My principal conclusion is that there will be an abundance of low-cost "logic and memory" for the remainder of the century. Potential applications will challenge our conventional thinking of how this logic and memory will interface with us in various classes of applications. A number of applications have been suggested, yet these applications that are talked about do not really present a coherent perspective of the full impact and ramification of this technology over the next 30 years or longer.

This coherent perspective was better described by Pat Haggerty, our Honorary Chairman of Texas Instruments, in a talk several years ago (1977):

> ... as his mind is aided and expanded by the inexpensive and increasingly complex elements of electronic logic and memory—elements known to us for a few decades in computers—man will be an even more different and powerful creature. Man so equipped, his muscles multiplied by his tools, his mobility extended to the boundaries of the planet and beyond, his mind and memory dynamically expanded by electronics, is in a completely different relationship with his environment from his predecessors. When he has been so equipped for generation after generation, he will, in a very real sense, be evolving into a different species.
>
> When the knowledge and the skill to use these extraordinarily powerful electronic tools are broadly dispersed and associated with the creation and the operation of the institutions to preserve, enhance, and transmit that knowledge and skill to succeeding generation after generation, they become a kind of evolutionary development that can have an impact on man and his environment of a scale we have customarily associated with the passage of eras of time measured in millions of years....

## REFERENCE

Haggerty, Patrick E. Shadow and substance, May 25, 1977, Semicon/West Annual Banquet, San Francisco.

# A Congressional View of the Coming Information Age

## The Honorable George E. Brown, Jr., Member of Congress

I would like to preface my remarks, which will attempt to give a Congressional view of the coming Information Age, with some general comments about technology and its role in our society. I begin with the premise, which I take to be self-evident today, that there are limits to material production and consumption, and that these limits are not nearly as remote as many of us once thought. Given this world of finite resources, the goal of improving the efficiency and productivity of our industry and commerce, while at the same time conserving energy and the environment, becomes paramount. It follows that any technological development must be carefully and thoroughly evaluated for its potential contribution to productivity goals.

Productivity, in its turn, is important because it is essential in achieving a still more fundamental goal—improving the quality of life of our citizens. Technology assessments, therefore, do not take place in a social vacuum, but in the atmosphere of a broadly shared vision of the future, a vision that reflects our highest concepts of the good life, in effect, our view of utopia. In seeking to implement this vision, we need to ask what technologies are appropriate to it and to determine the most effective way to use them.

It is false economy indeed to employ a certain technology for no better reason than that money and effort have been expended in developing it. In choosing which technologies to develop and use, important societal and environmental impacts, such as the degree of acceptability of the technology by the work force, or the amount of centralization or decentralization resulting from its application, must be carefully considered and anticipated.

In the past 15 or 20 years there has been no more spectacular technological development than in the ability to process, store, and transmit great quantities of information at an extremely rapid rate. My own vision of the future suggests that what we have come to call information technology will have effects on the way we live, and even on the way we think, that are truly deserving of the much overused term "revolutionary."

My principal reason for advancing this perhaps extravagant claim is the mounting body of evidence that many forms of information technology already meet the test I have proposed for technology assessment—increased efficiency and productivity, small inputs of energy for large outputs of product, and minimal environmental disruption. Although the track record of some of the newer forms of information technology, such as videodiscs and interactive cable television, is not yet established, I think that few here will quarrel with the general proposition that the anticipated economic benefits, which have been the driving force for the development of information technology, are being realized in a wide variety of settings. In industry, these technologies have resulted in enhanced productivity and in savings of precious energy resources. In the near future, individuals in their homes will benefit economically from such technologies as direct satellite broadcast and cable television, videotext and videodiscs, bringing news, consumer information, educational programs, films and a wide range of other entertainment into the home. There is increasing evidence that educational and health delivery systems will find cost-effective ways of reaching remote areas, and of augmenting existing instructional and clinical services, through the capabilities of new information technology.

I hasten to add, however, that increasing capital investment in information systems will not automatically result in productivity gains, partly because information techology can be used to *create* information, as well as to process information generated elsewhere. Increasing productivity through information technology will require the use of this technology by "knowledge workers" to assist in analysis and evaluation, not simply to process and transfer information.

In anticipating the "Information Revolution," we need to remind ourselves that every revolution has its victims. I want to reemphasize my earlier position that economic considerations cannot only be the only basis for evaluating the future of information technology. We must learn to deal with the information explosion equitably and humanely, not just efficiently. I will have more to say about this later, but I would like first to describe to you some ways in which Congress is attempting to deal with information questions and what I see emerging as the major issues of the next decade.

In the House of Representatives, the Committee on Science and Technology has the major responsibility for scientific and technological issues. My Subcommittee on Science, Research and Technology has jurisdiction over a large portion of federally supported scientific and technological research and development and over broad issues of science policy. Roughly speaking, our counterpart on the Senate side is Senator Stevenson's Subcommittee on Science, Technology and Space; the jurisdictions are not quite the same, but the overlap is considerable. During the life of the Ninety-sixth Congress, no issue has been more central to my subcommittee program than the need to increase the productivity and innovative capacity of U.S. industry. Part of our effort in this area has gone into strengthening the interactions among the three components of the research and development triad represented at this meeting—industry, academia, and government. We see a particular need for improving links between universities and industry, and we are beginning to address this problem through the programs of the National Science Foundation. The establishment of new institutions is also under consideration: a bill I have introduced, calling for the creation of a National Technology Foundation, would, in my opinion, encourage a fruitful interaction between industry and the federal government.

This need for new and more effective partnerships in scientific endeavors is equally evident within the Congress itself. Technological issues, and especially those related to information and communications, extend well beyond the concerns of a single subcommittee and even well beyond the view of the Science and Technology Committee. In April of 1980, my subcommittee joined with the Subcommittee on Select Education of the Education and Labor Committee to stage two days of hearings and a workshop for 150 participants on the use of information technology in education, an area that will have a great influence on our society's ability—or inability—to cope with the problems of the coming age. As another example, the development and operation of communications and remote sensing satellites, in which I have a keen interest, involves me both as a member of the Space Science and Applications Subcommittee, which oversees NASA and satellite research and development, and as a member of the Subcommittee on the Environment and Natural Resources, which oversees the National Oceanic and Atmospheric Administration's satellite programs. A different side of satellite communications, the regulatory question, is dealt with in another committee altogether.

There is another class of issues that impact heavily on scientific research and development. These are issues that our committee has addressed through legislative action and oversight hearings but in which the principle committee jurisdiction lies elsewhere. This range of issues includes, in addition to regulatory policies, such things as patent and tax policy. The precise effect of current and proposed statutes in these areas on productivity is a subject of considerable controversy, often resulting in much more heat than light, but obviously these are questions of importance. In addressing them coherently the Congress will have to learn to put important considerations of national economic well-being above the jurisdictional squabbles that sometimes hinder our approach to complicated issues.

We consider our approach rational, but we would do well to heed the words of Kenneth Boulding:

> The great danger of rationality is, of course, suboptimization; that is, finding and choosing the best position of part of the system which is not the best for the whole. Too many people, indeed, and especially too many experts, devote their lives to finding the best way of doing something that should not be done at all (1971, p. 32).

In assessing technological impacts, Congress now has an important resource to draw upon, the Office of Technology Assessment. OTA is now nearing completion of a major study in telecommunications, in which predictions are made for future technological developments and for societal impacts under several different scenarios for regulatory action. Other OTA studies almost finished are concerned with prospects for and impacts of electronic mail and electronic funds transfer. As a member of the Technology Assessment Board, I am anxious to see OTA develop its excellent promise as a major Congressional resource, a promise that, thus far in its rather young life, has not been completely fulfilled.

In addition to OTA's work, the Congressional Research Service recently prepared, at my direction, a study of communications and information technologies and their uses. As a result of all these studies Congress will soon have available to it a substantial information base, which will be useful in developing legislative initiatives.

In what areas are legislative initiatives likely to be forthcoming? I will offer you my personal view of some of the issues confronting Congress in the next decade in the information field, but I would not be so rash as to predict in detail what the Congress, in its infinite wisdom, will do about them. I have, rather arbitrarily, identified six principle issues of concern, most of them of course overlapping several others.

First is the major issue of the role of the government in research and development of information technology. The extent and nature of government-industry cooperation is a key aspect of this question. Some have cited the impressive advances of the Japanese in information technology as evidence that a closer government-industry partnership, or cooperative industrial research programs, is needed. In the semiconductor industry, for example, it has been argued that standardization of existing wafer fabrication processes is needed if U.S. firms are to remain competitive with foreign companies. Some help may be forthcoming here from the National Bureau of Standards, which plans to establish new standards for VLSI processes and measurement methods. Tax incentives for investment and a revised patent policy are seen by many as essential to the vitality of information technology R&D. (The Senate has now passed legislation making it easier for small firms to retain the rights to patentable government-supported discoveries; related legislation is now pending in the House.)

In the computer industry, the development of "supercomputers" utilizing VLSI technology and, further down the line, Josephson junctions, will require a considerable risk of capital for hardware design and development and will need substantial advances in programming techniques. This new generation of computers will be important for scientific research, for the development of low-cost home terminals—permitting self-directed exploration and investigation by the recipient—for teletext and viewdata, and for many other applications. Another very promising area of research and development is the videodisc, which, particularly in its digital form, offers immense data storage capabilities and, in combination with microcomputers, has great potential for educational applications. Exploiting the videodisc's capabilities will require the creation of complex and sophisticated access systems. In the telecommunications field, fiber optics technology, with its rapidly decreasing cost curve, will probably become cost-effective for short-range, high-capacity, two-way transmission systems.

In all of these areas, and others, we need to determine the adequacy of private sector research and development initiatives and to provide government support in places where private investment cannot do the job alone. This category will include, in particular, a good deal of basic research, including certain aspects of "human factors" research. Although there is intense private activity in "humanizing the man-machine interface" through audio input and improved graphics capabilities, there is much to be learned about how people organize and access knowledge and how they will interact with others and with machines in a highly automated environment.

Another problem of concern of government is the deteriorating position of the universities in research and development in computer science and systems development. The Feldman Report and other studies have made it clear that universities are experiencing serious problems in funding the acquisition and upgrading of computer systems and in attracting and maintaining highly qualified computer scientists. The maintenance of a healthy research effort in our universities in information science and technology is a serious concern. This year's budget for the National Science Foundation, if it survives the Congress, contains important funding increases in this area, and I am hopeful that the declining position of the universities can be arrested.

The second issue on my agenda for the 1980s is the role of the government in applications of information technology. The government may affect societal evolution by funding experimental demonstrations in information and communications technology that probably would not be developed without government support and that have the potential to effect significant change if they are widely adopted. For example, NASA's experiments with the ATS-6 and CTS satellites have been of great value, and current research aimed at opening the 20/30 GHZ frequency band offers the possibility of greatly expanding satellite communications capacity.

I am thinking here in particular of demonstration projects involving satellite transmission and other technologies in the public service sector—education, health care, and emergency services. Satellite technology affords an excellent means of moving large quantities of data very quickly, over long distances. It is already an economical means of one-way information dissemination over "thin routes." With larger and more sensitive antennae, combined with small, low-cost earth stations, two-way telecommunications involving small groups in relatively isolated environments could become cost effective (Resnikoff, 1980). The pattern in public service satellite transmission seems to have been that the projects are initiated mainly with government funds, with increasing private sector involvement and gradual government withdrawal as the technology matures and the market becomes dense enough to support private ventures on a profit-making basis. The experiences of the Public Service Satellite Consortium and the Alaska Telecommunications Project provide examples of this pattern. I believe, however, that an important role remains for the federal government here, particularly in aggregating a rather disparate user community and in developing multipurpose systems. I see an important opportunity for the relatively new National Telecommunications and Information Administration in market aggregation and funding of demonstration projects, and an opportunity for the even newer Federal Emergency Management Administration to create a unified emergency services communications system—using advanced satellite technology—which could serve as a useful prototype for other multipurpose systems.

Third on my agenda is an issue that has potential to become a major Congressional battleground of the decade—regulatory policy in the information and communications industries. One of the most obvious characteristics of recent technological advance is the convergence of information technology and communications. Computers now communicate, and communications networks now compute. The technological possibilities created by microprocessors and digital information transmission are immense. IBM is getting into communications, through its Satellite Business Systems venture with COMSAT and Aetna; meanwhile AT&T is entering into data processing. COMSAT, once content with satellite communications, is exploring possibilities for broadcasting television direct from satellites to homes and has just purchased a firm engaged in environmental data-gathering through satellite remote sensing.

These developments present policy makers with some hard choices. The postal and telephone monopolies will soon be threatened by competitive services combining these functions. The establishment and regulation of these monopolies was accomplished to assure universal, inexpensive service. Will the new competitors skim the cream of the market, leaving only the unprofitable services? And, with home information systems such as teletext soon to be available, is it in the public interest that the same company might not only act as a carrier, but also be responsible for the information content? The increasing indistinguishability of traditionally regulated communications services and traditionally unregulated data processing activities makes it painfully clear that the Communications Act of 1934, which has been the statutory underpinning for regulatory activity to date, is in need of major surgery. The FCC has already taken several steps to ease regulatory restrictions and to make the information/communications industry more competitive, but a comprehensive approach requires new legislation. My colleague Lionel Van Deerlin of California has been struggling for years to rewrite this Act; the difficulties he has encountered have been so formidable that the latest rewrite concentrates entirely on regulation of carriers and leaves broadcast regulation unchanged. Whatever the fate of this legislation, and it appears uncertain indeed at this writing, regulatory policy has a long way to go to catch up with today's technology.

Fourth on my agenda is the issue of computer networks and data bases. My interest in this subject begins with my subcommittee's jurisdiction over scientific and technical information. The progress made in science information systems over the past few years has been substantial, particularly in upgrading information systems in the various disciplines and in federal agencies. During the same period, scientific and technical information services have emerged in the for-profit part of the private sector. Computerized data bases have proliferated in every branch of science and technology, and on-line interactive computer networking systems are rapidly being developed. No doubt all of you are familiar with such examples as ARPANET, MEDLARS, and Lockheed's DIALOG, but there are many lesser-known successful examples, such as the Regional Energy/Environment Information Center in Denver, which uses data bases developed by the Department of Energy, and the Government Industrial Data Exchange Program, a data bank maintained by the Fleet Missile Analysis Center at Norco, California to provide information on materials characteristics to defense contractors.

Despite these encouraging developments, I believe we need to do much more in the way of linking data bases and encouraging the formation of networks, if we are to make economical and timely use of information and avoid wasteful duplication. I say this with some caution because there are some serious questions that must be addressed in the creation of networks. One such question concerns the possible usurpation by government of the legitimate function of private sector information transfer systems. This issue is not easily evaded, because information, in addition to being a resource in itself, is also a prerequisite to the development and allocation of other resources. As such government has an important stake in its dissemination.

Under what circumstances, then, should the federal government create information networks? According to the "Rockefeller Committee" report (*National Information Policy*, 1976), it should establish them only in those cases where they are needed but do not exist, where private entrepreneurs are not equipped to establish them, and where they are needed to further governmental missions and responsibilities. The report concludes that the determination of whether these considerations apply to particular cases will be difficult—but it needs to be done.

Another problem area in the creation of information networks is a basically healthy public distrust of too much centralization. Information is increasingly regarded as a resource convertible to political power, and the specter of a massive central data bank controlled by Strangelovian technocrats haunts many of those who think about these networks. The stillbirth of one proposed government network, the late FEDNET, is attributable in large measure to such apprehensions. Some even doubt the technical feasibility of creating large, reliable networks; recent disclosures of the inadequacies of the Defense Department's WWMCCS system have given skeptics much food for thought. It should be noted, however, that the WMMCCS system is not very interactive and does not embody the latest networking capabilities.

I don't believe that huge centralized data banks will have a role in our information future. Somewhere between the scenario of a single multipurpose network and the chaotic jumble of noninterconnected systems that is the likely result of continued inaction lies a more rational middle ground—a more or less coherent system of networks, each with many low-cost terminals, with protocols and interfaces to permit intersystem communication when necessary.

Achieving a sufficient level of coherence without sacrificing privacy and security will be difficult. It will require some governmental intervention in setting equipment standards and in developing adequate safeguards against unauthorized access. The National Bureau of Standards is beginning to address these problems through such steps as the development of encryption and decoding standards.

This brings me to the fifth item on my agenda. I have been describing a number of issues I think are proper and necessary concerns of Congress in the information field. What we do not yet have is any workable approach to bringing these threads together to plan a coherent national policy for the management of our information resources. Some elements of such a policy are coming into place; for example, in March, 1980, the House passed what could be a very important piece of legislation, the Paperwork Reduction Act, developed by my colleague Jack Brooks and the Government Operations Committee. Don't let the name fool you; it really should be called the Government Information Management Act. One of its features is the creation of a Federal Information Locator System to locate existing information and to identify duplication in agencies' reporting and record-keeping requirements. Another is the establishment in the Office of Management and Budget (OMB) of a focal point for information concerns, the Office of Federal Information Policy. This bill is a useful step toward developing a national information policy. But there are other information concerns, particularly in scientific and technical information, which are not addressed by the Paperwork Reduction Act. As with information management in general, approaches to the management of scientific and technical information have been ad hoc and piecemeal. Agencies have not considered in a systematic way the impacts of their actions on government-wide information problems. Other legislative initiatives are needed that address the storage, access, and dissemination of scientific and technical information obtained through federally funded research. An important component of such legislation must be the centralizing of responsibility for scientific and technical information policy activities in an appropriate governmental unit. The management functions of OMB under the Paperwork Reduction Act will have to be carefully coordinated with the actions of the Office of Science and Technology Policy, which has statutory responsibility for research, planning, and coordination of scientific and technical information activities.

I think that there are many reasons why such legislative initiatives have been slow in coming. One reason is that scientific information activities have traditionally been decentralized in this country; there is an understandable aversion on the part of the science information community toward top-down, imposed solutions, and a general distrust of federal control. Another is that high-level officials, busy with concerns other than information, are not yet convinced that national information problems are serious enough to require that something be done. It has been pointed out that in an information-rich world, the wealth of information implies the scarcity of that which the information consumes—the attention of the recipient. Attention is scarce at top levels of government: information is everybody's problem, hence nobody's responsibility.

Despite these difficulties, I think there are compelling reasons why we need to begin to plan for a national information policy. Information is an important national resource: the information industry, by whatever definition, has grown into a large and important sector of the national and international economy. By one estimate (Porat, 1977), approximately half of our work force is now engaged in information-related occupations, broadly defined. I have already described the important role played by information in improving the productivity and innovative capacity of U.S. industry. In addition to its economic impact, access to information has important consequences for social organization. Changing the available flow of information may alter traditional relationships among individuals and private and public organizations; for example, the collection of heretofore proprietary health and safety information has affected relationships between industry and the federal government. The social impact of information technology and its effect on information access is a vitally important and largely unstudied component of information policy.

I alluded briefly earlier to the last point on my information agenda for the 1980s—international information issues. As the information and communications sectors of the economies of the developed nations grow in importance and the information needs of developing countries increase, information policy is certain to play a major foreign policy role in the next decade. Developing countries realize the absolute necessity of access to information in a usable form if they are to attain true self-sufficiency and independence. The creation of an indigenous scientific and technological capability in the Third World is the only way these countries can deal with many of the problems facing them, and an adequate information base is the only way to establish this capability. Nevertheless, advanced information technologies are often viewed with suspicion as well as envy by the developing world, since they represent both fulfillment of a critical need and increased potential for domination by the developed world. The gap between "information rich" and "information poor" countries is potentially as dangerous as past economic inequities.

The apprehensions of the developing countries over the prospect of information inequity have found political voice in the call for a New World Information Order. There was considerable concern before the recent World Administrative Radio Conference (WARC) that the meeting would be polarized into a rhetorical confrontation between developed and Third World nations over information and communications policies. Fortunately, little of this occurred and WARC was at least moderately successful in achieving its goals. Nonetheless, we have a long and doubtless difficult road ahead in making our way through the series of specialized international conferences to follow WARC.

I consider our participation in these conferences, and more generally our role in helping to develop and manage information and communications systems in the Third World nations, to be a foreign policy matter of high priority. I believe that we have obligations, implicit in our technological leadership, and explicit in commitments made at the 1976 UNESCO meeting in Nairobi and since renewed, to ensure that the less developed countries will benefit from this technology in ways that meet their own needs. I see exciting possibilities here in the area of satellite communications systems; for example, these will allow some developing countries to leapfrog over the copper wire and microwave relay stage of communication development. Without an extensive infrastructure in place, these countries have the opportunity to plan from scratch and to avoid much of the costly retrofitting required in developed countries. The bold program in satellite communications being undertaken by the People's Republic of China with our assistance might serve as a model for the developing world. Communications satellites also provide the technological capability to make an international information system, like the UNESCO-proposed World Science Information System, a reality. Another area in which we can be of assistance is in training personnel to manage and interpret environmental data from LANDSAT and future remote sensing satellites. Such data is already of great use to developing nations in development and management of resources, and improved capability in using the data would be a valuable asset.

We need to approach these efforts with some care, however, in order to avoid the "technological arrogance" of many past technology transfer programs and to tailor our aid to meet the needs of developing countries. Initiatives must be chosen that meet the development needs of the Third World and provide benefits to the developed countries as well. We must also tread with care on the sensitive terrain of national sovereignty over data inflow and outflow. Already several European countries have adopted restrictions on transborder flow of personal data, and a number of developing nations have voiced apprehension over the remote sensing of their resources by U.S. satellites. On another front, the prospect of direct satellite television broadcast into foreign countries raises quite legitimate questions of cultural and political impact: the United Nations is presently trying to shape agreements for operation of direct broadcast systems, but the task will not be an easy one.

Apart from the foreign policy aspects of international information policy, there are narrower economic concerns that are of great importance. Traditionally, most of our scientific and technical information has been openly available to other countries. On the other hand, this information represents a valuable commodity that, many feel, must be protected and cultivated. The tensions resulting from the opposing forces of free information flow and practices aimed at recovering dissemination and development costs can no longer be ignored in the face of increasing foreign competition in all aspects of the information field. In remote sensing, the French, the Canadians, and the Japanese will soon be equipped to offer services, some components of which will probably be government-subsidized to enhance their competitive positions. The European Space Agency now has the capability to launch satellites and will be competing in communications services. The computer trade press is full of stories on increased Japanese competition for the 16K Random Access Memory market. All of these developments reinforce the reality that the information field is no longer a U.S. monopoly. The difficult international information issues confronting us make it all the more important that we begin work on a strategic national plan for the development and management of our information resources.

After this rather long-winded prospectus of information issues facing our government, and Congress in particular, I want to close by expanding a bit on my personal vision of our information future and on some concerns generated by the transition to an information society. At the beginning of my presentation, I stated my conviction that we need to assess technologies in terms of their ability to improve the quality of life and to ask the fundamental question: "Where do we want to go that this technology can help take us?"

I see the possibility that, through information technology, the whole community will become a learning environment. Satellite transmission and cable television will bring a wide variety of cultural and educational programs into homes and schools; students themselves will generate much of the programming of interactive TV systems, a prototype of which is already in operation in the Irvine, California school district. Schools, museums, libraries, and governmental units will be connected through computer and television networks and will have access to a wide variety of data bases. Inexpensive microcomputers in homes will be able to access, through rapid, reliable networks, an almost unlimited range of learning resources. In the workplace, information technology will be used in a wide variety of activities, from routine tasks like electronic mail and electronic funds transfer to sophisticated applications of computer-aided design and robotics. Updating of skills and learning of new skills through satellite transmission and computer-assisted instruction will be a standard feature of industrial and professional training. Videoconferencing and networking of hospitals and clinics will extend health care services to remote ares and improve patient care by easy access to medical knowledge bases and rapid transmission of records. Through home terminals, monitoring of outpatients and even monitoring of the health of the entire population will be possible. Advanced detection and information transmission systems will be able to give early warning of natural disasters and to coordinate evacuation and relief activities.

It is easy to get carried away with this rosy picture of what information technology might bring to our society. But we need to look beyond our visions of hardware utopias to probe a few of the cloudy areas in our information weather map.

Let us acknowledge at the outset that the existence of sophisticated networks, home computers, and all the other gadgetry of my hypothetical future, will not guarantee that the resulting systems will be used in socially constructive and equitable ways. Most of us remember how quickly the early educational promise of television bogged down in a swamp of endless and mindless pap, from which we are still struggling to emerge. Anyone who saw the vast array of electronic games that flooded the market last Christmas could not fail to wonder if home information technology was doomed to be trivialized in a television-like fashion. I think we need to recognize that authoring high-quality computer materials, or generating quality television programming, is, like writing a good book, a difficult undertaking. We need to recognize and support those rare individuals with talent for producing quality materials. The capability of new information systems to transmit greatly increased amounts of data offers the chance to free ourselves from the tyranny of lowest-common-denominator programming due to limited transmission capacity. In television, we now have the prospect of specialty programming of all types and of greatly extended public affairs programming, thanks to cable TV and satellites. In electronic networks, I think we will develop interactive user-system couplings so that the system can learn the status of the user's knowledge base and reorganize its response accordingly.

Earlier I mentioned the uncertain social impacts of information technology. Educational institutions may be among the first to be affected. If private schools are quicker to obtain and use information technology in creative ways in the educational process, private institutions may make further inroads into public education as parents seek better training for their children. The availability of education resources in the home through microcomputers may even threaten the existence of schools as we now know them. After all, the education of young people in a special institution set aside for that sole purpose has only been going on for about 100 years, not a large slice of time in human history; we cannot assume that it will necessarily continue forever. Surely some institution must evolve to provide coordination and guidance of educational resources, but it may bear little resemblance to what we—or teachers' professional organizations—usually think of as a school.

In the workplace also, there are some serious issues to be confronted. Dealing with an impersonal and often poorly understood technology can create distrust and even fear. The dignity and humanity of workers interacting with computerized systems must be preserved, and potentially dehumanizing features of the technology need to be altered or at least minimized to prevent feelings of alienation. We should take note of recent events in England and Norway, which have pioneered the establishment of "technology agreements" between unions and employers to provide a stable working environment in which innovation can be introduced without creating serious unrest. An important feature of these agreements is worker participation in prior consultations before technological innovations are introduced. It is too early to know how these experiments will turn out, but the result could be better, more effective systems with a minimum of worker alienation.

Finally, I want to discuss briefly the issue of critical importance for public acceptance of information technology—equity and personal liberties. Those of us in government have a special responsibility to see that the benefits of information technology are shared by all in our society and that we do not end up reinforcing current patterns of inequality. Nearly every home now has a television set, but it seems to me extremely unlikely that, even in ten years, nearly every home will have a microcomputer. I think that the presence or absence of computers in the home and in schools will have an important bearing on educational, and hence, social equality. I don't see any quick or easy solution to this problem; it may require substantial efforts on the part of government to bring the Information Age to all groups of society.

The implications of information technology for personal liberties are no less serious. Daniel Bell (1979) has identified three key issues of social control:

1. Expansion of the techniques of surveillance.
2. Concentration of the technology of record keeping.
3. Control of access to strategic information by monopoly or government imposition of secrecy.

I have already touched on some of these concerns in my earlier remarks about networks. In particular, the fear of unauthorized access to personal records is much on the public's mind these days. There is a technological issue here, namely, the construction of adequate security systems for data base access, but in the main, as Bell points out, the problem is not in the technology per se but in the social and political system in which that technology is embedded. Against the argument of centralization of power due to computer technology, one can argue that the increasing diversity of communication modes and rapidly decreasing hardware costs could result in decentralization—if our society chooses to use it in that way.

The third issue—control of access to strategic information—is likely to become a leading social issue. Free societies need to balance their legitimate security interests in protecting certain kinds of information against the damage done to democratic values in denying its citizens free and equal access to information. Sweden has recently drafted a "vulnerability act," which it hopes will make its computers and data bases less vulnerable. The act proposes that all nonmilitary publicly-owned computers be licensed, and it creates a "Vulnerability Authority" to investigate computer security, emergency planning, dependence of computers on other computers, and related matters.

In closing, I urge that, in our own views of the coming Information Age, we remain attentive to the fact that we are dealing, in the end, with human beings—their livelihoods, their aspirations, their dreams. In considering the future of information technology, or any other technology, we need to remember that people will not accept it unless they perceive it to be in their own best interests. As technology increases the availability and diversity of information, we need to carefully consider what market structures and pricing policies are most likely to give consumers inexpensive and convenient access to information. Finally, we need to be sympathetic to the plight of the individual, whose fixed and finite intellectual capacity contrasted with the exponential growth of information volume creates the "ignorance explosion" (Lukasiewicz, 1972)—a degradation of his relative ability to deal with information. It will take foresight and planning to avoid drowning in our own information flows.

I hope that the organizers of Houston Symposium 13 will not be so cruel as to invite me back in ten years to confront me with the fallacy of my clairvoyance regarding our information future. There is only one prediction I will make with no fear of contradiction—whatever happens in the next ten years in this field, things won't be dull.

## REFERENCES

Artandi, Susan. Man, information and society: New patterns of interaction. *Journal of the American Society for Information Science,* January 1979, 5, 16.

Bell, Daniel. Communication technology—for better or for worse. *Harvard Business Review,* May–June 1979, 57, 32.

Boulding, K.E. The economics of knowledge and the knowledge of economics. *American Economic Review,* 1966, 56 (2), 1–13. Reprinted in D.M. Lambertson, (Ed.), *Economics of Information and Knowledge.* Baltimore, Md: Penguin Books, 1971, p. 32.

Lukasiewicz, J. The ignorance explosion: A contribution to the study of confrontation of man with the complexity of science and environment. *Transactions of the New York Academy of Sciences,* 1972, 34, 373–91.

*National information policy,* Report to the President of the United States by the Domestic Council Committee on the Right of Privacy (Nelson Rockefeller, Chairman), Sept. 1976, p. 178.

Porat, Marc Uri. *The information economy: (1), Definition and measurement.* U.S. Department of Commerce, OT Special Publication 77-12, May, 1977.

Resnikoff, H.L. National information systems: Implications of new and anticipated technology advances. Paper presented to the *Third U.S.-India workshop on scientific and technical information: on modelling national science and techology information systems,* Agra, March 10–12, 1980.

# Data Processing:
# A View of the Future

## Richard P. Case, Roy Lachman,
## and Janet L. Lachman

Commercial information processing began, at least as we view its modern history, with a crisis application. It seems that the statistical summaries of the 1880 census had taken seven full years to complete. They were not published until 1887. Worse, the Census Bureau predicted that, with the country growing and the demand for information increasing, the 1890 census would not be done until about 1905. Even a hundred years ago, this situation presented an obvious productivity problem that had to be solved. Dr. Herman Hollerith invented several sorting and tabulating machines to help in the solution. As a result, the 1890 census was completed before 1894. One of Dr. Hollerith's machines incorporated an early, manually-operated punch-card reader on which a dedicated operator could process something like 15 cards a minute. The punch-card reader drove a bank of 40 clock-like dials that were the instrument's only output mechanism (see Figure 1). After processing a batch of cards through the card reader, the operator stopped and wrote down on a piece of paper the readings from each dial. Though it was a rather primitive concept compared to some of the things we do today, it represented a threefold to fourfold improvement in throughput productivity over the methods used a decade before.

The emerging information processing industry had at its technological core the idea of the punch card, the unit record, and the representation of numbers for primarily statistical and reporting purposes. A company that later became known as IBM developed, over the next 50 years, a line of punch-card accounting machines that were the mainstay of informa-

Editor's Note: This paper was delivered at the symposium by Richard P. Case. However, the final draft that appears here is the work of Mr. Case and Professors Roy Lachman and Janet L. Lachman of the University of Houston.

tion processing through the end of the 1940s. Typical of the equipment available at the end of the 1940s were sorters, tabulators, and keypunch machines, some of which can still be found.

Electronics was introduced around 1950, and in this presentation we are going to trace changes in information processing technology from the first electronic machines to the sophisticated devices available today, such as Very Large Scale Integrated Circuits, bubble memory, high density magnetic recording, and the like. Where possible, we will extrapolate these developments to the end of the present century. We propose to demonstrate that there are virtually no fundamental limits to the continued extension of the physical-science frontiers of information processing technology for the next quarter century.

Equipment in general is not the only thing that has undergone dramatic changes in the last 30 years. The range of applications in which the hardware is deployed has also expanded. Before reviewing the growth of technical capacity, let us look briefly at the expansion in range of information processing applications. Starting with the 1890 census, most applications of information processing technology were primarily numerical and statistical. The systems were generally used to report, summarize, and analyze events that had occurred in the past and had been previously recorded. For example, corporations tracked the previous fiscal year's employment and wage levels, inventories and sales experi-

**Figure 1.** Punch-card reader and tabulator developed by Dr. Herman Hollerith for the 1890 census.

ences, and the like. Little of this type of work was done on-line—virtually none of it in the sense that we understand "on-line" today. However, especially over the last 15 years, there has been an enormous increase in the kinds of use to which on-line and simulation technology has been put. We will examine three of these, to provide a flavor of computer uses other than typical applications of payroll, accounts receivable, inventory control, billing, and the like.

Engineering simulation is now a widespread application. For example, in a sizeable warehouse near Montreal, there is a computer-instrumented and computer-controlled facility that is interfaced to a physical simulation of a section of the St. Lawrence Seaway. With this facility, hydraulics engineers do expriments in resource management, flood control, erosion, and the like. This application supplies answers otherwise simply unavailable in the real world. One reason is that the model of the seaway can be exercised at least to the limits of its capabilities; for example, the engineers can subject it to the worst floods expected on the St. Lawrence Seaway in 200 years. Obviously, such conditions could not be modeled on the real seaway because of the impact on people's lives and property; but even if we wanted to do such a thing, it is physically impossible. There is insufficient energy available and insufficient control to create such conditions in the real seaway. It is only with the technology described in this paper that we can get answers to "what if" questions of this type in many areas of engineering design— answers that are prerequisite to prospective thinking and forward planning.

Another typical application is in public rapid transit. San Francisco's Bay Area Rapid Transit system (BART) and the Washington Metro are examples of modern, metropolitan transportation systems in which computers are used on-line at no less than two levels. One is the automatic train control system where central computers control schedules, speeds, and headways, start and stop the trains at appropriate stations, open and close doors, and insure that the trains don't collide or run off the end of the tracks. Computers are also used in the fare collection system. In BART, the fare structure depends on the length of the ride, unlike New York City's subway where 60 cents gets you anywhere in the system. Each BART passenger has a little fare card with a magnetic stripe on it. The card is purchased from machines located in each station for any amount of money that the passenger desires. The fare card is inserted into the turnstile when the passenger enters the system. A computer inside the turnstile reads the magnetic stripe and determines whether there are sufficient funds remaining on the ticket to cover the cost of the minimum ride from that station. The name of the entry station is recorded on the magentic stripe, and at the exit station the same fare card is inserted in the exit turnstile. The turnstile computer reads the magnetic stripe, discovers the station that was entered, calculates the fare between the point of entry and the point of exit, and deducts the fare from the remaining value on the ticket. The new remaining value is then written on the magnetic stripe (for the next computer) and printed in black ink on the face of the ticket (for the benefit of the passenger) and returned. It takes half a second to get the ticket in and out and to enable the exit turnstile. That half a second is about how long it takes a passenger at a dead run to cover the distance (about one meter) between the place where the ticket is inserted and the place where it comes back out again. If everything is right the gate opens just in time for such a passenger to race through. If everything is not right, and the gate doesn't open, then the passenger has a different kind of problem!

Information processing technology is also widely used in hospital settings. One example is the monitoring and maintenance of patients in intensive care units. In such an application, there is need for a backup system or some kind of procedure that completes the mission of the system even if there is a failure in its electronic parts. But as important as computer applications are in intensive care units, potential effects on the entire family of health care professions are even more significant. It is predicted that issues relating to the use of the computer as a diagnostic and therapeutic tool cannot be independently resolved by either information science or medical science alone. A new discipline called medical information science is emerging (Lincoln and Korpman, 1980).

Finally, no catalogue of applications of computer technology would be complete without including the space program and its absolute dependence on the development of information processing systems.

These examples highlight several factors of increasing importance as industries and agencies expand their use of computing equipment. There is a demand for greater reliability, associated in the hospital setting with the preservation of human life, but important also in preserving revenue or maintaining the continuity of socially necessary services such as public transportation. There is a demand for systems that can take on increasingly complex tasks. And there is an increasing demand for security-conscious installations. Fifteen years ago, large corporations liked to put their newest computer behind glass and stainless steel, on the ground floor of their corporate headquarters, preferably in the busiest metropolitan area they could find. The public was invited to come in and observe operation of the hardware through the glass walls, so they could see how advanced the corporation and its technology was. Today almost no computer installations are designed with such public exhibition in mind. Instead, most contemporary computer systems are installed in subbasements or block houses and equipped with sophisticated access mechanisms. Today's purchasers want to insure that nobody gets anywhere close to the central computing facility who does not have an absolute need to be there.

## THE REQUIREMENT FOR HUMAN INTELLIGENCE

We could fill the remainder of this chapter with descriptions of new applications that have been recently implemented or are in various stages of development. Instead, we wish to emphasize that in the many diverse applications, in many different walks of life, there is at least one thing that is common to all: the absolute requirement for human intelligence. It's the requirement for professional people—programmers, systems analysts, technologists, even psychologists—to translate jobs and problems into a form that can be acted upon by existing technology.

The ultimate technology is the use of human intellect in the reformulation of problems so the computer can work on them. Every government agency, and every commercial enterprise that we know of, has a drawer full of projected computer applications that are known to be economically justified. Such projects are just waiting for two to 20 smart people who can spend two to 20 months working on the systems, procedures, analyses, forms design, programming, and maybe even enterprise reorganization necessary to get the job onto the computer. In contrast, we know of *no* applications where all of that human intelligence has already been applied—programs written, forms designed, and everything checked out—but the project is waiting on the shelf for the cost of computing to come down, say, 25 percent.

The computer industry is unique. Its capacity to serve society is not limited by the factors that set the limits on other industries. It is unique, as the Congressman tells us in his paper in that prices are going down while capabilities are going up. It is also unique in that it does not use any significant amount of the nonrenewable natural resources that normally limit industrial growth and spin off other social problems. There is no excessive use of energy, little pollution, no intensive use of land. There is no long-term limitation from unavailability of capital or manufacturing capacity. The major limitation, over the long term, will be the effective use of human intellect—the emergence of a corps of professionals in the computer business who can communicate successfully with nonprofessionals. Such people are essential if potential applications are to be successfully implemented and the available equipment is in fact to be used in the solution of problems it is ideally suited to solve.

This inherent human limitation on the information processing industry realizing its potential is also based on the performance and attitudes of the noncomputer professional. Sometime during the next 25 years the industry will have to develop effective systems for delivering computer resources and information processing services to people who are naive about computers—people who have completed perhaps four hours of formal or semiformal instruction. If you ask such people to step up to a computer today and make it do something it was not already programmed to do, most would feel like David trying to program Goliath. We have all seen the familiar cartoons showing the large, giant "electronic brain" that fills the room while diminutive little people take answers out of the slot and puzzle over them. Such cartoons express a popular attitude that the machines are the masters—superior to their human operators and vastly smarter than those completely untrained in computer operation. This attitude is philosophically unacceptable and technologically wrong. Over the last 25 years especially, human mastery of information processing technology has been vividly apparent to professionals in the field. We know that there is no reason why people in all walks of life cannot understand and master the needed level of information technology if they are given the right data in the right form, at the right place and the right time. The persistence of the popular notions that the machines are in the driver's seat is perhaps suggestive of the gulf that exists between computer professionals and the public they must serve. Bridging that gulf is one of the significant challenges of our developing human technology.

## LOGIC CIRCUITS

For most of the remainder of this paper we will examine the numerous changes in information processing technology. Logic, memory, printing, software, magnetic recording, and the main technologies for building information-processing equipment will all be covered. We would like to begin with logic, the technology that makes computers add, subtract, multiply, and divide. Logic makes possible the execution of instructions and the conditional selection of instruction sequences that makes them simulate decision making.

In the early 1950s, logic was embodied in vacuum tubes. Figure 2 shows a large pluggable unit with eight vacuum tubes, typical of the technology upon which IBM built the 704, a computer dating back to about 1954 or 1955. The particular unit in Figure 2 is a one-bit slice out of a 36-bit adder. Thirty-six of those units stacked side by side could add two 36-bit numbers together, getting a 36— or a 37—bit sum, in roughly 11 microseconds (one—millionth of a second).

By the end of the 1950s, solid state transistors had come into use. IBM packaged a comparable amount of logical function on a printed circuit card (Figure 2, right side) with the resistors, capacitors, and diodes on the top part of the card and the transistors on the bottom. The

**Figure 2.** An eight vacuum tube pluggable unit is from a 1955 IBM 704. The same amount of logic is in a late 1950s solid-state printed circuit, right side. A middle 1960s hybrid integrated circuit also with the same amount of logic is shown at the bottom center.

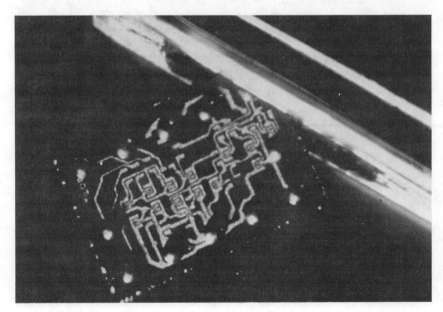

**Figure 3.** An early 1970s unit that handled as much logic as the eight-tube pluggable unit.

components were connected by printed wires, not visible in the figure, on the back side of that card. By the middle 1960s, about the same amount of logic was packaged in a hybrid integrated circuit device illustrated by the card in the middle and bottom of Figure 2. By the early 1970s a unit the size of a fly speck could do the job. The fly-speck sized unit, shown highly magnified in Figure 3, is an integrated circuit having about the same amount of logical function as the early eight-tube pluggable unit. The diagonal stripe across the upper right-hand corner of the figure is the eye of a sewing needle. It gives an idea of the level of magnification in the figure. A high speed computer today—such as IBM's 3033—is built out of silicon chips that each contain about three times as much logic and operate about a thousand times faster than did the eight-tube pluggable unit.

Figure 4 shows how miniaturization and increases in speed translate into performance improvements. Between 1952 and 1976, CPU (Central Processing Unit) speeds increased from an average of about 700 instructions per second to almost a million—an increase of approximately 120 times (See Figure 4A). During the same period, memory capacity increased 150-fold. These improvements were achieved for an increase of less than five times price. Figure 4A does not represent the fastest machine available in those years; rather, it shows the cost weighted average of all the machines built in a given year and thus reflects the capabilities of the entire industry. The unit-weighted average of all the

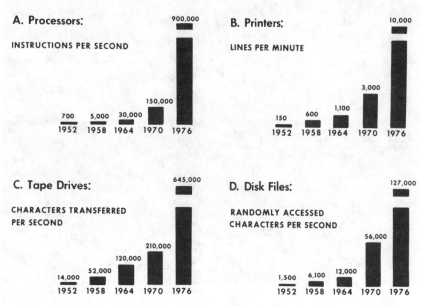

**Figure 4.** Technological improvements in data processing over 25 years (approximate values).

machines built from year to year may be flatter than shown because the 1970s were dominated by the minicomputers and microcomputers. But they also have a lower economic value, so the cost-weighted average of the industry is reasonably represented by the graph.

Progress did not stop in 1976. In 1980, machines were being delivered to customers in quantity with logic chips that are about 40 percent larger in each linear dimension than those of the previous generation but contain more than ten times the number of logical circuits. Each such chip contains more than 30 times the function that was on the original eight-tube pluggable unit.

These chips are mounted in modern technology on a ceramic substrate. Figure 5 schematically illustrates IBM's 4300 Processor's logic package, which holds up to nine of the chips. The ceramic unit is 50 millimeters square and about five millimeters thick. Internal to its structure is much wiring that can be seen only with a microscope. It contains about 20 layers of wire that connect the input-output pads of each chip to the other chips and to the pins at the bottom of the module. The pins in turn provide electrical connections to other units on a circuit board. That one 50-millimeter square module encapsulates within it what, in the previous technology, would have been about 150 to 200 meters worth of wiring and several thousand interconnections. Its speed of operation has been considerably increased by its smaller size, which

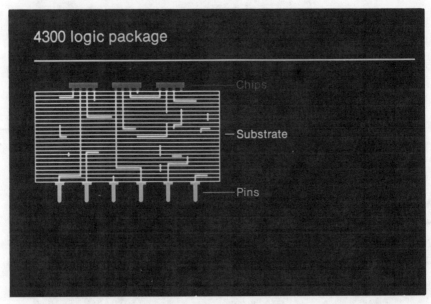

**Figure 5.** The IBM 4300 logic package is 50 millimeters square and five thick and contains up to nine chips with 30 times the logical function of eight-tube unit.

reduces the distance between components. The reliability has also been substantially improved. Finally, the cost of the logic available on the chip is significantly lower than it was in any previous technology.

Another way of looking at the effects of the technological advances is to consider the improvement they have wrought in the CPU product. The System/360 model 65 is the CPU product that was near the top of the line 15 years ago. The internal performance of a 1980 CPU product, the 4341, is 30 percent faster. It weighs about 11 percent as much and occupies roughly 10 percent as much floor space. It requires only about 20 percent as much power, puts out about 20 percent as much heat, and costs only about 20 percent as much as the 360-65 did 15 years ago. And that price is in 1980 dollars compared to 1965 dollars; the real cost may be as little as 10 percent when inflation is taken into account.

We confidently anticipate that circuit density is going to continue increasing well beyond 1980. All of the examples presented are from the so-called bipolar logic technology with several hundred circuits per chip today. By 1990 we expect several thousands of circuits per chip, or another tenfold increase in density for devices of this kind. Field effect transistors, used in wristwatches and hand-held calculators, are slower but much lower powered. Today they are an order of magnitude more dense than bipolar logic chips, containing several thousands of circuits each. By 1990 there will be several tens of thousands of circuits per chip.

The size of single transistor circuit elements has been cut in half every six years. Progress at that rate is expected to continue into the next decade, putting circuits with one-micrometer (micron, one-millionth of a meter) dimensions into mass production around 1990 (The National Academy of Sciences, 1979, p 219). Eventually the physical limits of miniaturization of the transistor will be reached, because of the atomic space problem. Semiconductors depend upon the presence of impurities and defects that allow conduction. At the level of about a quarter of a micron in the smallest feature, transistors would be built having only a couple of dozen impurity atoms or minority carriers in the base region. It cannot be made much smaller and remain a semiconductor.

There is another technology, however, that could supplant some aspects of transistor technology in the 1990s—the Josephson junction. This junction, discovered by Brian D. Josephson in 1962, is a superspeed circuit technology whose nonlinear elements can be made into and-gates, or-gates, and bistable state devices—the basic logic components of which computers are constructed. The Josephson circuit operates at the temperature of liquid helium, 4.2 degrees Kelvin (about -470 degrees Fahrenheit). Superconductive devices require no power except when switching. Each junction is normally superconducting and can be made resistive by the influence of a magnetic field, provided by passing a small current through a control wire. The speed and power dissipation of the device is of paramount interest. Each junction dissipates about one-thousandth the power of a similar transistor circuit, several microwatts rather than several milliwatts per junction. Each switches at a speed about one hundred times that of the transistor circuit, roughly ten picoseconds (one-trillionth of a second) rather than a nanosecond (one-billionth of a second). Each junction can eventually be made about several times smaller than the transistor in linear dimensions. Because the Josephson circuit does not depend on impurity atoms as does the semiconductor, it can be made physically smaller before the atomic spacing limits of the transistor are approached.

The disadvantages of the Josephson junction are that a cryostat and a refrigeration unit are required to maintain the liquid helium at a constant low temperature. The investment is substantial, and several million circuits must be placed inside the thermal protection system both to make the device cost-competitive and to amortize the initial costs. The technology, therefore, would most likely be used first in specialized applications for space, defense, or very large scale computers.

## MEMORY

For many years the technology of choice in mainframe memory was ferrite cores. But in the early 1970s, the technology of choice became

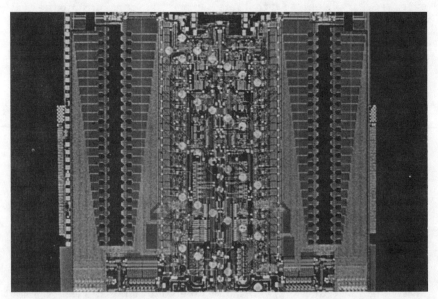

**Figure 6.** A 64,000-bit memory chip currently in mass production. The chip is about one-quarter inch square.

integrated circuits of silicon. The early silicon memory chips stored up to 2,000 bits of information. The latest in mass-produced IBM memory chips is shown in Figure 6. This little device stores 64,000 bits of information on a single chip not more than about one-quarter inch square. Each of the regular, symmetrical areas on the left and right store half of the total number of bits—32,000 bits in each array. And the rather irregular pattern down the center provides the support circuits for the memory: drivers, sense amplifiers, decode circuits, addressing, and two eight-bit buffers that synchronize information transfers between memory arrays and the CPU.

The Josephson junction also has applications in advanced memory technology. A memory device using the Josephson junction "remembers" that a binary 1 has been stored at a given position by capturing magnetic flux within a circle of superconducting current broken by the junction. The zero flux state corresponds to a binary 0. Reading the contents of memory is made possible by switching and other properties of the junction. A voltage is produced at the output when a read signal is sent to a loop holding magnetic flux. Presence or absence of the voltage output thus corresponds to presence or absence of flux, thereby permitting memory for one bit. Cache memory is the fastest component of a computer's main memory. A cache memory chip to be built from this technology is expected to have a retrieval access time of 500 picoseconds (Matisoo, 1980). Such a chip for main memory has been built and operated successfully that stores a bit of information by capturing within the circle of superconducting current exactly one quantum of magnetic flux. There is some theoretical basis to believe that the physical limits have been reached and we can do no better.

In contrast, progress in density of memory is going to continue. Although the 64,000-bit chip in Figure 6 is a bit above the line for 1980 products, by 1990 or sooner several hundreds of thousands of bits per chip are expected in the main memory array, with correspondingly lower prices.

## MAGNETIC RECORDING

Magnetic recording on cassettes, reels of tape, disks, or drums has been the technology of choice for years and probably will be for the foreseeable future. It represents the lowest cost permanent storage available in information processing equipment.

Advances in magnetic recording, like the above-described advances in circuitry, have been predicated on the objectives of cramming more and more into smaller and smaller spaces. The more storage obtained per square unit of area, the lower the cost for each unit of storage. Given a fixed amount of magnetic recording surface at an almost fixed cost, forcing ten times more bits onto that surface reduces the cost of each bit to nearly one-tenth of its former cost.

The first magnetic recording instruments of 20 years ago recorded about 100 bits per inch. Within about five years, information was being recorded at about 1,000 to 2,000 bits per inch. Recording densities of around 7,000 bits per inch were obtained by the middle 1970s. By 1980 commercially available products could record at 15,000 bits per inch. The next step should be the introduction of products recording 25,000 to 30,000 bits per inch. Each increase in density of recording has provided a lower and lower cost per bit and a sharply lower cost per megabyte of storage. Over the entire period of the last 20 years, the compound rate of decline in mass storage cost has been about 40 percent per year. In other words, in spite of inflation, the cost of storing information on magnetic media has been halved every two years of the last 20. Improvements in the performance of disk files from 1952 to 1976 is shown in Figure 4D. Randomly accessed characters per second has increased 84-fold, and storage capacity has increased about a 100-fold, while prices have actually decreased. The comparable plot for tape drives is shown in Figure 4C. Tape drives transferred approximately 46 times as many characters in 1976 as in 1952, and had about 16 times as much capacity for less than two times the price.

Experimental plate models of magnetic recording devices are today recording at various higher densities. The cost per megabyte, however, would be considerable, and the devices are as yet unreliable. But they have been useful in demonstrating that factors such as magnetic domain wall size or inherent energy may set physical limits on the recording of information at that density. It will require basic scientific inquiry coupled with a substantial engineering effort for continuing progress in magnetic recording devices over the next ten years. But consider the progress that has been made: magnetic recording technology on a hard disk file gives more than 80 times the performance of 30 years ago and costs less, and that same technology on flexible media, such as a magnetic tape drive, yields 40 times the performance for less than two times the price.

A more recent form for magnetic recording is little cylinders of magnetic tape about five centimeters in diameter and about ten centimeters long. The cylinders are stored in honeycomb walls with hexagonal pigeonholes. A mechanical arm moves vertically and horizontally between two honeycomb units to fetch a cylinder, deliver it to a read-write station, and then return it to its hexagonal hole. Each cylinder holds about 50,000,000 bytes of information, and access time to a cylinder is of the order of ten seconds. If an application requires that substantial amounts of information be available on-line to a computer, this is the cheapest way.

Another new storage technology is magnetic bubbles. Although magnetic bubble memories are not semiconductors, the manufacturing process is not too different from that of semiconductors. A thin film of magnetic material is first placed on top of a sheet of crystal. Under controlled manufacturing conditions, most of the magnetic material is biased with the north end of the magnet up, while little local areas are biased with the north end down. Each of the local areas is roughly cylindrical in shape, about two microns in diameter, and two microns thick. The discrete regions of reversed magnetic fields are stable but can be moved along precise paths under the influence of an external magnetic field. The locally reversed magnetic regions (the bubbles) are used to store information in a way that is analogous to the magnetized spots on a tape or floppy disk. The device is like a very long shift register, in that the stored magnetic spots are moved magnetically so the physical substrate is stationary. Since it is entirely electronic, it has no moving parts, which allows for much greater reliability and faster data motion. Today, the cost per bit of storage is about the same as for semiconductor memories, but it has the additional advantage of retaining information when the power is turned off. Future developments may reduce the cost per megabite to one-quarter of today's costs, or less. If these costs could be reached, the technology could dominate all fixed-head files, and the parts of the data base that require high access rates, such as indexes or paging stores, could be placed in this kind of technology rather than on the rotating mechanical media of drum or disk.

And, of course, some storage technologies never worked out, for example, lasers. There was considerable excitement a decade ago for the prospects of laser holography; it was going to be the storage wave of the future. Numerous laboratories went to work on lasers trying to realize their apparent potential, with disastrous consequences for some enterprises. IBM also went to work, building red, green, blue, purple, and yellow lasers. The color of one model could even be changed with the turn of a knob. High and low powered lasers, gas lasers, solid state lasers—all were built, but none were developed into a commercially acceptable product.

The reason has nothing to do with science; laser holography works. There are quite a few laboratory models of laser-based storage devices that work satisfactorily sitting in the warehouse. The reason is that they were always more costly per bit, by a factor of two or three, than the best available magnetic devices previously described. Of course, in the early 1970s it was obvious that their cost would drop significantly. The prediction was correct. But the predictions totally missed the mark on the actual rate of cost reduction for magnetic technology, which was thought in the early 1970s to have more or less reached the end of its development. The cost per unit of magnetic storage was expected to be fairly flat for a decade at least, while the cost of laser technology was expected to come rapidly down. We have already seen what really happened to the cost of magnetic storage; and today laser storage is still more expensive in cost per bit by a factor of two or three than magnetics.

There is an interesting principle here. Whenever competing technologies differ by a cost factor as little as two, it is not science that calls the winner, it is engineering. The outcome is not determined by fundamental characteristics of the device, the idea, or the physics involved. It is determined by the economics of mass production and potential achievements in cost reduction. Many technologies can change by a cost factor of two in ten years. In the computer industry most things change by a cost factor of two in two or three years. The occasional failure of prediction, such as occurred with lasers and magnetics, is thus an occupational hazard.

## PRINTING

The massive investment in lasers was not a total loss. At least two products in IBM's line use lasers. One is the supermarket scanner that reads universal product codes—the small rectangles of black and white bars on grocery products. The other is high speed printers, in which a laser beam is used to expose a drum, which then captures toner and fuses it on paper to produce a printed record.

Printers probably come in more varieties than anything else in the information processing industry. There are impact and nonimpact printers, plain-paper and special-paper printers, electro-erosion printers, and so on. Despite the variety, the hammer method has clearly been the technology of choice for most of the last 25 years. A reverse image of an alphanumeric character is engraved on the end of a slug of metal and positioned close to a piece of paper. An inked ribbon is located between the print head and the paper, and the back end of the slug is hit with a hammer. Faster printing was accomplished by use of a bigger hammer. Printing increased from 150 lines a minute to several thousand lines per minute, always by increasing the energy of the hammer. Eventually, it became impossible to build a larger hammer and still package them ten to the inch, the spacing of standard pica type. That marked the end of speed improvements in the mechanical printer. Only a nonimpact printing device, for example, the laser printer mentioned above, can achieve as much as 10,000 lines per minute. Although some impact printers can run at between 3,000 and 5,000 lines a minute, the cost performance characteristics are poor when the mechanical technologies are pushed to their limits. Thus, increased speed is no longer a real goal in impact printing. However, cost reduction is, and the cost of impact printers continues to drop despite inflation.

The 25-year growth in printer performance is plotted in Figure 4B. Between 1952 and 1976, printers achieved an increase of 66 times the performance in lines per minute, for less than 15 times the price. The price/performance improvement in printers is less than the corresponding price/performance improvement in logic, memory, and magnetic recording. That is typical, not only of printers, but of all technology that is directly used by human beings. As long as human eyes must read displays, or human fingers must operate keyboards, microminiaturization and batch fabrication cannot be pushed to the limit in creating a smaller and smaller product. Hence, performance and cost/performance improvements in this section of the industry are not as dramatic as those in logic, memory, and magnetic recording.

One very promising new printing technology is ink jets, which involves the controlled spraying of ink droplets from small orifices onto paper. The essential problem in perfecting a jet printer is nicely illustrated by the problem of using a garden hose to water flowers that are a little farther away than the hose will reach. A stream of liquid traveling through the air does not hold together; the situation is one of unstable hydrodynamics. Normally, no variation in the shape of the nozzle or the pressure of the fluid will prevent the liquid from breaking up; the liquid stream separates into randomly-sized and randomly-spaced droplets. The ink-jet invention is to make the stream break up into uniformly sized and spaced droplets.

After that, it is all engineering. An electric charge is put on each droplet, and the stream is passed between a set of charged deflection plates much like in a TV tube, though not in a vacuum. Pulses of the right voltage are passed from a rather complicated electronic system to the deflection plates. The droplets are then deflected as they fly through the air into the shape of characters—letters or numbers. Some of the droplets do not hit the paper but are deflected into a trough for recirculation into the system.

A jet printer is offered by IBM. It's a device that produces correspondence-quality output about seven or eight times faster than the mechanical typewriter. Ink-jet technology can yield printers of either low resolution and high speed or high resolution and low speed. There is a tradeoff between the size of the drops selected and the number of drops per character. If only 50 or 100 drops per character is used with dot matrix printing, a very-high-speed printer is possible. The use of very tiny drops, up to tens of thousands of them per character, permits a graphic-arts quality printer with multiple fonts, but it is slower. It would be ideal if we could combine the high-speed, low-resolution and the low-speed, high-resolution printer in the same product. This is probably not feasible, because paper handling requirements are so much different in the two cases. But at any combination of speed and resolution, a jet printer is inherently quiet: there are no hammers hitting the back end of metal slugs, which usually makes the printer the noisiest instrument in the computing center.

## TERMINALS

Let us, briefly, consider computer terminals. Fifteen years ago the only terminals that were available were typewriters. Today IBM is offering dozens, and the industry is offering hundreds, of individual terminal types, customized for particular work stations, environments, or for specialized jobs. In 15 more years, the industry will undoubtedly be offering thousands of customized terminal types for a variety of different applications whose value we might not recognize today, even assuming we could understand them. That calls to mind another principle. Computer designers have seldom anticipated the scope of application that users would eventually find for the technology. Those familiar with the internal workings of computers are rather poor at estimating how they are going to be used five or ten years after they become available. Characteristically, the extent and variety of terminal use has not been adequately foreseen. Nevertheless, it continues to develop. Terminals are being connected together across plant sites and university campuses by wideband communication networks—and there has been talk in this symposium about connections across continents or oceans by the emerging satellite technology.

## SOFTWARE

Software has also undergone a rather significant change in the last 25 years. As recently as 20 years ago, all the software for a major computing facility could be held in one hand. The rest of it was up to the user. Today, system software defies measurement; there are 20, 30, or 50 million lines of code provided by the manufacturer at every major computing installation. A factor of ten can be added for the code provided by the individual user. The complexity is almost overwhelming. At major computing facilities, the software element has been running at the limit of human capacity to deal with complexity for the last 15 years. There seems to be no end to the demand for additional software, from operating systems to discrete applications. If the code were written that permitted management of a software system ten times the size of the ones now in service, it would immediately be put to work.

At IBM, we are finding that there is a shift in the type of software that is most in demand. Whereas in the early 1960s we spent 95 percent of our time developing what might be called *systems disciplines*—multiprogramming, data base management, programming languages, and software support for the CPU and the peripheral devices—today we are spending about 40 percent of our time on what might be called *implementation disciplines.* This latter category includes software that simplifies installation, increases the reliability and ease of operation of the system, and affords greater security. Advances in systems disciplines result in new entries in the "capabilities" section of the system manuals. Advances in implementation disciplines do not result in additions to the manual that tell the user his machine will do something new; but users are discovering the value of these advances all the same, and demand for this type of software is on the upswing. Implementation discipline development represents another of the technological challenges for the future, to which we shall return shortly.

## PRODUCTIVE BANDWIDTH

That completes the technology survey. As Figure 4 illustrates, there have been tremendous advances over a 25-year period in logic, memory, magnetic recording, and printing. Moreover, the advances have not slowed over the five years since 1976. And perhaps most interesting, there is room for further improvement in every one of the existing technologies. Even in cases where there are established limitations to the existing technologies, for that matter, where there are no known, important limitations, there are alternative technologies available to take over where presently implemented technologies leave off. So we confidently predict that the next 25 years in the computer industry are going to be just as exciting as the last 25 years have been.

For that prediction to be justified, we must deal successfully with the complexities of putting the hardware to work. The price/performance improvement (cf. Figure 4) in devices produced using the physical technologies we have previously described have increasingly outstripped the price/performance improvements in fully implemented systems. Figure 7 illustrates that point and the effect over time. The performance per unit cost at the device level is higher at any given time than the performance per unit cost at the systems level; or put another way, the productive bandwidth of devices is several years ahead of the productive bandwidth of the systems in which the devices are contained. The productive bandwidth of systems reflects delivered end cost to the user, such as cost per transaction, cost per invoice, or cost per calculation.

Now, if we had to pick one number to represent the improvement in performance relative to price, over the last 25 years, as a result of the findings of the science laboratories, that number would be roughly a factor of one thousand. That is, there has been a performance increase of

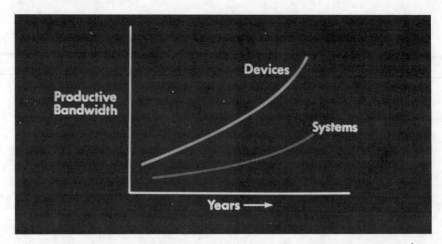

**Figure 7.** The relationship between productive bandwidth of devices and the systems in which they are components.

a thousand times for each unit increment in price. In some of the technologies the factor is a good bit more; in others it is somewhat less. But assuming a factor of a thousand, the delivered end cost to the ultimate user is a factor of about 50—perhaps a factor between 50 and 100. As we have said, miniaturization and increased speed will be the source of the next factor of a thousand with respect to devices over the next 25 years. That much improvement in device technology, we estimate, will produce another factor of 50 to 100 in price/performance improvement in systems. But whether it is 50 or 100 or even 25, that is sufficient change to make the next 25 years just as exciting as the last 25 have been. But more important, it will make the shape of the industry and the utilization of this technology just as different 25 years from now as today is from 25 years ago.

One of the upper limits for the productive bandwidth of devices is the speed of light. It is an increasingly significant factor in the internal cycle times of the large scale computers. The IBM System/370, model 168, a top-of-the-line computer of about six years ago, had an 80-nanosecond cycle time. About 25 percent of that, roughly 20 nanoseconds, is accounted for entirely by electromagnetic propagation at the speed of light from point to point within the computer. The other 60 nanoseconds is capacitive loading, transistor switching, and other circuit effects that cause delays. A top-of-the-line computer of today, such as the 3033, is faster. But now one-third of its faster cycle time is accounted for by the speed of light. If you perform a theoretical calculation taking the transistor circuit to the physical limits of miniaturization, one-half to one-quarter micron in size, the estimated cycle times of the resulting processors will be very much faster. But, by then, more than two-thirds of the total cycle time will be accounted for by the speed of light. When as much as half of the cycle time is accounted for by the speed of light and a research laboratory comes up with magic in terms of a new circuit family, improvement by a factor of two is all that is possible. So, computer circuits are going to become smaller and smaller not only because of the element of cost reduction in batch fabrication and microminiaturization, but also because of the desire for faster operation. If information cannot be transmitted faster between two points, at least the two points can be brought closer together so that the time required to move signals between them is reduced.

## AGAIN, HUMAN INTELLIGENCE

While the speed of light is one absolute limit on the productive bandwidth of devices, we know of no comparable absolute limits peculiar to systems. Yet as Figure 7 shows, the productive bandwidth of systems has lagged considerably behind that of devices over the years. Many of the factors that account for this lag involve the human element—the same human intelligence that must achieve implementation of the physically available technology to solve problems in industry and society in general.

Software development, particularly in the implementation disciplines, often calls for an understanding of human intellectual capacities and social requirements rather than those of physical technology. We touched only slightly, if at all, on such matters as information systems management, high order languages, security, search strategies, and so on. It would take another paper at least the size of this one to do justice to these topics. These areas, where much less is known than in the physical realm, provide the greatest challenges for the future. Unfortunately, they also provide the greatest potential for disaster. If a major new facility or application is created, but the system design is planned wrong, five years or so of new technology will bail it out. But if the human interface is a failure, or the security is impossible to maintain, or the information structure is wrong, or the search gets in the way, the trouble will get worse in five years rather than better.

The implementation disciplines make computer systems more usable for the information processing specialist and nonspecialist alike. The intangible nature of such software problems and their solution taxes the conceptual ability of the problem solver in a rather different way than do the tangible problems involving physical hardware. For the specialist, these disciplines involve development of software that is devoted to system installation, automatic recovery after crashes, general reliability, and the like. For the noncomputer specialist, they involve the development of software and documentation that make computer systems usable, or increase their usability, in solving problems of a profession, industry, or political entity. The development of "very high level" languages that permit the programmer to work with problem level concepts rather than lower level code is likely to help both. Efforts at the standardization of computer languages, e.g., the use of Ada in real-time applications for the Department of Defense (Broad, 1981), is likely to be specially felicitous to the nonspecialist, because it makes the mastery of just one computer language sufficient for the task of locating, mastering, and putting to work an enormous quantity of applications software.

We understand the major limiting factors on physical technology for computers. We do not know what the limiting factors deriving from human intelligence might be. While limits might be set for any single individual's intellectual achievements, no one knows what the collective intellectual potential of the human species might be, or even if there are any limits at all. Yet, our poorer understanding of the human element is in large measure responsible for the gap between the development of cost-justified devices and the development of cost-justified systems using those devices. An increase in our knowledge of human capacity, and our ability to solve conceptual problems whose only pragmatic limit derives from that capacity, must thus occupy a significant place in industry priorities over the coming years.

## REFERENCES

Broad, W.J. Pentagon orders end to computer babel. *Science*, 1981, *211*, 31—33.
Lincoln, T.L. and Korpman, R.A. Computers, health care, and medical information science. *Science*, 1980, *210*, 257—63.
Matisoo, J. The superconducting computer. *Scientific American*, 1980, *242*, 50—65.
The National Academy of Sciences. *Science and technology*. San Francisco: W.H. Freeman, 1979.

# Coping with Complexity

## B. A. Sheil

By way of beginning our exploration of the psychological and sociological impacts of information technology, let us consider why we expect there to *be* any. Or, since there will undoubtedly be *some,* why do we expect them to be particularly interesting? The calling of this symposium clearly presumes some such shared expectations. However, we can distinguish two very different rationales underlying this apparent consensus, which, in turn, suggest very different perspectives on the behavioral impacts of information technology.

## THE ACCELERATION OF CHANGE

The most straightforward reason for expecting information technology to wreak major social change dwells on the rapidity with which this technology is being developed and introduced. A typical presentation of this point of view contains a number of graphs that plot some unit of progress against time. The prototypical such graph is shown in Figure 1. As each of these graphs shows progress *accelerating* over time, the conclusion is drawn that great and dramatic things, either good or bad depending on the viewpoint of the presenter, are in the offing.

This argument is a descendent of a rhetorical device to which most of us were first exposed in an undergraduate course entitled, perhaps, "Introductory Western Civilization." This consisted of a presentation that expressed the recorded history of humanity in terms of a single year, at the rate of about 80 years of history to each day. In this metaphor, one finds that the Stone Age lasts essentially to the end of September, the Bronze Age occupies most of October, Rome started and finished in late

77

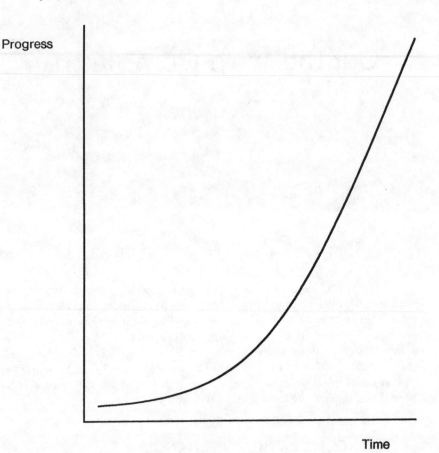

**Figure 1.** The general purpose progress graph

November and early December, and most of the history that is salient to us happened in late December. The twentieth century, in particular, has to be expressed in terms of the hours and minutes of the last day of the year. The conclusion typically drawn from that presentation, like that drawn from graphs of technological development, is that we are in a period of accelerating change and the effect of such continued acceleration can only be convulsive change.

That's one interpretation. Another interpretation is suggested by Steinberg's famous *New Yorker* cover, which shows a "perspective" view looking down and to the west from the *New Yorker* offices. In the foreground, Ninth Avenue is shown in great detail; then Tenth Avenue, a little smaller; the Hudson River, smaller still; New Jersey; then wilderness (with Texas a small smudge in the distance). The interpretation of *this* exponential change (in perspective) is very clear—one's perception of "space" (size, speed, importance, *etc.*) is very egocentric.

This in turn suggests that one could interpret the apparent acceleration of change *not* as evidence that change is in fact accelerating, but as an effect of the much greater precision with which one perceives things that are near than those that are far away. The number of circuit elements per square centimeter is definitely changing. Whether that appears to be an *extraordinary* change or a normal one is a function of what we pay attention to. Because the number of circuit elements per square centimeter is changing, we pay attention to it. Because we pay attention to it, we become more aware of it changing. Because we are then aware of very frequent changes, change appears very rapid.

This suggests that we adopt a fairly sceptical point of view on the implication that, because one can draw sharply accelerating graphs, it is therefore the case that something unusual is happening. Steinberg's cartoon tells us that our immediate environment will always loom so large in our perceptions that any change in it will appear to be revolutionary. Throughout history, people have always been in the throes of what *they* regarded as overwhelming change. The fact that *we* don't regard those changes to be as rapid as those that surround us is as likely to be simply a difference in perspective as a qualitative difference in velocity.

Furthermore, even if technical change were accelerating, it does not follow that change measured in *technical* terms will have sociological effects of corresponding magnitude. One reason for this is that most manifestations of technical innovation are *functionally* equivalent to some artifact, object, or procedure that antedates them. The Xerox copier, for example, while a major *technical* innovation, was not fundamentally different in function from the carbon paper/blueprint/photographic technologies that it replaced. It induced a minor adjustment in some cost parameters (with a consequent opportunity for commercial profit!), but its introduction has not changed its users' world in any fundamental way.

Further the ubiquity of change itself suggests that both individuals and societies have a wide range of adaptive mechanisms for coping with it. Thus, in the absence of any argument to the contrary, we should assume that these mechanisms, which have buffered the effects of many changes in the past, will probably prevent there being any drastic social response to the introduction of information technology. In short, our perceptions of the rate of change are very tenuous grounds on which to predict extraordinary behavioral consequences.

## DISTINGUISHING CHARACTERISTICS OF INFORMATION TECHNOLOGY

The principal other reason for expecting information technology to have significant social impact is a belief that it is in some way different in kind from previous technological innovations. This argument has considerable face validity, as information technology does have some characteristic qualities that set it apart from the technologies that have preceded it. Further, any hypothesis as to the critical difference provides not only a reason for expecting significant social impact, but also some indication of what that impact is likely to be.

## Complexity

The crudest form of this argument is the claim that information technology is simply more complex than previous technologies and that coping with this complexity will itself cause (or be!) social trauma. Clearly, this argument is a first cousin of the argument from the acceleration of change (substitute "complexity" for "progress" on the same graphs). The same criticisms of egocentrism apply. There are many complex objects in the world, and dealing with their complexity has always been a characteristic human activity. Technology, of whatever form, accounts for neither the majority nor the most extreme of the complex objects with which people must deal. At the very grossest level, understanding other human beings is incomparably more difficult than dealing with any artifact that we are likely to make, yet this does not (always) seem insuperable. Put this crudely, the argument from complexity has little force.

## Fabrication

Various specific attributes of information technology can be advanced as reasons why information technology is different in kind from other technologies. One of the more striking is that information technology artifacts have close to zero fabrication cost. The cost of producing and using an artifact can be broken down into three categories—design, fabrication, and service and other postimplementation costs. For information technology, the second of these terms is either very low (for hardware) or zero (for software). Consequently, the limits of application of information technology are imposed entirely by design and maintenance issues. This is quite different from most other technologies, where fabrication complexity is a major barrier. For example, the construction of a large conventional artifact, such as an airplane, is a very substantial part of the cost of using that artifact.

Information technology's relative freedom from fabrication limitations can be expected to lead to both more complex artifacts (as complexity is only loosely constrained by fabrication considerations) and their more rapid and widespread dissemination to users. It is less clear, however, that these attributes constitute a difference in *type* of technological innovation.

## Routinization

Another characteristic of information technology is that it concentrates decision making by separating out what is algorithmically decidable from what requires judgement and treating that which is algorithmically decidable as a problem in *automatic* information processing. Eventually, this will have a degrading effect on the perceived worth of clerical labor. In the much longer term, it may also change our ideas about what are the central characteristics of human beings, in much the same way as the introduction of machines that displaced people from craft labor changed our perception of the importance of such labor as a distinguishing quality of human beings. However, such changes take time—time enough for society to absorb them fairly gracefully.

## Reactivity

At least in the short term, a much more important characteristic of information technology is that it is extremely *reactive.* The information processing that information technology functionally replicates is usually intricately related to existing structures that are often very sensitive to change. As a very simple example, in order to use a computer to control the ignition system of an automobile, one has to factor the existing engine design into *effector* and *control* parts, so one can replace the control function with information technology. Unfortunately, in the typical conventional engine, these two functions are completely confounded; e.g., the shaft that transmits the power is also used to control the ignition cycle. The reason for such confounding is that, until very recently, information per se was not thought of as a separable component. However, the result is that, in order to apply information technology, one often has to redesign practically the entire system rather than just the part one is interested in affecting. Even relatively simple systems can present major problems when an attempt is made to repartition them along lines that do not reflect their original design.

Social and cultural institutions are particularly resistant to such partitioning. The engineer who attempts to introduce technology into some process that is being carried out by a group of people, quickly finds that she has a substantial problem separating out the activity that is the target of the technology from the myriad of social and group maintenance activities with which it is interwoven. Further, such a separation will itself be seen as a political act, which can elicit resistance from the people involved. Thus, the engineer finds herself cast as an actor in the very social uncertainties that the technology is often designed to remove.

This is all very familiar to anyone associated with the practice of engineering. But there is a much more subtle and profound twist to the introduction of information processing technology in that the information engineer is typically making a cut through the problem that is quite foreign to the people who are currently involved. As a result, it is extremely difficult both to obtain a precise description of the current activity in a form that is useful for information engineering purposes and to control the political reaction to the introduction of the change.

The magnitude of this problem was forcefully brought home to me during some field work in which we tried to obtain precise descriptions of the office procedures used in some typical local control offices, such as a branch sales office. The obvious way to obtain such descriptions is to sit down with each of the people who do the work and ask them to tell you what they do. After you do this with all the people who are involved and you go away and try and match up all the information you've been given, you'll find various discrepancies, e.g., that some document is supposed to be sent from person A to person B, but one of those two people doesn't seem to be aware of it. So you go back with diagrams and flowcharts and try to link all the loose ends together. This is, of course, an iterative process of questioning, talking, and adjusting, which can last for several weeks, if you're conscientiously trying to get a complete picture.

Well, a funny thing happens somewhere along this path to precision and completeness. Sometimes, after $N$ iterations on some topic, such as the number of times some form is handled by somebody, when you're pushing for more precision, trying to resolve the last nagging inconsistency, all of the sudden a very upsetting thing happens—the person you're talking to starts to *giggle*. That is *very* distressing. It is not *seemly* to have one's informants giggle at you when you are playing scientist. What happens next is even worse. After having giggled, the person will say to you, "Look.... I'm sorry.... That's not what really happens. What *really* happens is...." and then give you some completely different story. The first couple of times this happened to me, I regarded it as a psychological aberration of the person I was talking to or, perhaps, a deliberate effort to confuse us. But it's not so. What was happening reflected a fundamental clash of world views.

I had approached those offices convinced (with the confidence that comes of not having realized that there might be an alternative) that office procedures were, at least in principle, clearly defined methods of processing information. Programs, in other words. Things that could be transcribed, analyzed, maybe even reprogrammed for a different "machine." But, above all, I assumed that they *existed*, independently of my enquiries. And that is fantasy. The office worker was under no such delusion. When confronted with my request, she said to herself, "This person wants a description of what I do. Why does that person want that description and what does he want to do with it?" And then she *constructed* something that she thought would be a "good" description for me to have. Of course, I treated that as a description of reality and pounded away at it logically until it fell apart, leaving the office worker very embarrassed. She had told me something, and I had gone over it like a lawyer and caught her fibbing. That's not what she had expected me to do with it. What had she expected me to do with it? She had expected me to use that description *as a model for conducting a social interaction* with her. To an office worker, such descriptions are *social tools* that are constructed and used to shape the behavior of others. One such use is that office workers construct different descriptions of what they do, around a common core of fact, for consumption by different groups of outsiders. By controlling those groups' beliefs about her work, the office worker can cause them to interact with her in a way that she finds advantageous. For example, the sales representatives in one office were led to believe in the existence of a phantom procedure, which took much longer than the real one actually did, in order to provide legitimacy for a requirement that sales representatives initiate their interactions with that part of the office well before their own (sales) deadlines.

The important point about this example is *not* resistance to rationalization, which is a common reaction to any technical innovation. Our office-worker informants, with the best will in the world, simply had no reasonable model of what we were after and thus no idea how to respond to our inquiries. Without a basic notion of information processing as distinct from the social processes that embodied it in their environment, their *only* interpretation of a request for how information was handled was as a sociopolitical request. They will be no better prepared to understand what is happening when their entire work environment begins to be reshaped according to just that notion.

This conceptual separation of information processing from other functions is both central to information technology and fundamentally foreign to most of those that it will impact. It is *this* characteristic of information technology that provides good reason to expect its introduction to have significant social and psychological effects. The high level of reactivity, coupled with a basic lack of understanding of the underlying rationale on the part of those who have to adapt to its changes, strongly suggests that this innovation is a significant social and psychological issue, rather than a normal case of technological change. In order to anticipate its consequences, we must examine the novel concepts that underlie this technology more closely.

## PROCEDURAL REASONING

Beyond the simple realization that information processing is a separable activity, the key idea underlying information technology is the notion of *procedural reasoning*. Procedural reasoning is the process by which one determines the effect of a set of instructions or, alternatively, the set of instructions that will achieve a particular effect. It presumes not only the notion of information as a distinct entity, but also the separation of processor and instructions, a distinction between instances and general rules, and specialized versions of a whole collection of concepts (such as *closed and open forms*) otherwise encountered only in mathematics. Procedural reasoning is the fundamental skill underlying both programming itself and any appreciation of programmed artifacts.

## Symptoms and Consequences

Procedural reasoning is a fundamentally new way of thinking. Formally, it introduces new types of logic; psychologically, it requires the development of a new and different set of skills. Over the next 50 years, this intellectual revolution will fundamentally change the way we think about many problems, in the same way that the introduction of Newtonian mechanics did. Psychologists can already see the impact that a principled way to describe procedures has had on psychological theory, both in the terminology we use and in the kinds of explanations that we find acceptable. In the 1930s, it was fashionable within certain schools of learning theory to lampoon cognitive learning theories, as Guthrie did with his famous remark that Tolman's theories left a rat that was solving a maze sitting in the maze "buried in thought." To the modern psychologist, that does not even seem to be an argument, much less a lampoon. After all, the rat is solving a problem, so what else is it supposed to be doing other than thinking about it? Something that was laughable 40 years ago is no longer laughable. It is standard, conventional, mainstream academic psychology. Over the next 40 years a similar change in thinking will spread throughout most of the populace.

Unfortunately, as one might expect of a recently developed way of thinking, procedural reasoning is currently very poorly understood by people who are not professional "thinkers of procedures." It is easy for an information technologist to forget quite how fundamental that lack of understanding is. The problems I encountered attempting to describe the "information handling procedures" of an existing office are just one example. An information technologist's preconceptions about such procedures are quite different from those of the people who are currently carrying them out, who have not been subjected to the training that a technologist has.

Even worse, this lack of understanding does not manifest itself as a perceived lack of information but as fairly deep misconceptions. The reason is that people who have not internalized the information technologist's view of procedures *do* have a model of something fairly similar, the giving of instructions to another person, which they carry over and apply to programmed devices. This anthropomorphic model, while a useful pedagogical metaphor, has fundamental limits as a predictive or explanatory model of mechanical procedures. Such a model inevitably encourages its users to rely much more on their expectations of the hypothetical *agent* (the person following the instructions) than on the instructions themselves, whereas the mechanical reality is just the reverse.

One of the most striking examples of misjudgement based on anthropomorphic procedural models is the usual reaction of naive observers to even the most sophisticated natural language under-standing system. As many an (embarrassed and frustrated) computa-tional linguist can attest, such naive observers are usually much more impressed by trivia such as the left and right justification of typewritten text than by any ability of the system to understand it! The reason for this (to the expert, incomprehensible) reaction is that the naive observers *themselves* would find it very difficult and tedious to left and right justify typewritten text, but they don't have the least problem understanding natural language. So they think of these problems as comparably difficult, which they fundamentally are not.

We will later argue that programming, or activities very much like it, will become an essential competency in a world full of very complex devices. However, even for people who will never write a program, an appreciation of procedural reasoning is basic to the utilization of information technology. The reason is that, for complex, programmed devices, a procedural theory is the *only* theory that is of any use in explaining why the device does what it does. An object whose behavior is very simple can be "understood" as a list of facts. But for more complex devices, the list-of-facts approach collapses from memory overload. For devices of this type, one has to have a *theory* to represent one's knowledge of its behavior. Unfortunately, if the device is programmed, the odds against finding a nonprocedural theory with any predictive power are very slight.

Failure to understand this is one of the root causes of the dissatis-faction many people feel with programmed technology such as word processors and data processing systems. Without some elementary notions of programming, there is simply no way of making sense of the behavior of such devices. The common result is that most users restrict their interaction with the device to some small part of its repertoire that can be accommodated by a list-of-facts approach. This puzzles the system designers, who cannot understand why their users don't make use of all the facilities that are provided. A rarer, but more spectacular, resolution is that the user falls back on an outrightly anthropomorphic model. Then, of course, the user starts expecting the device to do things that it can't possibly do, and the typical manifestation is a secretary in tears at a word processing machine saying, "Why doesn't it *realize*...?" The information technologist, of course, simply dismisses such behavior, but it is important to recognize it as a symptom of a fundamental misunderstanding.

The introduction of technology that requires new ways of reasoning for its effective utilization is particularly difficult because its users get very little transference from their established skills. Most previous major technological innovations, like the introduction of the automobile, although they may have been profound changes in artifacts, did not require a change in any basic patterns of *thinking*. The conceptual skills needed in order to understand an automobile are the same patterns of reasoning needed to understand any other mechanical object. All mechanical objects can be understood in terms of a naive, qualitative mechanics that enables reasoning of the form, "that rod is broken, so it won't push the warble, and so the fronz won't go down." This type of reasoning was widely distributed in the population before the introduction of most major mechanical innovations such as the automobile. For programmed devices, on the other hand, there is no equivalent base of preexisting skills, except for anthropomorphic models that fundamentally do more harm than good.

## The Use of Procedural Skills

Beyond an abstract need for a first order theory for programmed devices, procedural reasoning skills have an important role to play in their application. The introduction of any complex device poses an immediate problem to its users—how to get the device to do what they want. Their ability to do this, to give instructions to a machine, may not seem to be a particularly deep or fundamental skill and, indeed, for classical machines it has not been such. However, as the variety of machines and their individual complexity increases, it becomes increasingly less trivial. Sheer proliferation causes confusion because the user's cognitive representations for devices with similar behaviors interfere with each other. Devices with very complex behavior can require equally complex specifications. The number and complexity of the devices spawned by the revolution in information technology will simply outrun the simple, linear strategies we presently use to control machines. Consequently, we are about to be in desperate need of a better understanding of mechanisms of specification and control and the underlying cognitive skills.

To make this more concrete, let us examine some ways in which machines can accept instructions. The first type of machine is the *single instruction device*. A single instruction device has exactly one free parameter: you either turn it on or you don't. A simple Xerox copier, once again, provides a good example of a device that, from the user's point of view, has exactly two states. The problem is that many tasks don't have that simple a description—the instructions needed to describe them require more complexity.

The next level of complexity is the *multiple function device.* The essential idea underlying the multiple function device is that of *selection.* The multiple function device provides a fixed set of different tasks (or variants on a task) from which the user *selects* the appropriate one. Selection is a very powerful specification technique and is the basic interface technique by which the vast majority of existing software is parameterized and controlled. However, although a wide variety of techniques (such as menu driven selection schemes) can be used to reduce the cognitive load of recalling the choices available at each point, the primary problem with selection is that it does not scale. A ten-blade Swiss army knife (the paradigm example of selection in conventional technology) is a wonderful idea, but a ten thousand-blade Swiss army knife would be an absurdity: you'd never be able to find the blade you wanted; it would be so heavy that you'd have to carry it behind you in a wagon, and it would break your foot if you dropped it!

Devices whose behavior cannot be characterized by a reasonable number of choices bring us to the class of *open devices.* Since open devices have a behavioral repertoire that is inherently more complex than any enumeration of their instructions, they introduce the new notion of *combinatoric specification*—the composition of several elements from a device's instructional repertoire to create new behavior.

Open devices can be divided into two categories. One category is that of *guided devices,* such as an automobile. The basic characteristic of a guided device is that it has a human being in the control loop, and the device essentially acts as an amplifier or transducer of the human's actions. That's fine for applications in which a person can be left in the loop. One of the promises of information technology, however, is to take people out of a lot of loops in which they are now required! The second type of open device, those without an active human guider, requires instructions that provide the control that a guider would have provided. This introduces a basically new problem for the user, whose specifications can no longer be couched entirely in terms of some *specific* problem but must now be abstracted to deal with some *class* of possible problems. How complex an abstraction this is, of course, varies widely from one application to another. But, however minimal the abstraction, it requires the user, for the first time, to consider her intentions separately from any extention description of what is to be done. This separation of intent from action is the essential characteristic of *programming.*

So, in addition to the elementary notions of programming, which are required for even a rough theory of complex programmed devices, we find that programmatic reasoning also forms the basic skill required to *apply* such devices to more complex tasks. The need for programmatic specifications results from their being the only specification technique for tasks of a certain level of complexity. Since the promise of information technology is largely in coping with just such complex problems, the demands of this complexity will slowly force procedural literacy on all of us. The development of calculators provides an ideal example of this evolution. Calculators began with four arithmetic functions and progressed by adding more and more functions until they outran the number of buttons that would fit on a calculator that was to be carried in a pocket. Presto, the programmable calculator! Other devices can be expected to follow the same route, progressively being forced to provide programmatic specification mechanisms as the only bounded method of increasing their functionality.

## Procedural Reasoning and the Nonprogrammer

If procedural specification is so important, one is drawn to ask if there is anything wrong with the relevant existing technology, such as programming languages, programmable calculators, *etc.* The answer is that it is difficult to use! As anybody who has ever taught a programming course will attest, it's simply not self-evident how to program—a significant fraction of the populace can't seem to "get it." In light of the previous discussion, it should be clear that this is a problem of major proportions. The question of *why* programming is difficult, which will concern us for most of the rest of this paper, is a *psychological* research issue of major importance to the utilization of information technology. A significant simplification in programming would be a psychological result that would have a major effect on minimizing the turbulence of the introduction of information technology.

To begin our exploration of why programming is difficult, I'd like to ask you to introspect while formulating a procedure which, given a set of $N$ numbers, finds the largest. Informal studies show two typical responses to this problem. One pattern of response, if you've never programmed before, is to get confused. The other response is to produce the following algorithm, which, notational variance aside, is the standard programmer's response to the problem of finding the maximum of a set of numbers.

$m \leftarrow 0$

**for** $i$ **from** 1 **to** $N$ **do** (if $m < a_i$ then $m \leftarrow a_i$)

Basically, this algorithm works by initializing a temporary variable (here, $m$) to zero and then, for each element of the set (here, written $a_i$), if the temporary variable is less than the current element, setting the temporary to the current element. After all the elements of the set have been examined, the temporary will be the maximum of the set. Essentially a trivial program, but it provides the basis for a number of interesting observations. First, observe that the procedure has a bug in it. It assumes that at least one of the numbers is nonnegative. If they are all negative, the answer will be (incorrectly) zero. A small point, but one which illustrates the very major problem data processing professionals have with the consequences of the seemingly innocent remark made earlier about "determining one's intent"!

There are some deeper issues though. There are exactly two ways in which you could either have generated that procedure or having been presented with it, could have understood it. One way, the way that you would *believe* you did it if you read any of the literature on programming that is written by computer scientists, is to formulate a loop invariant. For this loop, the appropriate invariant is that, at the end of the $k$th pass through the loop, $m \geq a_j$ for $j \ \varepsilon \ [1, k]$. Having formulated that invariant, one can proceed to prove it by induction. Having proved it by induction, you can instantiate it for $k = N$, and you have now a complete proof that $m$ is a maximum of the set, which is what you want.

The problem is that nobody does it that way. The reason nobody does it that way except in introductory programming courses is that it takes too long and it's far too complicated. If you know how to program, you neither wrote this program, nor did you synthesize an understanding of it. You *knew* the answer. You *recognized* the problem, keyed directly into that knowledge, and pulled out a working procedure. The working procedure that you retrieved is a version of the *iterate, test, and exit* program schema that is one of the very large number of program schemata that any practicing programmer carries around in her head. Such schemata consist of program fragments, abstracted to various degrees, each associated with a variety of propositions about the behavior of the schema and indexed so it can be quickly applied to broad classes of problems. The expertise of the expert programmer is made up of hundreds and thousands of schemata like this, each with extremely detailed and specific rules for its combination with others to produce complex programs.

This analysis of programming skill has very sobering implications for our prospects of being able to produce programmable artifacts for people without programming training. Such people clearly cannot be expected to carry out the mathematical analysis required for the induction proof; they simply don't have the formal reasoning skills. But it is equally unreasonable to expect them to have the complex knowledge network of the expert programmer, as such knowledge is the product of long, costly training. How, then, will we produce devices with the flexibility needed, for example, by clerks doing office work?

## SOME PUTATIVE SOLUTIONS

Most of the commonly suggested approaches to "simplifying" programming simply do not speak to this formulation of the problem. For example, the problem is often claimed to be one of incomprehensibility of programming notations, but notice how little the problem of comprehending the procedure changes when it is rephrased on domain-specific English:

> The maximum ledger entry is initially zero.
>     Each line of the ledger is examined in turn. If the entry on the current line is larger than the maximum ledger entry found so far, consider the current line entry to be the maximum ledger entry.

Even given the ability to use completely unrestricted English (which is far from current technical feasibility), the skills required to understand this procedure are *exactly* the same. Natural language, and other interface concerns, are *not* a solution to this problem. There's a fundamental concept that one has to grasp, a fundamental set of knowledge that one has to have. The notation, while it can degrade performance, does not speak to that problem.

Neither can the issue be finessed by a language which has "find the maximum" as a primitive. The maximum is an instance of a problem *class* whose combinatorics generate an open-ended set of problems. For example, a typical data processing operation that might be encountered by an office clerk:

> Given a pile of invoices, sorted by name, find the name that appears most frequently in the pile.

This has almost the same structure as the maximum problem. Any programmer will use the same program schema to produce a procedure that has *two* temporary variables (one to count the frequency of each name, one to keep track of the current maximum) rather than one. But if *that* operation is a primitive in your language, it's easy to come up with one that needs *three* temporary variables. Shades of the Swiss army knife! Sooner or later you have to deal with the issue of how the users generate *new* operations from the primitives with which they have been provided.

Nor can one wish the procedural literacy problem away by hoping for some radical technical solution such as automatic programming. Not only are such techniques (both now and forseeably) technically infeasible, but they suffer from a more fundamental limitation. It is virtually impossible to have a reasonable conversation about some task without having a basic understanding of that task. It is equally difficult to specify, describe, or evaluate a program produced by some such automatic process without having some notion of what a program *is*.

This problem has haunted the designers of declarative notations intended to avoid the need for computer users to program. Many such notations have been constructed only to find that, without an appreciation of how its expressions are translated into programs, users have no semantic model of the notation. Consequently, only programmers aware of the system's internal operation, or users who acquire this knowledge, can make effective use of it. The same problem would arise throughout one's interaction with an automatic programming system. In order to have any idea either how to describe a problem, when the description is complete, or whether the product satisfies one's intentions, it is necessary to engage in a logical analysis that is essentially similar to (although presumably much less detailed than) that carried out by a programmer. Thus, procedural understanding would still be a central skill, even were automatic programming to be completely successful.

In the interim, note that the paradigm of completely automatic programming is particularly *fail hard*. When an automatic programming system encounters a problem it can't deal with, a user whose model is that the machine will somehow understand what to do can not even engage in a meaningful conversation about what the problem was. For this class of user, automatic programming is not amenable to partial solutions. Thus, neither partial or complete forms of automatic programming provide any escape from the necessity of the user having a basic level of procedural understanding.

Another way we will not solve the problem of procedural literacy is by seizing on some surface defect of existing systems (candidates abound!) and blaming all our problems on it. It is easy to lampoon the human interface designs of existing systems, many of which are indeed poor. But it is downright dishonest to suggest, on the basis of several such examples, that the difficulty of using computer systems reflects simple incompetence or insensitivity on the part of their designers. Equally unfair is the suggestion that these problems would simply not arise were those designers as intelligent (sophisticated, learned in human factors, *etc.*) as "we" are. Often, poor user interfaces reflect economic and logistical contraints, rather than design decisions made in their own right. Often, some fragment that can be made to look absurd in isolation is quite reasonable in the context of the whole system or is entailed by constraints therein. Some systems that are easy to lampoon are used effectively by very large numbers of people, which raises the question of what evidentiary weight one ought to assign to one's own snickers! The fundamental issue is that criticisms based on an appeal to absurdity are entirely unprincipled. They appeal to one's "common sense" (and arrogance and snobbery) without giving the slightest useful indication of what a designer is supposed to do in response. They are both sloppy science and a maximally ineffective way to conduct a dialogue with a technical community.

Scarcely better is the variant that attributes all the faults of existing system interfaces to failure to observe some grand, but very vague, design philosophy. One example is the oft-made claim that the essential problem with existing software systems is lack of "uniformity." Existing systems, it is argued, are baroque and needlessly ad hoc; if only they were "cleaned up" and made more "principled," there would be no further problems. There is some truth to this argument. The design of many existing systems is very ad hoc, and the value of organizing principles, both for learning and for retaining information, is well established. However, its principal appeal is the suggestion that computer literacy problems are amenable to relatively simple solutions, such as the adoption of a few basic design principles. Unfortunately, *effective* principles for large systems are very hard to come by, and without such principles the argument leads nowhere. Even worse, the same reasoning also strongly suggests that choosing the wrong principles would be disastrous.

And so it turns out to be. Some time ago, a major computer manufacturer released an operating system that was deeply influenced by the claim that the key to having users accept a complex system is that it be completely "uniform" in its interpretations. One of the areas that was made subject to this dictum concerned the recognition of file names. In common with most large computer systems, this one allowed its users to maintain several different, numbered versions of each file. Typically, such systems use different versions in different contexts. Thus, when the user deletes a file, the system selects the oldest version, but when one is created the system will use a new (higher) version number. In this system, it was decided to eliminate this context sensitive nonuniformity and use the same version number in all cases. As you might expect, this ran very badly afoul of the fact that users have very strong expectations about which version is appropriate in which context. The wrong uniformity may be very simple to describe. However, running counter to the "obvious" interpretation does *not* simplify things from the point of the user, who now has to remember whether the artificial convention is appropriate in each situation. The point is that notions like "uniformity" and "simplicity" simply have little or no context independent meaning and thus do not constitute useful design principles.

This harsh evaluation of approaches that dwell on the surface characteristics of existing systems should not be taken as an endorsement of the current state of such systems. Curiously persistent historical oddities, inappropriate technology, and simple poor design combine to make many contemporary computing environments hostile to, rather than supportive of, the fledgling user. In addition to eliminating the human factors outrages, there are a number of facilities that could be provided using existing technology that would significantly ease many of these problems. However, these tools simplify things for the procedurally literate; they do not create procedural literates.

## A DIGRESSION ON LOW LEVEL ISSUES

Analysis in terms of surface task characteristics (how it is done, rather than what is done) is an inappropriate response to the principal problems of information technology; the level of analysis is just too low. However, even if one chooses to discuss mechanics, rather than content, there is still a desperate need to raise the level of discussion from that found in the standard system design and human factors literatures. For example, rather than debate the mechanics of detecting and reporting errors, it is far more constructive to consider using the *constraints* the environment will sooner or later impose to provide constructive *advice*, rather than hostile reprimands, to the user. The most straightforward application of this idea is to devices, such as programming language processors, that only accept instructions in certain highly constrained formats. Our current technological "solution" to this problem is to have the user prepare an incantation, which is presented to the device for its consideration, the result of which is, almost always, WRONG! It is currently fashionable among technologists to exult in this depressing state of affairs as a desirable error-detecting property of the redundancy (potential for internal inconsistency) in the specifications for incantations. Users, strangely enough, are less charmed and would like to minimize the frequency of this dolorous result.

The response of the human factors psychologist has been to explore different syntaxes for incantations in the hope of finding one that is easier to learn. Highly significant results can be obtained following this approach, if for no better reason than many syntaxes are virtually impossible to learn. But surely it is more productive to consider whether one should ever put a person in such a situation of almost certain failure. One should *surely* not allow failure to be the dominant characteristic of a person's initial experience. However, for the average person who starts to learn programming, her first $N$ interactions with a computer are of the form WRONG! And that turns people off! In fact, it makes one seriously wonder about the psychology of the people who survive that experience and go on to design the next generation of systems. They were either very lucky the first time around, or they have been selected for a very strange set of personality traits. The knowledge that was used to say WRONG! can be turned around and used to help *guide* somebody through the syntax of an interaction (e.g., Hansen, 1971). Such reversals of the current technology–first thinking constitute the higher level human factors paradigms, which should be the focus of future research on interactive systems.

## ALTERNATIVE PROCEDURAL FORMALISMS

Leaving aside environmental issues, another approach to procedural literacy is the claim that the problems are a result of the way technologists have come to think about computing. As distinct from the criticisms of syntax and low level semantic that were dismissed earlier, this argument is that the *conceptual* structure of existing programming formalisms is both ineffective and needlessly foreign to the noninitiated user. The exemplars of this point of view are the LOGO (Papert, 1971) and SmallTalk projects (Goldberg, 1980). Their claim is that, if we think about computing in some better way, then programming will no longer be particularly difficult. The problem is seen not to be people's inability to acquire procedural skills, but the arcane formalisms within which those skills must currently be practised. Both LOGO and SmallTalk (and others) present different, unconventional approaches to programming, LOGO emphasizing the use of recursion and SmallTalk the use of message passing, which are alleged to remove the problems that confront the novice programmer.

Unfortunately, the strong form of this position is as yet unconfirmed. While people can be *taught* computing in these terms, there is no evidence that it is a spontaneous skill. Consequently, this position is often paired with an educational position to the effect that it is important that procedural notions (in particular, the new ones being advocated) be made a basic literacy skill on the same level as elementary mathematics. It should be clear that the whole thrust of this paper supports the case for this kind of education. However, adopting such a program of education confronts one immediately with the problem of exactly what is to be taught, which raises again the question of what makes programming difficult. Neither the urgency of beginning an educational program, nor the clear advantages of languages like LOGO and SmallTalk over those of conventional programming practice, implies that procedural literacy is simply a matter of changing our programming languages. The sugar-coated environments of LOGO and SmallTalk have more than enough attractions to provide real advantages over conventional technology.

That the languages alone are sufficient to eliminate the problems of acquiring procedural skill has simply not been established.

Indeed, the Gedanken analysis of programming presented earlier provides strong reason for suspecting otherwise. To see this, consider a recursive solution (of the form one might write in LOGO) to the maximum problem. Expressed in English, such a solution might be:

> The maximum of a set containing no numbers is zero. For $N > 0$, a set of $N$ numbers has a maximum that is the larger of any random element selected out of it and the maximum of the rest of them.

As a sometime mathematician, I find this solution simple, elegant, and beautiful, but how does one understand it? One way is by formulating a recursion induction, similar to the loop induction we examined previously. Another way is to understand it by virtue of having been told, learned, and internalized this particular schema, which is known as *tail recursion*. Both methods present the *exactly* same problems as the loop version did. Perhaps, more elegantly stated, but the same problem.

Furthermore, the claim that recursive (or message passing, or whatever) notations are good naive programming metaphors because of their simplicity and/or elegance is a subtle version of the same fallacy that underlies the advocacy of "uniformity." (At least, I find it more subtle because it appeals to my prejudices.) Qualities like "simplicity and elegance" are *not* properties of objects but properties of their evaluation within some other cognitive framework. The reason I find the recursive solution so "simple and elegant" is not that it *is* simple and elegant, but rather that it *appears* so in the context of my mathematical training. When you consider the amount of extra information that has to be supplied in order to interpret that concise solution, its inherent "simplicity" becomes a great deal less clear.

## LIMITED FLEXIBILITY NOTATIONS

A completely different conclusion that can be drawn from the analysis of the maximum problem is that programming really is inherently complex. But if programming is an activity of considerable complexity, comparable perhaps to mathematics, it suggests that we abandon the search for a globally "simple" solution. There may be none, no more than there is a simple way of doing mathematics. If programming is inherently complex, any attempt to simplify it must be based on some property of the programs that some class of people actually want to write, which allows a simpler approach. Arbitrary programming would remain complex, but simpler forms would allow nonprogrammers to formulate most of the complex instructions that they need to cope with complex information technology. At the very least, we might expect to be able to construct programming notations that exclude programs whose properties are undecidable. Whether or not this formal restriction improves subjective ease of use, it simplifies many of the technical problems associated with providing programmer support facilities such as program analyzers. This in turn makes it possible for the programming environment to provide significantly more advice and assistance to the programmer.

The essence of this approach is to treat the problem of providing procedural tools as one of matching the flexibility of those tools to the types of programs that specific classes of users want to write. To see why this is a source of significant leverage, consider a card player sorting a bridge hand into order. Has it ever occurred to that person that one day she might be dealt a set of cards such that the sorting would not terminate? So that no matter how many times individual cards were exchanged, the hand was always out of order? I can report from experience that if you raise this with the average card player, she will look at you as if you were mad! The problem simply does not arise in the average person's procedural space. However, reformulate her card sorting procedure as a programming problem and it arises in spades (so to speak). The question of whether one's program goes into an infinite loop is a primary concern of every programmer. Somehow, when we map simple procedural problems into existing programming environments, we put our users in a larger, more complex and more difficult, space than they really need.

What would a limited flexibility procedural environment look like? The domain of social science data analysis is a familiar context in which one approach to this problem has been developed to the level of a complete prototype. In many ways, this is an ideal domain in which to explore this problem. Social scientists are heavy users of computerized data analysis, yet few have either the expertise or the time to program their analysis software themselves. As a result, nearly all their data analysis is done with software that uses the *selection* paradigm discussed earlier—the system provides a long list of analyses from which the scientist chooses one to be applied to the data. Unfortunately, the number of conceivable analyses is essentially unbounded, so social scientists will also recognize the classic symptoms of a selection system approaching overload. The task set of the packages is closed but the logical structure of data analysis allows an open-ended set of tasks, so the task set never completely covers the users' needs. No matter how much effort is invested, there are always some analyses that are not available, despite being clearly related to some that are. The constant pressure for adding them makes the system large and clumsy. It becomes so difficult to find what you want in a manual the size of a telephone book, that a class of experts evolves to interface users to the system. Data analysis instructors begin to teach data analysis as a set of separate and unrelated operations. They have little choice. Since the statistical relationships between different analyses are not reflected in the computing environment, any principled instruction will generate demands for analyses for which no computational support exists. In short, data analysis is in exactly the position, between where a selection system breaks down and short of the need for arbitrary programming, where an intermediate procedural environment would be most effective.

The IDL data analysis system (Smith and Sheil, 1975; Kaplan, Sheil, and Smith, 1978) is an attempt to provide a restricted programming environment for this domain. The structure of IDL reflects the logical structure that underlies data analysis tasks, rather than the separate analyses that are frequently used. The key idea is that the large set of analyses can be generated by simple combinations of a very much smaller set of basic data analytic ideas. Thus, the system provides a small set of operators, each of which provides the computations associated with one of those basic ideas (e.g., removing the variance associated with one variable from a variable space). In addition, a *simple* set of operations is provided for composing the operators together to carry out analyses. Thus, the underlying structure both of the domain and of the system is reflected out directly to the user. A geometric analogy is to view the design as a set of basis vectors for the analysis space such that any point in that space can be described straightforwardly in terms of them.

The claim for simplicity (as perceived by the user) has two parts: the basic data analytic ideas are considered to be (at least latently) part of the expertise the user has by virtue of being a data analyst; the combinatoric operators are required to be of absolutely minimal complexity. Specifically, IDL provides exactly one composition primitive, *functional composition*. Functional composition allows the output of one operation to be given as input to another. That is the *sole* programmatic construct in IDL—there are no assignment statements, loops, recursions, or anything else that would require procedural sophistication. Yet, although functional composition is the sole combinatoric tool, it generates an open-ended task set, specifically the entire space of linear statistics. On the other hand, the system can be described very concisely, the manual is very thin, and the combinatoric power is very weak. At least in its surface characteristics, it seems plausible that this system might provide the requisite flexibility without also providing a programmatic complexity with which its users could not deal.

IDL has been in use as a research prototype for several years, during which time we have learned something about the strengths and the limitations of this approach. It *does* allow people to formulate new data analysis procedures, including many computations that no task–list system could feasibly have provided. Its users seem generally comfortable with the composition scheme it provides. IDL is also a valuable instructional tool because its computational structure is very close to the conceptual structure of linear statistics, so that knowledge of one reinforces the other.

The basic weakness of IDL is that there are sharp limits to how deep a chain of composition users find comfortable. Sometimes, in order to obtain some particular analysis, one has to apply one operator to the results of another, applied to a third, to a fourth, to a fifth, to a sixth, and so on. For example, computing some quantity of interest might require inverting some matrix, extracting its diagonal, dropping out one element, and summing the square roots of the positive ones that remain. It turns out to be a nontrivial skill to predict the result of composing six or seven operators in this fashion. The effect of such a series, even if it does not involve any deep statistical intuition, is simply not transparent.

What has therefore happened is that most users remain fairly "close" to the basic operators that are provided and rely on a small cult of wizards to provide simple expressions to get them to nonstandard places. It was simply not the case, unfortunately, that reducing the combinatoric power or "glue" of the procedural system, made it straightforward to construct a path to any point in its space. Complexity arises simply from the *length* of the chain of reasoning. One of the consequences is that the builder of such a system is more or less constrained to put the basic operators as close as possible to certain analyses that are known to be used with high frequency. For example, linear regression has a very beautiful treatment in terms of a set of operators that manipulate variable spaces (see Dempster, 1969). Analysis of variance, on the other hand, does not have a similarly compact description in terms of independently motivated operators. It can be obtained by a composition of replication and accumulation but in a very nonobvious way. In such cases, the designer feels obligated to provide an operator whose sole motivation is to facilitate the frequently used task, in order to enhance initial user acceptability. But that is in some sense a concession that long chains of reasoning are becoming almost as difficult as conventional programming.

Furthermore, many domains do not lend themselves to such a spare, elegant decomposition. Consider Figure 2's short excerpt from the procedure manual for a fictitious operational office, which describes in a very terse and abbreviated form the jobs of some of the people therein. None of these procedures requires any judgement, and no part of them is particularly complex, so they should be describable in some simple notation. On the other hand, it is not at all clear exactly *what* it is about

**Time card processing**

**All Employees**

Each week fill in your time card for the previous week and send it to your supervisor. The card should be in by Wednesday of the following week. Its not being in by Friday of the following week constitutes grounds for dismissal.

**Supervisor**

1. Verify and sign the time card for each employee in your group. Send the signed card to the bookkeeper. Send *each time card as soon as you have signed it - do not hold up operations by waiting until you have all the time cards for your group.* Use the time card log sheet to keep track of time cards. Sign your own time card.

2. You are responsible for assuring that all time cards have been completed. If you do not receive a time card by Wednesday, mail a reminder form to the employee.

3. If you do not receive a time card by Friday, initiate dismissal of the employee. Notify the bookkeeper if you do this.

4. Process vacation requests. Each employee may request vacation. You must assure that the duties of your group are met, by assigning others to cover for them; use the Cover Assignment form to do this. Use the vacation log sheet to coordinate vacations.

**Bookkeeper**

1. You will receive time cards from the supervisors. Check the totals and the signature. Use the pay rate scale to compute the gross pay and enter it on the time card. Use the tax rate scale to compute the tax and enter it on the time card. Compute the net pay and enter it on the time card. Mail each time card to the cashier as soon as possible in each week.

2. Maintain an up-to-date estimate of the pay expenditures for your division and send these each week to each supervisor.

**Cashier**

You will receive completed time cards from the bookkeeper. Check that the pay computations are correct. Complete and sign a pay slip for each time card. Mail the pay slip to the employee and file the time cards.

**Figure 2.** Extract from a set of office procedures

such procedures that makes them significantly simple; they certainly do *not* have the clean, mathematical structure of linear statistics. Further, unlike the domain of data analysis where the requirement was for descriptive power, the procedural nature of these examples (i.e., the "do this then that" flavor of the instructions) is so dominant as to make highly restricted procedural structures, such as IDL's restriction to functional composition, unnatural.

## THE PSYCHOLOGICAL AGENDA

The first step towards providing descriptive tools for procedures such as these is to explore the conceptual models their users have of procedures. Despite the previous criticism of the tendency of naive procedural reasoning to fall into anthropomorphic interpretations, the use of quasi–procedures such as job instructions, recipes, directions for how to get from one place to another, etc. provides evidence that there is *some* kind of procedural framework that is widely used to formulate, follow, and reason about procedures. Anthropomorphic intrusions may weaken the degree to which this framework can be productively applied to mechanistic devices, but the utility of naive procedure descriptions does suggest some underlying effective reasoning power. Were it possible to characterize this framework more precisely it would provide us with a model for procedures that is both widely distributed within the population and that maps directly onto the class of procedures that people actually *do* want to express to machines. Such a *naive procedural semantics* will probably be very different from the formal procedural semantics of computer science. Its study is both an important topic for cognitive psychology, because of its clear relations to planning and other kinds of reasoning, and a critical contribution that psychologists could make to the effective utilization of information technology.

The last point makes explicit a thread that has run throughout this discussion—these are all *psychological* claims. Among others, we have considered claims that recursive thinking leads to better programming; that specification by selection is easier than by composition, which is easier than closed form induction; that programming is a knowledge based skill, in the same sense that we now understand chess to be; that the length of a chain of functional composition is a major source of difficulty. As a sometime psychologist, I feel embarrassed that, despite these all being psychological claims, I've offered nothing but anecdotal evidence for any of them. Their central importance to the effective use of information technology makes it vital that these psychological hypotheses should be examined as such, rather than left to the anecdotal and stylistic arguments of the technical community.

However, having ceded the field, there are a few concerns that I would like to urge on those who conduct this examination. Most importantly, it is critically important that the empirical and theoretical questions be phrased at a high level. It's very easy to focus in too narrowly on issues that are specific to a particular combination of technology and application. Nearly ten years ago, Nickerson (1969) observed that computing environments were changing sufficiently rapidly that psychologists often studied problems motivated by practical concerns that were obsolete by the time their data was collected. The pace has not slowed. I have argued that the study of the behavioral impact of variations in programming language syntax is a contemporary example of such misguided concern. Our research must address the basic issues in human–machine interaction, rather than ephemera that depend on volatile characteristics of their current configurations.

Lest that sound too much like an appeal for the obvious, let me point out that this can only be done at considerable cost in experimental control. Contrasting the effectiveness of, for example, two programming formalisms that are identical except for some minor variation achieves control, but at the price of embedding any findings deeply within the context of the controlled language features. In the context of real programming, language features almost certainly have major interactions with each other. Thus, the results of such a closely controlled study have limited generalizability outside the particular situation studied and as a result have *neither theoretical nor practical significance.* Psychologists are, rightfully, extremely reluctant to surrender experimental control. On the other hand, how compelling does one find a psychological study of novice programming (Sime, Green, and Guest, 1977) that found novices' fears of dealing with a teletype so overwhelmed their effects that they studied "programming" in the context of a bizarre game, which involved feeding a mechanical rabbit! The authors of that study make a plausible case that their game taps the same mental skills as programming. One the other hand, if one has to control things that tightly in order to detect any effects, they are probably not very interesting to an engineer who has to apply them in a world in which such other influences abound.

It's somewhat of a cliche, but I would once again like to urge that we adopt a very sceptical attitude in evaluating our own findings. It's very easy in this domain to get statistically significant effects. *Everything* has an effect. But significance in that sense is not useful. The only statistical methodology that will detect findings of interest to technologists is the methodology that Edwards dubbed the "intra-occular traumatic test," i.e., does the effect hit you between the eyes! If you need a mass of statistics to prove to me that some technique is useful, I'm not interested. The problems are sufficiently large that a half a percent of the variance will not make much of an impression on them. The significance of such results is confined to the statistical.

Another, fairly depressing, requirement of work in this area is that it will require very complex theories. This is probably characteristic of the study of any knowledge–based skill. The theories that one might sketch on the back of an envelope simply are not complex enough to deal with a highly learned skill, like programming, or mathematics, or anything of that level of complexity. This is the reason why the classic experimental paradigms are not all that useful. The numbers of variables and configurations that affect any one task are so huge that it is infeasible to use nomothetic techniques, which require subjects to be stratified into relatively homogeneous treatment groups. The only alternative is the detailed study of individual behavior, using cross–task or within–task consistency as the evidentiary principle by which construct validity is demonstrated.

$$
\begin{array}{r} 41 \\ +9 \\ \hline 50 \end{array} \qquad
\begin{array}{r} 328 \\ +917 \\ \hline 1345 \end{array} \qquad
\begin{array}{r} 989 \\ +52 \\ \hline 1141 \end{array} \qquad
\begin{array}{r} 66 \\ +887 \\ \hline 1053 \end{array} \qquad
\begin{array}{r} 216 \\ +13 \\ \hline 229 \end{array}
$$

$$
\begin{array}{r} 446 \\ +815 \\ \hline \end{array} \qquad
\begin{array}{r} 201 \\ +399 \\ \hline \end{array}
$$

**Figure 3.** Some addition problems [*Source:* Brown and Burton, 1978]

Evidence of this form is more familiar to linguists than psychologists. Therefore, as an example, I would like to discuss one approach to the study of a (semi) complex skill that might at first sight seem far removed from programming. Earlier, I claimed that people have an elementary understanding of procedural constructs from a variety of procedures they have mastered in other contexts. One of the most important experiences of this sort is learning the procedures for elementary arithmetic, which children are taught in school. These are among the very few standard procedural skills that we all learn and that we all learn to do essentially the same way. The displacement of this teaching by calculators is unfortunate, not because of the utility of mental arithmetic, but because of what is learned about *procedures.* It is ironic that this loss should be occuring now, just when we have learned enough about procedures to train teachers to use this experience to develop some more generalized procedural skills.

Consider how one might study the development of these simple arithmetic skills. Figure 3 contains the answers given by a primary school child to a series of place value addition problems, abstracted from Brown and Burton (1978). One's first impression is that the answers are more or less random, but it's not too difficult to find a pattern. According to Brown and Burton's analysis, the child is reliably following a procedure, but the procedure has a bug in it. One buggy procedure that would generate this behavior is that, when the child is carrying an overflow from one column to the next, she is accumulating all the carries all the way across. Rather than just adding the carry to the next column and forgetting about it, she is acting as if she has a carry register (to use a piece of computer jargon). Every time a carry takes place, she adds the carry into it so the effect propagates all the way to the leftmost column. If this diagnosis is correct, one should be able to predict what the child will answer for the next two problems. If the answers are in fact 1361 and

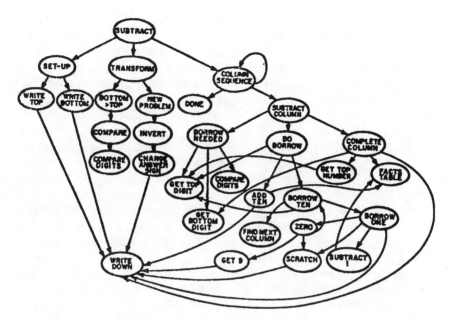

**Figure 4.** A procedural network for subtraction [*Source:* Brown and Burton, 1978]

700, that's a very impressive piece of confirmation. What kind of nomothetic data could be so compelling? When one is studying skills that have this much individual variability, individual predictive models of this form are exactly what one wants and as much as one could reasonably hope for.

One might object that all that could come of such research would be a typology of arithmetic bugs, and what kind of theory is that? Well, for a start, it is a very useful theory for a teacher, because it provides significant insight into how to diagnose and correct childrens' misunderstandings. The theory itself can be represented as a procedural network of the form shown in Figure 4, which is a model of place value subtraction taken from Brown and Burton (1978). The network is composed from a set of skills that are considered primitive, such as looking up in a table of facts the value of a basic operation on two digits.

The success of these models as descriptive techniques then raises the next scientific question: what underlying procedural mechanism admits exactly the observed bugs and no others? For example, children never show a systematic pattern of getting the digits of the right answer but in the reverse of the right order. One's theory must explain the absence of that bug just as cogently as it accounts for the presence of those that do occur. The simplest theory of bug generation is random alteration of such networks (e.g., random addition and deletion of paths). The set of all networks generated by such random changes constitute one prediction (not very accurate, as it turns out) as to which bugs will occur. In later work, Brown and VanLehn (1980) develop a more sophisticated theory of the process by which partially formed and erroneous procedural skills are repaired by a set of heuristic repair strategies, which have the property that they generate the systematic bugs that are observed in children's behavior.

This example has illustrated two important points. The first is that it illustrates a methodology that can be used to investigate complex cognitive skills, such as the comprehension of procedures. The second point, however, has disturbing consequences for us. This model of subtraction is *appallingly* complex. It is, after all, a theory of what children learn about subtracting numbers in second grade. The study of procedural reasoning demands a theory of what adults learn in four years of programming courses in college. I am appalled when I think of how complex that theory will have to be. On the other hand, feeling appalled and feeling challenged are simply different reactions to the same perception of reality!

## THE CHALLENGE

Psychology has already adopted much of its modern theoretical language from information technology. The problem of understanding how people reason about procedures, while clearly motivated by the pressing needs to make effective use of that technology, constitutes the complementary area of empirical research. Like problem solving, information science's other gift to empirical psychology, procedural reasoning is a deep enough problem to join the classical areas of cognitive research, such as learning, memory, and perception, in shaping psychological theory. I hope that psychology will take up this challenge and help technologists cope with the problem of coping with complexity.

## ACKNOWLEDGEMENTS

These ideas originally emerged during extended research collaborations with Ron Kaplan and Martin Newell, both of whom have had a profound influence on my thinking about these problems. My initial formulations were both encouraged and polished by interactions with colleagues in Cognitive and Instructional Sciences at Xerox PARC. The final form profited immensely from detailed commentary by Ron Kaplan and Joanne Martin.

# REFERENCES

Brown, J. and Burton, R. Diagnostic models for procedural bugs in basic mathematical skills. *Cognitive Science,* 1978, *2,* 155–92.

Brown, J. and VanLehn, K. Repair theory: A generative theory of bugs in procedural skills. *Cognitive Science* 1980, *4,* 329–426.

Dempster, A. *Elements of continuous multivariate analysis.* Reading, Mass.: Addison-Wesley, 1969.

Goldberg, A. SmallTalk: Dreams and schemes. Xerox Palo Alto Research Center, 1980.

Hansen, W. Creation of hierachic text with a computer display. Ph.D. thesis, Stanford University, 1971.

Kaplan, R., Sheil, B., and Smith, E. The interactive data analysis language reference manual. Xerox Palo Alto Research Center, SSL-1978-4, 1978.

Nickerson, R. Man-computer interaction: A challenge for human factors research. *IEEE Transaction on Man-machine Systems,* 1969, *10,* 164–180.

Papert, S. Teaching children thinking. MIT Artificial Intelligence Laboratory, Memo 247, 1971.

Sime, M., Green, T., and Guest, D. Scope marking in computer conditionals: A psychological evaluation. *International Journal of Man-machine Studies,* 1977, *9,* 107–18.

Smith, E. and Sheil, B. An interactive data analysis language. *Social Science Information,* 1975, *14,* 139–46.

# Computers and the Common Man

## Alphonse Chapanis

It's safe to say that technology has advanced more in the last 100 years than it has in the entire history of man up to a century ago. Indeed the scientific and technological accomplishments of the last 100 years are so many that they almost defy enumeration. But if I were to pick the two technological creations that have had the most profound effects on our civilization I would nominate the automobile and the computer.

### THE AUTOMOBILE AND THE COMPUTER

The automobile has changed our way of living, of doing business, and of enjoying our leisure time. Vast new industries have been created because of the automobile. It has given us enormously greater mobility and contributed to changes in family structure and social cohesiveness. It has been responsible for new forms of crime. It has changed the way we design cities and organize our society. And it has made us so dependent on fossil fuel that it could potentially lead to the disintegration of civilized life as we know it now.

The computer has had no less profound effects on society, on our ways of living, and on our ways of doing business. Computers help manage our finances, our checking accounts, and our charge accounts. They help schedule our rail and air travel, book our theatre tickets, check out our groceries, diagnose our illnesses, teach our children, and amuse us with sophisticated games. Computers have made it possible to erase time and distance in our telecommunications, thereby giving us the freedom to choose the times and places at which we work. And like the automobile, computers have created new industries and have spawned new forms of crime. In fact, computers have become so intricately woven into the fabric of our daily lives that without computers our civilization could not function as it does today.

## Attitudes

Despite these similarities between the two kinds of machines, there are, it seems to me, at least two very important differences between them. The first has to do with people's attitudes toward them. Almost everyone likes automobiles, and a substantial proportion of people actually love them. People coddle their vehicles, wash them, polish them, decorate them, and, according to some psychiatrists, treat them subconsciously as projections of their own egos. During the 1979 gasoline crisis in the United States, one newspaper columnist observed, not entirely facetiously, that Americans are willing to give up their children and their wives more readily than their automobiles. These days, happiness is being able to drive into a service station and drive out with a full tank of gasoline.

Computers, on the other hand, evoke quite different attitudes. In a factor analysis of attitudes and beliefs about computers from interviews of some 3,000 persons aged 18 years and older, Lee (1970) found two factors that were virtually independent of one another. One factor was a positively-toned set of beliefs centering on the notion that computers are beneficial instruments for man's purposes—helpful in science, industry, space exploration, and in freeing man from boring and tiresome tasks. The other factor in Lee's opinion was a more science-fiction view of the computer. This factor was loaded with beliefs that the computer is a relatively autonomous machine that can perform the functions of human thinking—functions previously thought to be the unique province of the human mind. That in turn was viewed as a downgrading of humans—a depreciation of man's previously unique significance in the order of things. Some statements that correlate highly with this second factor are:

- With these machines, the individual person will not count for very much anymore.
- They sort of make you feel that machines can be smarter than people.
- Someday in the future, these machines may be running our lives for us.
- These machines can make important decisions better than people.
- They are going too far with these machines.

This second set of attitudes and beliefs about computers is quite different from those that characterize the friendly, warm feelings people have towards automobiles. Cars give people freedom and an identity; computers restrict people and strip them of an identity.

Although Lee's study was published in 1970, his data were collected in 1963—about 17 years ago. Computers have become quite common-place in those 17 years. Have attitudes changed in the meantime? To test current attitudes about computers, Miss E. Zoltan of my laboratory has just completed another attitude survey. Her questionnaire contained 64 items as compared with Lee's 20, but her sample of subjects was smaller—521 versus 3,000. The subjects in Zoltan's study were profes-sional persons—certified public accountants, lawyers, physicians, and pharmacists.

Seven factors emerged from Miss Zoltan's factor analysis of her data. The first two are strikingly similar to Lee's. The first accounts for 15.3 percent of the variance and is characterized by a positively-toned set of words and statements: efficient, precise, reliable, dependable, effec-tive, systematic, fast, organized, and cooperative. Miss Zoltan's second factor accounts for 10.1 percent of the variance. It is characterized by such words as dehumanizing, depersonalizing, impersonal, cold, and unforgiving.

To sum up, then, it doesn't appear that attitudes towards computers have changed very much in the past 17 years. The best way of saying it is that people appear to be ambivalent about computers. They have some strong positive and some strong negative attitudes about them. All of which may partly account for public statements such as the following attributed to Jeffrey A. Rochlis, president of Mattel, Inc.'s electronics division: "The very word 'computer' scares most consumers, so we deliberately avoid using it as much as possible" (Sansweet, 1980).

## Costs

A second major difference between automobiles and computers concerns their costs. Automobiles, and their operation, have increased in cost over the past several decades. Indeed, some automobiles today cost as much as some small houses did just a few years ago. Operational costs have also increased, even if one discounts those costs for inflation.

Computing costs, on the other hand, have decreased dramatically over the past few decades. Since several participants in this symposium have already made this point dramatically, there is no need for me to dwell on it at great length. Figure 1, however, shows that the costs of disk storage over a 20-year period have decreased by roughly two orders of magnitude. Figure 2 shows the costs, and the processing time, required to do a mixture of about 1,700 computer operations, including payroll, discount computation, file maintenance, table lookup, and report preparation. Over the 20-year period shown here, not only have costs plummeted, but processing time has also dropped commensurately. Robert W. DeSio, director of IBM's Systems Research Institute, said recently that if automotive technology had advanced as much as computer technology had during the past three decades, we would now be able to buy an automobile for about $20 and travel around the world on a tankful of gasoline.

## THE RELATIVE COSTS OF PEOPLE AND COMPUTERS

The dramatic decrease in computer costs has some implications for the human use of computers. Figure 3 shows computer costs versus user

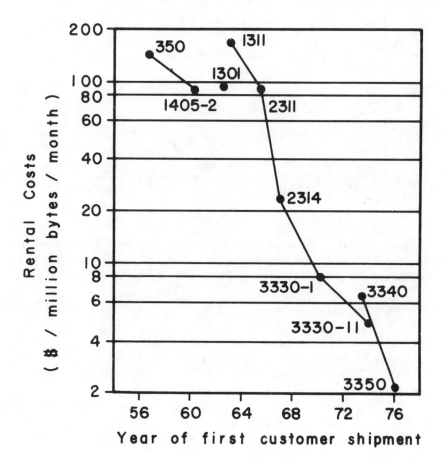

**Figure 1.** Rental costs of disk storage over a 20-year period. The numbers on the curves refer to various IBM products [*Source:* Doherty, 1979]

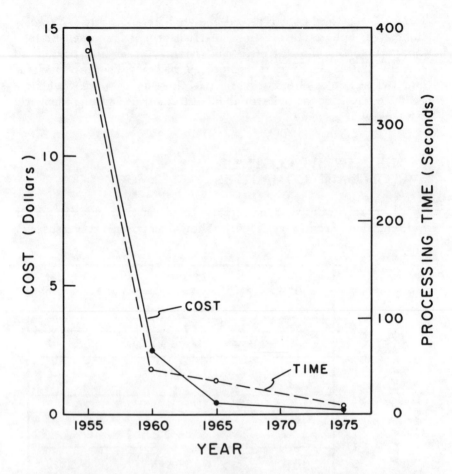

**Figure 2.** Data processing costs and data processing time to do a standard mix of about 1,700 computer operations [*Source:* International Business Machines Corporation, 1976]

costs at the IBM Computing Center over a four-year period. In 1973, computer costs and human costs were very nearly equal. These costs have since diverged until in 1977 the human costs were from four to six times those of the hardware.

The lesson to be learned from data such as these is that the really significant cost savings are to be made, not by reducing computer costs, but rather by reducing the human costs of using computers. And that, of course, is a human factors problem.

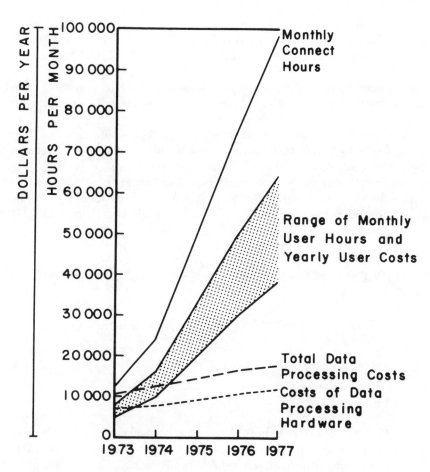

**Figure 3.** Computer costs versus user costs at the IBM Thomas J. Watson Computing Center over a four-year period [*Source:* Doherty, 1979]

## THE HARDWARE-SOFTWARE VERSUS USER POINT OF VIEW IN DESIGN

Recognizing the need to improve the efficiency of the human element in computer systems leads us to a new kind of design philosophy—one that starts not with hardware or software, but with people. In the past, computer systems seem to have been designed and marketed from a hardware point of view. By that I mean that computer designers and manufacturers designed and built a system that they thought had new, unique, or more useful characteristics than competitive equipment on the market and then sold the computer on that basis. Reduced to its essentials, the sales argument was: "Here is a computer that is faster, cheaper, more versatile, or has some other more desirable characteristics than its competitors. Buy it and put it to use." The implicit assumption was that the users—whoever they might be—were adaptable, could learn to use the computer, and could adapt the computer to their particular needs.

That kind of philosophy and point of view is gradually changing, particularly as computers become cheaper and extend into areas of application that now involve almost all segments of our population. The proliferation of computers is making us realize that they must now be designed from the reverse point of view. Instead of starting with the hardware or software, we need to start with the user, with his requirements, and his needs.

## THE ESSENTIAL ELEMENTS OF MAN-COMPUTER SYSTEMS

The basic building blocks of man-computer systems are:

- Hardware.
- Software.
- The work environment.
- The user.

Interactions between these elements are the places in which human factors can contribute to increased effectiveness. Many of these interactions draw on rather conventional areas of human factors, although the specific applications may differ from those that are generally treated in textbooks and handbooks of human factors.

### User-Hardware Problems

User-hardware problems are those that arise from interactions between the user and the actual pieces of machinery or equipment that make up the computer. Mostly these are interactions between the user and such things as the keyboard, the display unit, and the work surface on which the computer is placed. Keyboard layout and design; workplace layout; the size, shape, and design of characters on display units; access to the internal parts of equipment for repair, maintenance, or just routine operations such as changing ribbons—all these fall properly in this category of user-hardware problems.

## User-Software Problems

User-software problems are those that originate from the language of computer programs, the concepts and strategies that computer programs impose on users to solve problems, and the documentation, that is, the instructions and manuals, that explain how computer systems and programs are supposed to be used.

## User-Environment Problems

User-environment problems include such things as noise, lighting, temperature, and crowding. Glare from screens and ambient illumination, noise from terminals and printers, the physical arrangement of work spaces—all these and more fall into this category of problems.

## THE AIM OF THIS PAPER

In this paper I am entirely concerned with some user-software problems associated with computers. That is not to deny the importance of the interactions between the user and the hardware or between the user and the environment in which computers are located. However, it is in the area of software that I feel the really significant gains are to be made in improving the efficiency of man-computer interactions. I emphasize the word "some" in the introductory sentence of this paragraph. User-software problems are so many, and so complex, that it would be impossible to treat them all in a presentation as short as this one. My aim here is rather to discuss a few software problems that interest me. Additional details and a discussion of our research program at The Johns Hopkins University can be found in the Appendix of this volume.

## WHO IS THE USER?

In attacking user-software problems, the first human factors question that needs to be answered is: "Exactly who is the user?" The answer, more often than not, is that there is no single user, but that every system has multiple users and that all of them need to be considered, although perhaps to differing extents.

Take, for example, a computerized banking operation. One group of users is, of course, the customers, the broad spectrum of people who want to use banking facilities and services. A second group of users consists of bank employees, such as tellers, data input operators, and accountants. Still another group of users is the system operators and maintenance personnel, who are not involved with banking operations per se, but are concerned with keeping the system operating and insuring that it does the job it is supposed to do. Still other possible groups of users are the bank managers and boards of directors.

Comparable multiple user groups can be identified for virtually all computer systems, for example, with those in information-retrieval systems (Goldstein and Ford, 1978), postal operations, manufacturing, and education. The important point is that diverse user groups have different characteristics and needs. Bank customers represent a much broader cross section of the population than do the other users of a computerized banking operation. Customers are generally infrequent users and so are much more likely to be unfamiliar with the operation of the system and with financial operations. Bank tellers, on the other hand, are generally better trained than customers in both respects. Neither customers nor bank tellers, however, need to get into the actual programming of the system. Maintenance personnel do. As a result, maintenance personnel have special requirements because they need to diagnose and to correct difficulties when they arise.

All these diverse groups of users have legitimate claims on the system. To ignore any group is almost certain to result later in problems with the operation of the system. While acknowledging the diversity of user groups for computer systems, I intend to concentrate on one particular group—the very large group of what have been referred to as end users (Dolotta, et al., 1976), discretionary users (Bennett, 1979), casual users (Eason, 1979; Schilling, 1979), or "anybody" (Block, 1980). These are users such as small businessmen, shopkeepers, managers, physicians, lawyers, scientists, newspapermen, trade unionists, students, housewives, or, in other words, just about anybody who will work with computers.

The most important single characteristic of these people is that they will not be computer professionals. It is this class of users that many experts (see, for example, Bennett, 1979; Coulouris, 1979; Eason, 1979; Sackman, 1979; Schilling, 1979) see as constituting the large potential market for computing services in the coming decade. These users, incidentally, are collectively the *common man* that I referred to in the title of my article. At this point it should be abundantly clear that I have used the words *common man* loosely, and that I do not mean to say that the people who make up this group are common in any more literal sense of that word. I mean only to say that we are concerned here with a very broad spectrum of the general population.

## What Are the Characteristics of this User Group?

How can we characterize this large group of users? What are their distinctive attributes? Unfortunately, I don't know of any data to which I can turn for an answer to those questions. There has been, so far as I know, no systematic human factors research on the descriptors of this large body of potential computer users. I have, however, formulated a tentative list of characteristics for our target audience based on what experts in the field have hypothesized; from general articles; from complaints voiced in newspapers, journals, and magazines; and from some introspection. The users that we are concerned with:

- Are not computer professionals.
- Are occasional users of computers.
- Are not interested in computers per se.
- Are not willing to communicate with a computer in computer terms.
- Are not willing to undergo extensive training to learn how to use a computer.
- Are not highly motivated to use computers.
- May not be capable of learning complicated procedures or of understanding complex languages.

Let me elaborate on a couple of these points.

**The computer as a tool.** One thing on which most experts agree is that computer users of the future will be using the computer as a tool—as something that will help them do their real work, which may be ordering supplies, prescribing medicines, making travel arrangements, balancing checking accounts, planning meals, making up payrolls, or preparing inventories. These users will not be interested in learning how a computer works, nor will they be interested in learning any programming or special computer language. Many of these users will be first-time users, and, after that, only occasional users. As a result, even if those users learned some simple computer language, many of them would use computers so infrequently that they would probably not be able to maintain a high level of proficiency in that language.

Because many of our users will use computers by choice rather than by necessity, computer interactions must be made sufficiently rewarding that the user can immediately see the utility of the computer. If the user does not see that the computer has any utility, or if the utility as he perceives it is not sufficiently great to balance the human costs of using the computer, we can anticipate that most of our users will refrain from using it.

**The intellectual capacity of the user group.** Our user group includes a large number of professional people who are clearly very well trained and intellectually skilled. As we broaden the spectrum of users to include more and more of the general population, however, we cannot expect that all users will be of that intellectual caliber. After all, half the population is below average in intelligence! I say this not in any pejorative sense, but rather as a simple statement of fact. I think it is especially difficult for computer designers and computer programmers to understand that most people do not think as they do. Many people have difficulty with abstract concepts, with numerical calculations, and even with statements in the English language that exceed a grammar-school reading level.

According to the U.S. Office of Education, some 23 million adults in the United States read at less than the eighth-grade level. Many cannot read, much less understand, newspaper want ads listing jobs for which they might qualify. An estimated 39 million U.S. adults cannot interpret a payroll earnings statement well enough to find out how much was deducted for social security. Government agencies frequently encounter adults who cannot understand instructions on food labels, tax forms, or job applications. And an estimated 52 million U.S. adults cannot handle the simple arithmetic required to verify whether they have received the correct change when they see a cash-register total and hand over a bank note to pay for a purchase.

In addition to that sobering characterization we must also take note of what appears to be a general decline in the quality of our education these days. Students graduating from our high schools and colleges today do not seem to have the communicative skills and basic intellectual tools that comparable students did a decade or two ago. This is certainly the impression that comes through to many of us who have been in the business of collegiate or university education for at least a couple of decades. And our impressions seem to be substantiated by objective test performance data from such organizations as the Educational Testing Service.

The conclusion to be drawn from the foregoing is that if computers of the future are going to serve the common man, we are clearly going to have to design much simpler software packages and interactive languages. The common man is not a person of great intellectual skills, and there is no reason to expect that our educational system will be capable of making any appreciable improvements in that situation within the foreseeable future.

## THE EASE OF USE

What is it that the common man wants of computers or, for that matter, of any tool, machine, or device? I think it can be summed up in

**Figure 4.** Ease-of-use considerations in 17 advertisements appearing in *Infosystems* and *Modern Office Procedures* during 1979 and 1980.

three simple words: "ease of use." This is the message that comes through loud and clear from consumers as expressed in consumer surveys and in newspaper, magazine, and journal articles (Figure 4).

We are all being engulfed by complicated technology in our places of work, in our homes, and even in our recreational activities. Life is much too complicated for many of us. We want things to be easy to use.

What makes computers easy to use? Here are some of the features that I think are important:

- Reliability and availability. The computer should be at least as reliable and as available as, say, the telephone.
- Familiarity of the entire user interface. By this I mean that the keyboard and display unit should, insofar as possible, look like familiar things in our environment, say, for example, typewriters and television sets.
- Understandability of the entire interface. Keyboards, displays, documentation, and programs should make use of simple, readily understood symbols, words, instructions, and rules. Insofar as possible all these should be in the user's own natural language.

- Smoothness and naturalness. All operations and functions should be easy to carry out, and they should conform to the user's natural ways of doing things.
- Friendliness, forgiveness, and robustness. Simple human errors should be forgiven. By that I mean that programs should accept common kinds of keying errors, spelling errors, and errors in grammar. In the case of those terrors for which error-correcting routines cannot be prepared, errors should be reported to the user before a catastrophe occurs. Moreover, when an error occurs, the user should be told as nearly as possible what the error probably was and how he might extricate himself.

## Tools versus Tasks

At this point I think it is important to forestall a question that I'm sure would otherwise arise. It is a question that I almost invariably hear from professional data processing personnel and computer programmers whenever I talk about ease of use in connection with computers. The question goes something like this: "Isn't it possible that you will end up making computers so easy to use that no one will want to use them? You will make them dull, boring, and uninteresting."

My answer to that question is that you have to make a distinction between tasks and tools. When I'm busy fashioning something in my home workshop, my task may be to build a shelf or repair a cabinet. Now that task may be challenging, and, in fact, part of the fun of doing things in one's own workshop is the challenge of designing something. In carrying out those tasks, however, I want my tools easy to use. I don't want to have to fight with my power drill, saw, or plane.

That analogy holds for intellectual jobs as well. When I'm trying to figure out how to do a complex analysis of variance with a set of data, that's my task. It's challenging and intellectually taxing. But I want my computer to be easy to use, because it's only a tool. I don't want to have to struggle with the computer program. The same is true whether we are preparing our income tax returns, making travel arrangements, or preparing an evening meal. These are our tasks; and these tasks command our attention. We don't want to have to worry about the tools that we use to get those tasks done.

To sum up, computers are challenging and should be challenging to professional data processing personnel and to programmers, because computers are their task. To the common man, however, the computer is a tool and he wants that tool easy to use.

## HOW EASY IS IT TO USE PRESENT-DAY COMPUTERS?

Let's now compare modern computers against my short checklist of features that make computers easy to use. It would be misleading to claim that I have seen or tried many different computers or computer programs. I will say only that I have seen and interacted with a substantial number of them, among them some of the most sophisticated and advanced systems that certain large organizations are developing. Every single computer, computer program, or computer interface that I have seen fails to measure up to my standards of being easy to use. I can think of no exceptions to that sweeping statement. In this connection, I think it is very important to understand that the developers or designers of computer programs are understandably ego-involved with their creations and highly enthusiastic about them. That very ego-involvement and enthusiasm, however, blinds them to design faults that are immediately apparent to the first-time user. The designer of a software package has worked intimately with every detail of that package, he knows what it is supposed to do, he knows how it is supposed to work, and he usually rationalizes away the "silly little difficulties" that first-time users get into when they sit down at a terminal and interact with the system. But it is precisely those difficulties that are the heart of the whole usability issue.

## What's Wrong with Modern Computers?

A good place to start in a search for more usability is to ask: What's wrong with what we're doing now? I see at least five main things wrong with computers and computer programs. They:

- Are explained in words that are difficult or impossible to understand.
- Don't forgive simple human errors.
- Don't tell you what you did wrong when you do something wrong.
- Give you "help" messages that don't help.
- Make use of thought processes and languages that are unnatural, or at best unfamiliar.

Let me illustrate each of these in turn.

## Explanations that You Can't Understand

You don't have to search far to find examples of poorly written computer instructions, manuals, and books. One of my favorite examples starts with what I call "the promise."

Learning how to use a computer can be compared to learning how to drive an automobile. Thanks to many successful innovations in automotive development, the new driver is confronted with the rather simple process of learning how to steer and to recognize which buttons and pedals control, say, the lights or the driving speed.... Many people who have no detailed knowledge of how an automobile runs have become excellent drivers. In much the same way, a number of people have learned how to use the computer....

This is from the foreword to the programmed instruction course in FORTRAN IV for the IBM System/360. The promise held out to the potential user is that learning how to operate a computer is no more complicated than learning to drive an automobile. What's the reality? Thumb through these four booklets and you are confronted with page after page of such literary gems as the following:

87 The variables listed as arguments in the *function-defining statement*, then, are *dummy arguments*, meaning that they are not variables in the usual sense but rather are used to show what is to be done with the values of the *actual arguments* as indicated in the function notation elsewhere in the program.

127 Repeat: a FUNCTION that has a dummy argument which is an array *must* have a DIMENSION statement containing that name (even if specified array size is *different* from that of the calling program) to permit subscripted use of the variable.

Here's another gem from a current manual that "... provides the end user community with a simple and unified approach to manipulating data stored on a Query-by-Example data base":

With a single shared data base, the data base administrator is userid A and userids B and C are the sharing users. Userids B and C may simultaneously access the data base if both are read mode; however, only one userid may have access at a time in write mode. The data base administrator userid A has unlimited access to all tables in the data base. Userids B and C only have access to tables they create or have been granted authority to use.

With the shared and private data bases, userid A is the data base administrator for the shared data base and userid B is the data base administrator for the private data base. Userid B is also a user of the shared data base but can only access one data base at a time. Userid C is a sharing user of the shared data base. Again, the data base administrators A and B have unlimited access to their respective data bases. Userids A, B, and C can operate on the shared data base simultaneously in read mode or serially in write mode.

I could go on and quote other instructions written in the same general style, but I don't really think there's any need to do so, because I'm sure you have your own favorite examples. It is writing of this kind that was undoubtedly responsible for the following excerpt from a letter written by a university student to a computer manufacturer: "Damn you!

Damn you! Damn you! I spent $100 on your user manuals and I can't understand a thing they say!" (Maynard, 1979). If university students can't understand manuals, pity our common man.

The documentation associated with computers and computer programs is, to my mind, an indication of a kind of computer mentality that is far removed from our ordinary ways of talking, thinking, and reading. Consider something as simple as the index words that are used to identify features of a computer terminal. The IBM 3270 (and other terminals too, of course) has a key that can be used to lock the terminal so that it cannot be used by unauthorized persons. The key is similar to a house key or car key. Yet if you look in the index to the 3270 manual you will find no entry under "key," nor under "lock." What index word did the writer of this manual use? Where do you find this feature in the index? Under "security keylock!"

Another example: Some terminals can be used with a light pen. You've all seen them. You hold the pen up against the face of the CRT, activate the pen, and the computer will select out or act on the item you were pointing to. Once again, look in the index of the manual to find out where this feature is described. If you describe or demonstrate this piece of equipment to a first-time user and ask him what he would call it, you get such names as "pointer," "pen," or "stick." Needless to say, none of these words can be found in the index to the manual. A more sophisticated user would undoubtedly think of "light pen." But those words can't be found in the index either. What index words did the writer of this manual use? "Selector light pen!"

These, I insist, are computerese. They are illustrations of what I think is a general kind of mentality in the computer industry, a mentality that is enmeshed in its own jargon and that is unwilling, or unable, to translate its jargon into familiar words.

The difficulties I have just illustrated do not require sophisticated research for their solution. All they require are three rather simple things:

1.   An appreciation that good clear writing is important.
2.   A willingness to translate computer jargon into ordinary understandable speech.
3.   The patience to test translations to be sure that they are indeed understandable and usable by their intended audience, and if they are not understandable, to try again.

## Computers Don't Forgive Simple Human Errors

In my laboratory we have just concluded an extended program of research that has investigated conferencing face-to-face and teleconferencing through various electronic media. Groups of two, three, or

```
SK:    Need information .  Use form of a list for clarity. Present info on
       all candidates in the area of research each has done..

       end my typing go.


SO:    A: The Eskimo as a Minority Worker in Alaska
            Sikudaruty  (Ignore)     Solidarity Fornation Between Blue and
       White Collar Workers in Adverse

SK:    wait/////////////              ignore info about topics ... Can you give
       data of 1. quantity of research done as manifested in # of publications
       etc.  If not, move on to (past experience in teaching) present in same
       fashion..... Please give SYNOPSIS of material for efficiency/////±±±±±±

SO:    A: 3 publications
       B:none
       C:  3 pub.
       D:  4 publ.
       E: Dissertation research: The Existance of a Pecking Order in Penal Cloonies


SK:    Information on AWARDS RECEIVED BY ANY OF CANDIDATES OR HINT OF QUALITY
       OF RESEARCH ?    Then move on to teaching

SO:    A: Best Paper, honor graduation, member of 2 Honor Societies
       B:Phi Beta Kappa, most promissing grad, cited for contribution to science
       C:Top 5%of  class, Phi B K
       D:

SK:    from what institutions      ?    TYPE FASTER TURKEY      go


SO:    First change above AC  A, B, C to B, C, D  Sorry


SK:    ok   go


SO:    B: Grad from Duke Unev.
       C: Harvard and Oxford
       D:Univ. of Montana, Cornell
       E:U. of Calif at Berkeley , UCla
```

**Figure 5.** Start of the interchanges between two persons who communicated in the teletypewriter mode to solve a faculty selection problem. On the original protocol one person's messges (SK) were in black type, the other person's (SO) in red type. In this reproduction only the vertical spacing has been altered to make the typing somewhat more regular than it really was [*Source:* Ford, Chapanis, and Weeks, 1979—unpublished protocol]

four persons were typically required to solve realistic problems cooperatively while communicating face-to-face, through linked teletypewriters, through voice channels, through slaved telautograph systems, or through closed-circuit television. One of the most impressive things to us was to discover how unruly normal interactive communication can be. We all know that when we talk we often don't talk in sentences. We also

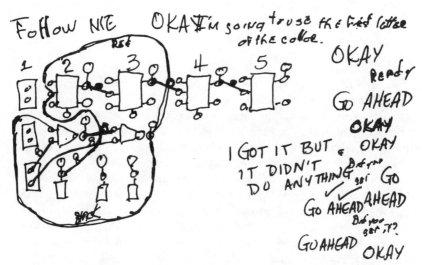

**Figure 6.** One segment of a telepen protocol made by two persons who solved a wiring task. This black-and-white illustration does not show that messages from one person were in blue ink, by the other in red ink. There are 14 separate consecutive messages here, with each communicator in turn adding to previous messages [*Source:* Hoecker, 1979—unpublished protocol]

knew that before we started our research, but what we didn't know was how disorganized normal human communication could be—no matter whether it was spoken, written, or typewritten. Words are misspelled; punctuation is omitted, repeated, or used incorrectly; and virtually every rule of grammar is violated. Many of our protocols have not a single grammatically correct sentence. Figure 5 is a short segment of a typewritten protocol from one of our experiments in which two persons communicated by slaved teletypewriters to solve a faculty selection problem. Figure 6 is an illustration of a frame recorded in an experiment in which two persons communicated through slaved telautograph terminals to solve the task of wiring up an electronic laboratory board.

Another impressive thing to us was that, despite the unruliness of their communications, people solved their problems—and usually expeditiously at that. We normally accept each other's mistakes—the slips of the tongue, the spelling errors, the grammatical errors—reading through the errors to the underlying meanings.

Our recent work has centered on man-computer interactions, and here once again we find many mistakes—even when people are deliberately trying to be correct. In contrast to what we found in our person-to-person communications, however, our computer is most inflexible about these unintentional human errors. But this, of course, comes as no surprise to anyone who has worked with or interacted with a computer.

## What Did I Do Wrong?

The inflexibility of computer programs would be much more acceptable if the user could at least be told what he did wrong when the computer refuses to accept his input. If you have ever interacted with a computer you have, I'm sure, encountered situations in which you can't figure out why a computer responds in some way, or refuses to respond at all. The inability of computer programs to accept simple human errors and their unhelpfulness when errors are made are illustrated very nicely in the sequence of interchanges in Figure 7. This is a genuine series of interchanges between a computer and a learner in my laboratory who was trying to get access to a program that teaches APL programming. As you may infer from the interchange, the learner had finished Lesson 1 and was trying to go to Lesson 2.

In the first line, the learner knew that he had to begin with a reverse parenthesis and then type LOAD 45 LESSON2. However, the learner unintentionally typed an extra lowercase "d" after the 2. The computer response was a noncommittal INCORRECT COMMAND. Recognizing his mistake the learner tried again, but this time misspelled LOAD unintentionally. The computer response was again the same noncommittal INCORRECT COMMAND. On the third attempt, the learner thought he had everything correct. Yet the computer came back with the

```
Learner:    )LOAD 45 LESSON2d
Computer:   INCORRECT COMMAND
Learner:        )LAOD LESSON 2
Computer:   INCORRECT COMMAND
Learner:        )LOAD 45 LESSON 2
Computer:   INCORRECT COMMAND
Learner:        )LOAD LESSON2
Computer:   WS NOT FOUND
Learner:        ))LOAD 45 LESSON2
Computer:   INCORRECT COMMAND
Learner:        )LOAD 45 LESSON2
Computer:   SAVED 13.28.24   09/21/78
            SYSTEM? 1=APLSV, 2=VSPC, 3=VM/370,
            4=TSO: KEY NUMBER, HIT ENTER
```

**Figure 7.** Interchanges between a learner and a computer. The learner was trying to access a program that teaches APL programming.

same dreary INCORRECT COMMAND. At this point, the learner sought help from an expert. The latter told him that the error this time was that he had left a space between the LESSON and the 2. This is, by any human standard, a trivial matter, but, of course, the computer would not accept it. On his fourth attempt, the learner carefully left no space between the LESSON and the 2, but the computer still would not accept his input, coming back this time with a different response, but a response that was just as uninformative as previous responses had been. The learner took the abbreviation to mean that the lesson WAS NOT FOUND. By this time the learner was becoming frustrated and confused. Why wasn't the lesson found? What had happened to it? Consultation with the expert revealed that the abbreviation really meant WORK-SPACE NOT FOUND and that the reason the workspace had not been found was that the learner had omitted the "45."

The learner's fifth attempt was marked by another trivial error. This time he typed in two reverse parenthesis marks, again unintentionally. A trivial mistake, from a human standpoint, but not for the computer. Once again, the computer came back with its familiar, but uninformative INCORRECT COMMAND. Consultation was required again with the expert to clarify the source of the new difficulty. As you see, finally, after the sixth attempt the learner was able to get a response showing that he was on the track. But what a response to give a learner! Can you deduce what the learner is supposed to do next? This particular learner decided that it wasn't worth the trouble and turned the computer off.

That is only one illustration, and a rather small one, from a collection of similar ones that I have made from computer systems of all kinds, in a variety of applications, around the country. In my opinion, there is no excuse for this kind of rigidity. For example, most people would naturally leave a space between LESSON and 2 in typing or writing. Why is it so important that no space be left?

Why give the learner an ambiguous response like WS NOT FOUND? There's plenty of room on the display unit. There's no reason at all to abbreviate "workspace."

More important, why not tell the learner why the workspace was not found?

If people are prone to add extra characters, such as a close parenthesis mark unintentionally, why not have the program accept it?

And so on, and so on, and so on.

## Help Messages that Don't Really Help

There are, of course, many computer programs that try to be more helpful than the one from which I got the illustration in Figure 7. Typically, these programs respond with what is supposed to be a helpful

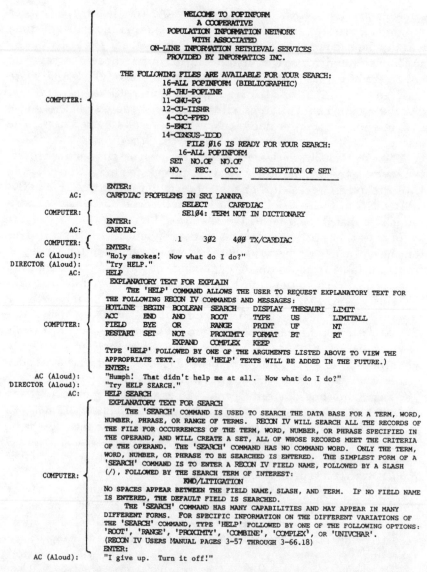

|  | |
|---|---|
| COMPUTER: | WELCOME TO POPINFORM<br>A COOPERATIVE<br>POPULATION INFORMATION NETWORK<br>WITH ASSOCIATED<br>ON-LINE INFORMATION RETRIEVAL SERVICES<br>PROVIDED BY INFORMATICS INC.<br><br>THE FOLLOWING FILES ARE AVAILABLE FOR YOUR SEARCH:<br>16-ALL POPINFORM (BIBLIOGRAPHIC)<br>1Ø-JHU-POPLINE<br>11-GWU-PG<br>12-CU-IISHR<br>4-CDC-FPED<br>5-EWCI<br>14-CENSUS-IDDD<br>　FILE Ø16 IS READY FOR YOUR SEARCH:<br>　16-ALL POPINFORM<br>SET　NO.OF　NO.OF<br>NO.　REC.　OCC.　DESCRIPTION OF SET<br>——　——　——<br>ENTER: |
| AC: | CARFDIAC PROPBLEMS IN SRI LANNKA |
| COMPUTER: | 　　　　SELECT　　CARFDIAC<br>　　　　SE1Ø4: TERM NOT IN DICTIONARY<br>ENTER: |
| AC: | CARDIAC |
| COMPUTER: | 　　　1　3Ø2　4ØØ TX/CARDIAC<br>ENTER: |
| AC (Aloud): | "Holy smokes!  Now what do I do?" |
| DIRECTOR (Aloud): | "Try HELP." |
| AC: | HELP |
| COMPUTER: | EXPLANATORY TEXT FOR EXPLAIN<br>　THE 'HELP' COMMAND ALLOWS THE USER TO REQUEST EXPLANATORY TEXT FOR THE FOLLOWING RECON IV COMMANDS AND MESSAGES:<br>HOTLINE　BEGIN　BOOLEAN　SEARCH　DISPLAY　THESAURI　LIMIT<br>ACC　END　AND　ROOT　TYPE　US　LIMITALL<br>FIELD　BYE　OR　RANGE　PRINT　UF　NT<br>RESTART　SET　NOT　PROXIMITY　FORMAT　BT　RT<br>　　EXPAND　COMPLEX　KEEP<br>TYPE 'HELP' FOLLOWED BY ONE OF THE ARGUMENTS LISTED ABOVE TO VIEW THE APPROPRIATE TEXT.  (MORE 'HELP' TEXTS WILL BE ADDED IN THE FUTURE.)<br>ENTER: |
| AC (Aloud): | "Humph!  That didn't help me at all.  Now what do I do?" |
| DIRECTOR (Aloud): | "Try HELP SEARCH." |
| AC: | HELP SEARCH |
| COMPUTER: | EXPLANATORY TEXT FOR SEARCH<br>　THE 'SEARCH' COMMAND IS USED TO SEARCH THE DATA BASE FOR A TERM, WORD, NUMBER, PHRASE, OR RANGE OF TERMS.  RECON IV WILL SEARCH ALL THE RECORDS OF THE FILE FOR OCCURRENCES OF THE TERM, WORD, NUMBER, OR PHRASE SPECIFIED IN THE OPERAND, AND WILL CREATE A SET, ALL OF WHOSE RECORDS MEET THE CRITERIA OF THE OPERAND.  THE 'SEARCH' COMMAND HAS NO COMMAND WORD.  ONLY THE TERM, WORD, NUMBER, OR PHRASE TO BE SEARCHED IS ENTERED.  THE SIMPLEST FORM OF A 'SEARCH' COMMAND IS TO ENTER A RECON IV FIELD NAME, FOLLOWED BY A SLASH (/), FOLLOWED BY THE SEARCH TERM OF INTEREST:<br>　　　KWD/LITIGATION<br>NO SPACES APPEAR BETWEEN THE FIELD NAME, SLASH, AND TERM.  IF NO FIELD NAME IS ENTERED, THE DEFAULT FIELD IS SEARCHED.<br>　THE 'SEARCH' COMMAND HAS MANY CAPABILITIES AND MAY APPEAR IN MANY DIFFERENT FORMS.  FOR SPECIFIC INFORMATION ON THE DIFFERENT VARIATIONS OF THE 'SEARCH' COMMAND, TYPE 'HELP' FOLLOWED BY ONE OF THE FOLLOWING OPTIONS: 'ROOT', 'RANGE', 'PROXIMITY', 'COMBINE', 'COMPLEX', OR 'UNIVCHAR'.<br>(RECON IV USERS MANUAL PAGES 3-57 THROUGH 3-66.18)<br>ENTER: |
| AC (Aloud): | "I give up.  Turn it off!" |

**Figure 8.** Interchanges between the author (AC), a computer system called POPINFORM, and the program director. Aside from the legibility of the print, which is much better here than on the record printed by the computer, this figure captures faithfully the substance of our interactions.

message when the user types in the word HELP. Although most such programs are well intentioned, they still fall far short of providing the help that users need. Once again, I would like to illustrate with a genuine interchange between, in this case, me, and a computer system called POPINFORM.

POPINFORM is a computerized, on-line information system that provides citations and abstracts of journal articles, book chapters, published and unpublished reports, government and United Nations documents, and other population and family planning data. It is a worldwide system, with remote terminals in many foreign countries, designed to be used by public health personnel, physicians, and government officials. The system is supported by AID, the United States Agency for International Development.

My colleague, Dr. Gerald D. Weeks, and I were introduced to POPINFORM when we were invited to confer with the director about a problem she had. The problem, as it was put to us, was a motivational problem. What could be done to motivate public health officials in places like New Delhi, Sri Lanka, and Manila to use the system? Perhaps it was, we suggested, that the users didn't speak or understand English. We were assured that that was not the problem. Finally, after some gentle insistence, I was offered a chance to interact with the system. That interaction is shown in Figure 8.

By now, the pattern should be familiar. A couple of unintentional misspellings in my first input got me into difficulty immediately—a difficulty from which I could not extricate myself without help. I don't need to take you through the whole exchange. It's evident what happened. What I would like to call to your attention, however, are the so-called help messages. You will have to agree that they are singularly unhelpful. In passing, notice, too, the abbreviations, the esoteric jargon, and the enigmatic responses—all of which are inexcusable. If I, an American, couldn't make any sense of the interchange, how could we expect any better performance from persons with perhaps a less complete understanding of ordinary English?

## Thought Processes, or Languages, that Are Unnatural

So much has been written about the esoteric nature of computer programming languages that it seems almost unnecessary to comment on them here. Programming languages such as APL, FORTRAN, and COBOL are totally incomprehensible to the uninitiated (see, for example, Figure 9). The length of time needed to master them is proof enough of their difficulty. Surprisingly little research has been done to try to identify the features of programming languages that make them difficult or easy to learn and to use. One of the very few studies of this kind has been reported by Reisner (1977) who made systematic comparisons of two programming languages, SQUARE and SEQUEL, by students with no prior programming experience and by students with some knowledge of programming. Her work has revealed a large number of features in

```
∇SUPERPROC[□]
    ∇ Z←SUPERPROC VEC;□IO;A;B;C;I;N;IN;VX;RHA;TE;T1;C1;C2;TMP
[1]    TE← 1,0/TMP←ι0,0/T1←21ρ0,0/□IO←1
[2]    A←SUBCAT VEC
[3]    L05:I←0,0/RHA←1↑ρA←'REPMAP' TFIND5 CATVEC
[4]    L1:→(RHA<I←I+1)/G1
[5]    IN←1+B,0/N←1↑B,0/B←(B≠0)/B←,A[I;]
[6]    IND[1+IN]←0
[7]    CATVEC[1↑IN]←N
[8]    →L1
[9]    G1:CATVEC←IND/CATVEC
[10]   CAT←IND/CAT
[11]   VMAT←IND≠VMAT
[12]   IND←(ρCATVEC)ρ1
[13]   →(~TE←TE+1)/L05
[14]   I←0,0/RHA←1↑ρA←'OPMATTIME' TFIND5 CATVEC
[15]   L2:→(RHA<I←I+1)/G2
[16]   N←(,CAT[3;(CAT[1;C]=1)/C]),0/C+1↓(C≠0)/C←,A[I;]
[17]   C1[((¯4↓C1)>10)/ι19]←0,0/C1←C1←(,PCODE[(1↑,A[I;]);])
[18]   C1←((C1≠0)/C1←C1[(ι6),(7+ι5),14+ι5]),0/C2←((¯4↓C1)≠0)/ι19
[19]   ↓((ρC2)≠ρN)/'→(1↑1,ρ□←''ERROR EXISTS, N='',(↑N),'''', C2='','',↑C2)/L2'
[20]   →(∨/T1[C2]≠0)/L2
[21]   T1[4 11 18]←T1[4 11 18]+(0.1×C1[20 21 22]),0/T1[C2]←N[C1],0/IND[C]←0
[22]   T1[B]←C1[B←((¯4↓C1)>10)/ι19]
[23]   ↓(∨/T1[14+ι7]≠0)/'T1[14+ι7]←0,0/TMP←TMP,(1↑C),T1[14+ι7]'
[24]   →L2
[25]   G2:→(0=ρTMP)/END
[26]   TMP← 2 8 ρTMP,99,7ρ0
[27]   TMP← 0 1 ↓TMP[⍋TMP[;1];]
[28]   T1[A]←,TMP[1;A←(T1[ι7]=0)/ι7]
[29]   T1[A]←,TMP[2;(A←(T1[7+ι7]=0)/7+ι7)-7]
[30]   END:Z←T1
[31]   VMAT←IND≠VMAT
    ∇
```

**Figure 9.** Part of an APL program that supports our natural-language interactions.

both the SQUARE and SEQUEL programming languages that were particularly troublesome to both groups of students. These were features that seemed unnatural or confusing to the students.

Here, for example, are some kinds of errors that were made by 50 percent or more of subjects on one or both of the programming languages in a final examination at the end of a two-week training program:

• Ending errors: For example, subjects used "names," "supplied," or "number dispatch," whereas the computer program would accept only "name," "supplier," and "number dispatched."

• Spelling errors.

• Synonym errors: Subjects used synonyms and other subtitles for table names, column names, operators, and function names even though they had data bases and their own reference notes available. For example, they used "ave," "average," or "avg." but the computer program would accept only "avg," or they used "employee," whereas the computer program would accept only "personnel."

• Quotation-mark errors: Subjects either omitted quotation marks around data values where the computer program required them, or inserted quotation marks around values that the computer program would not accept.

Even the best and the simplest programming languages still leave much to be desired. Consider BASIC, for example. Figure 10 contains an example of a very simple program to ask interviewees the following:

Please answer Question 1 and either Question 2 or 3.

   1. Do you own a television?    Yes——    No——
   2. If you don't own a TV, are you planning to buy one in the next year?   Yes——    No——
   3. If you own a TV, how often do you watch it in the daytime?
       ——Often
       ——Seldom
       ——Never

I hasten to explain that the program illustrated in Figure 10 was copied literally from an introductory book on BASIC, whereas the questions above are the way I would ask them if I were administering a paper-and-pencil questionnaire.

```
10    REMARK -- INTERVIEWING PROGRAM:  TELEVISION
11    REMARK -- VIEWING HABITS
13    DIM A(3)
15    PRINT "HELLO.  I WOULD LIKE TO ASK YOU SOME"
16    PRINT "QUESTIONS ABOUT YOUR T.V. VIEWING."
17    PRINT
18    PRINT "IF YOU OWN A TELEVISION, PLEASE TYPE"
19    PRINT "A 1.  IF YOU DONT, TYPE 0 ";
20    INPUT A(1)
30    IF A(1) = 1 THEN 50
40    PRINT "IF YOU PLAN TO BUY ONE IN THE NEXT YEAR"
41    PRINT "TYPE A 1.  IF NOT, TYPE 0 ";
42    INPUT A(2)
43    GO TO 60
50    PRINT "DO YOU WATCH YOUR TELEVISION DURING THE"
51    PRINT "DAYTIME:"
52    PRINT "  1   OFTEN"
53    PRINT "  2   SELDOM"
54    PRINT "  3   NEVER"
55    PRINT "TYPE A 1, 2, OR 3 ";
56    INPUT A(3)
60    PRINT
62    PRINT "THANK YOU."
63    STOP
```

Figure 10. A BASIC program to ask an interviewee a question about his viewing habits. The legibility of the print here is much better than on the record printed by the computer, but this figure is otherwise a faithful copy of the original [*Source:* Sharpe and Jacob, 1971]

The point I want to make, however, is that the BASIC program doesn't look familiar and, simple as it might seem to you and me, it is completely incomprehensible, and beyond the comprehension, of a great many potential users.

Even in the case of so-called natural language programs, computer programmers often phrase things in ways that are not natural. Consider the following interchange with a system called ROBOT (Harris, 1979)— a system that is illustrative of the best available today. The user types in:

> WHAT IS THE FAMILY STATUS OF THE AREA MANAGERS
> THAT LIVE IN NEW YORK
> The computer responds with:
> REQUEST AMBIGUOUS, IS IT:
> NUMBER 1
> PRINT THE FAMILY STATUS, STATE, AND CITY OF ANY
> EMPLOYEE WITH STATE = NY AND JOB = AREA MANAGER
> NUMBER 2
> PRINT THE FAMILY STATUS, STATE, AND CITY OF ANY
> EMPLOYEE WITH CITY = NEW YORK AND JOB = AREA MANAGER
> PLEASE TYPE THE NUMBER 1 OR THE NUMBER 2

I submit that although this is pretty good, it is not natural communication. What common man would ask a question with the words "STATE = NY" or "CITY = NEW YORK"? A natural way of phrasing the question might be something like:

> I'm sorry, but I don't understand what you mean by New York. Do you
> mean the city or the state?

There is no technical difficulty with making the computer respond in that way. All it requires is an awareness on the part of the programmer that it is important to make the computer program communicate with the user in the user's own words.

## CONCLUSION

The dramatic decrease in the cost of computer hardware and software over the past several decades means that the important cost savings in man-computer usage in the future are to be made by decreasing the human costs of using computers, not by decreasing computer costs per se. Some of the greatest potential gains in reducing the human costs of using computers are to be found in the improvement of computer software. Many computer programs today are explained in words that are difficult to understand, are unforgiving of simple human errors, don't tell the user what he did wrong when he does something wrong, give "help" messages that don't help, and make use of thought processes and languages that are unnatural or at best unfamiliar. Although these are all psychological problems, psychologists have not been particularly active in working on them. Most of this work has been left to engineers, computer programmers, and technical writers. Perhaps the explanation for this state of affairs is that the solution of most of these problems does not require any extensive new basic psychological research, or the application of any sophisticated psychological theories. What it does require is a sensitivity to the needs of users, a willingness to make computer software meet those needs, and the patience to try out solutions empirically to be sure those needs are met. Although this may not seem as glamorous as some other kinds of psychological work, it is an activity that constitutes an opportunity and a challenge to psychologists. Making computer software meet human needs is essential if we are ever to meet our goals of making computers truly available to the common man.

## NOTE

[1]Additional details of Professor Chapanis' research program are provided in Appendix A.

## REFERENCES

Bennett, J.L. The commercial impact of usability in interactive systems. In *Infotech state of the art report: Man/computer communication. Volume 2: Invited papers.* Maidenhead, Berkshire, England: Infotech International Limited, 1979.

Block, V. Network outlook: sociology a growing concern. *Infosystems*, 1980, 27(3), 20.

Coulouris, G.F. The personal computer in the office of the future. In *Infotech state of the art report: Man/computer communication. Volume 2: Invited papers.* Maidenhead, Berkshire, England: Infotech International Limited, 1979.

Doherty, W.J. The commercial significance of man/computer interaction. In *Infotech state of the art report: Man/computer communication. Volume 2: Invited papers.* Maidenhead, Berkshire, England: Infotech International Limited, 1979.

Dolotta, T.A., Bernstein, M.I., Dickson, R.S., Jr., France, N.A., Rosenblatt, B.A., Smith, D.M., and Steel, T.B., Jr. *Data processing in 1980–1985: A study of potential limitations to progress.* New York, John Wiley & Sons: 1976.

Eason, K.D. Man-computer communication in public and private computing. In *Infotech state of the art report: Man/computer communication. Volume 2: Invited papers.* Maidenhead, Berkshire, England: Infotech International Limited, 1979.

Ford, W.R., Chapanis, A., and Weeks, G.D. Self-limited and unlimited word usage during problem solving in two telecommunication modes. *Journal of Psycholinguistic Research*, 1979, 8, 451–75.

Goldstein, C.M. and Ford, W.H. The user-cordial interface. *Online Review*, 1978, 2, 269–275.

Harris, L.R. Man/machine communication in natural language. In *Infotech state of the art report: Man/computer communication. Volume 2: Invited papers*. Maidenhead, Berkshire, England: Infotech International Limited, 1979.

Hoecker, G.D. Problem-solving in five communication modes as a function of verbal and spatial abilities, Ph.D. dissertation, The Johns Hopkins University, 1979. *Dissertation Abstracts International*, 1980, (University Microfilms No. 80-6928).

International Business Machines Corporation. *It was to have been the nuclear age. It became...the computer age. The evolution of IBM computers*. Armonk, New York: Author, 1976.

Lee, R.S. Social attitudes and the computer revolution. *Public Opinion Quarterly*, 1970, 34, 53–59.

Maynard, J. A user-driver approach to better user manuals. *Computer*, 1979, 12(1), 72–75.

Reisner, P. Use of psychological experimentation as an aid to development of a query language. *IEEE Transactions on Software Engineering*, 1977, SE-3, 218–229.

Sackman, H. The public interest in mass computer communication networks of the future. In *Infotech state of the art report: Man/computer communication. Volume 2: Invited papers*. Maidenhead, Berkshire, England: Infotech International Limited, 1979.

Sansweet, S.J. Mattel tries to lure skeptical consumers by selling computer as high-priced fun. *The Wall Street Journal*, March 14, 1980, p. 15.

Schilling, D.E. Coping with the casual user. In *Infotech state of the art report: Man/computer communication. Volume 2: Invited papers*. Maidenhead, Berkshire, England: Infotech International Limited, 1979.

Sharpe, W.F. and Jacob, N.L. *BASIC: An introduction to computer programming using the BASIC language*. (Revised Edition) New York: The Free Press, 1971.

Zloof, M.M. Query by example—language design considerations. In *Infotech state of the art report: Man/computer communication: Volume 2: Invited papers*. Maidenhead, Berkshire, England: Infotech International Limited, 1979.

# Training in the 1970s:
# A View toward the 1980s

## Irwin L. Goldstein

This paper is designed to review the training literature with a particular focus on topics and information relevant to the development of high technology in the 1980s. High technology is likely to affect the development of training programs in at least two different ways. First, it is likely that job requirements will change. If this is the case, then instructional programs will be necessary in order to train individuals to perform these new job functions. Also, however, the development of high technology may itself result in the design of new training methodologies and techniques.

These new high technology developments bring a particular danger. There appears to be a belief that instructional efforts based upon new technological toys will result in enhanced job performance and increased productivity. Indeed, most of the recent financial awards are for the development of expensive new techniques (e.g., flight simulators) and very little attention is given to need assessment techniques or evaluation efforts to determine the utility of these approaches.

Training analysts are somewhat unique in their treatment of need assessment techniques. For some reason, they have tended to focus their attention on instructional techniques rather than a consideration of the need and a determination of which instructional technique is likely to best fit that need. Thus, as described by Campbell (1971), the training field is dominated by a fads approach. Children go from yo-yos to hoola hoops to skate boards, and training directors move from sensitivity training to organizational development to behavioral role modeling. Probably, each of these techniques has a place (for the children, also), but analysts never seem to find out very much about their approach before they are off examining another type of program. This type of fads approach places a heavy emphasis on the development of techniques without consideration of needs assessment followed by a matching of the technique to the needs. It is interesting to note that machinists examine the job they must perform before choosing their tools, and a gardener usually chooses a sprinkling system rather than a bucket to water a half-acre lawn. Yet analysts still have to be warned about selecting tools and finding something they fit through advice like the following:

> If you don't have a gadget called a teaching machine, don't get one. Don't buy one; don't borrow one; don't steal one. If you have such a gadget, get rid of it. Don't give it away, for someone else might use it. This is a most practical rule, based on empirical facts from considerable observation. If you begin with a device of any kind, you will try to develop the teaching program to fit that device (Gilbert, 1960, p. 478).

Gilbert is not saying that teaching machines or sensitivity training or CAI or any other technique doesn't work. He is saying that the design of change programs cannot begin with instructional media. Instead, it is necessary to use need assessment procedures to determine the objectives of instructional programs so that the criteria for evaluation and the employment of programs are based upon sound decisions.

The consequences that occur when need assessment approaches are not utilized were amply demonstrated in an investigation (Miller and Zeller, 1967) of 418 hard core unemployed trainees in a program to train highway construction machinery operators. The authors were able to obtain information from 270 graduates. Of this group, 61 percent of the graduate were employed and 39 percent unemployed at the time of the interview. In addition, more than half of the employed group said they were without jobs more than 60 percent of the time. Some of the reasons for the unemployment situation were inadequacies in training, which included not enough task practice and insufficient training time. The details showed that the program was not based upon a consideration of the job components. One trainee noted that "the contractors laughed when I showed them my training diploma and said 'come back after you get some schooling buddy'" (ibid., pp. 32–33). In a now familiar lament, the authors of the report wonder how a training program could be designed without a thorough analysis of the skills required.

The reason for this state of affairs is probably rather complex. Training analysts appear to have adopted the fads approach based upon a forlorn belief that the next toy they purchase will provide the answers to their training problem. This situation appears to have resulted in an approach dominated by anecdotal testimonials rather than research.

Similar problems concerning evaluation methodology can be presented. As described by Goldstein (1974) evaluation is considered to be an information gathering process that should not expect to reach decisions that declare a program as all good or poor. Instructional programs are never complete but instead are designed to be revised on the basis of information obtained from evaluations that examine relevant multiple criteria that are both free from contamination and are reliable. The better experimental procedures control more variables, permitting a greater degree of confidence in specifying program effects. While the constraints of the training environment may make laboratory-type evaluation impossible to achieve, an awareness of the important factors in experimental design make it possible to conduct a useful evaluation even under adverse conditions.

If this particular philosophy is reasonable, then the early state of training evaluation has been absolutely deplorable. Over 25 years ago, French (1953) found only one company in 40 made any scientific evaluation of supervisory training programs. In 1971, the Civil Service Catalogue of Basic Education Systems listed 55 basic reading programs for educationally disadvantaged employees. For these programs, four publishers listed some type of validation program, two publishers offered case studies, and the other 49 indicated that validation data were not available. Similar commentary on the lack of sound empirical data for managerial training programs has also been offered (Campbell, et al., 1970) and a recent analysis of the Department of Defense training effort (Orlansky and String, 1977) suggests that efforts to examine the cost-effectiveness of major simulation efforts are minimal.

Additionally, examinations of type of criteria utilized to provide evaluation data are consistent with the above commentary. For example, Catalanello and Kirkpatrick (1968) found that of 154 companies surveyed, the largest number (77 percent) stressed studies related to reactions of trainees rather than learning or on-the-job performance. Even in those instances where reaction data were collected, some investigators (Mindak and Anderson, 1971) have suggested that most of these measures were *eyeball* attempts to measure reactions.

Authors who have commented about evaluation methodology concerning specific training techniques are equally concerned about the state-of-the-art. For example, in 1961, McGehee and Thayer reached the following conclusion concerning the use of business games: "For all we know, at this time, there may be a negative or zero relationship between the kinds of behavior developed by business game training and the kinds of behavior required to operate a business successfully" (p. 223).

Unfortunately, the development of high technology appears to promise more of these problems. For example, Adams (1978) presented some of the major principles that underlie simulator development, including the importance of knowledge or results, stimulus-response learning, and motivation. He argued that systems that are built on these sound scientific laws require less concern with evaluation because a good scientific law produces accurate prediction. From his perspective, when the outcome is predictable, it is redundant to conduct an evaluation. I strongly support the use of all scientific laws in the design of simulations or any other device. However, the lack of knowledge in the formulation of these laws and in the areas of need assessment as well as the difficulties in designing systems that effectively transfer performance into the organization make any statement advocating less of an emphasis on evaluation efforts difficult to support.

Fortunately, there appears to be a growing concern about training programs that do not achieve their potential. Further, there are researchers who are concerned about constraints within the work organization that prevent effective training programs from producing changes on-the-job. These concerns probably reflect a growing emphasis given to the following premises of instructional design:

1.   The development of instructional techniques and evaluation models must be based upon a careful and thorough need assessment of the organization.
2.   The systematic development of any training or change technique is dependent upon thoughtful evaluation, which provides the information necessary to suggest revisions in our techniques.

This paper will focus on what we have learned in the 1970s about these issues.

If we turn to research on training, including needs assessment and evaluation, we can almost trace a path toward understanding the effects of our interventions. In the most primitive stage, appropriate methodology is ignored and decisions are based upon anecdotal trainee and trainer reactions. This is also the stage where appropriate needs assessment is not done and where the fads approach to training is dominant. While most analysts realize the limitations of this approach and apologize, there are still far too many efforts of this type. In the next stage, which could be just as unproductive in providing relevant information, the evaluation strategy is dependent upon strict adherence to the basic experimental methodologies of academic laboratories. This stage is characterized by designs that do not recognize the constraints imposed by the environment or the influence of the multitude of organizational variables. Often researchers find these type of studies come to a screeching halt because of organizational constraints or because a technology has been applied that does not answer the questions being asked. A good illustration is the use of traditional "do nothing" control groups in situations where it is clearly not the appropriate comparison. Since the researcher has faith in the results precisely because experimental methodology has been employed, these type of efforts can be particularly misleading.

A third stage is observed when methodologies are matched to the constraints of the environment. It is characterized by careful consideration of threats to validity and the creative application of design methodology to the questions being investigated. While these type of efforts are few, the work of Komaki, Waddel, and Pierce and their colleagues (1977), which employed time series designs with small sample sizes, provides a fine illustration of the creative possibilities. A fourth stage, which interacts closely with the third stage, is the development and understanding of the philosophy of intervention. The work here recognizes that the instructional program itself, including the evaluation effort, interacts with the organization to produce a variety of effects. An illustration of these issues is provided by Hand and Slocum's (1972) study, which speculated that decrements in control group performance occurred as a consequence of their being upset over the results of the more favorable treatment given to the training group. While it may be possible to control for the results in the Hand and Slocum study, it is also necessary to understand these types of behaviors in organizational environments. For example, it may be very beneficial to determine for which conditions and for what kinds of organizations subjects in control groups become upset over being excluded from treatment.

During the 1970s, there have been a number of important developments concerning needs assessment and evaluation methodology. The next section of this paper reviews some of these developments and explores their implications for the 1980s.

## NEEDS ASSESSMENT

Influenced by McGehee and Thayer's (1961) classic text, most training analysts consider organizational analysis, operations or task analysis, and person analysis to be the three critical components of needs assessment.

### Organizational Analysis

The original purpose of organizational analysis was to provide input that specified where and when training could be utilized in the organization. Thus, manpower and skill inventories along with various indices such as accident, turnover, and absenteeism rates were collected. While these measures provide important information, recent discussions of organizational analysis reflect a concern that the fit between the training function and the organization to which it belongs is less than perfect.

Several authors have lamented that training programs are often judged to be failures because of organizational constraints that were not originally intended to be addressed by the instructional program. Salinger (1973) reported on disincentives to effective employee training such as supervisors who do not accept the practices taught by the training program or supervisors who can not meet their required production norms while their employees are in training. Another study (Baumgartel and Jeanpierre, 1972) noted that managers only utilized skills developed in training when the organizational climate was favorable.

Allen and Silverzweig (1976) approach the disincentive issue by discussing the influence of group norms on training effectiveness. They suggested that it is necessary to determine the effects of behaviors such as bringing a new way of performing a task back to the work setting. Negative reactions from supervisors or other employees should make most training analysts reconsider their instructional plans. Research is needed to develop an understanding of the variables that could predict the likelihood of positive transfer from training to the on-the-job environment. In a humorous but pointed example, McGehee and Thayer (1961) described a situation where the most effective approach was not to hold a formal training program. In other instances, researchers might well find that other organizational development activities are necessary alternatives or additions to the instructional program. Research is needed on these types of systems relationships.

## Task and Person Analysis

Specification of tasks to be learned provides critical input to the design of the instructional process. Yet, little attention is given to the design of task and person analysis systems, specifically for training input. As Prien (1977) notes, there has been little effort to systematically relate particular procedures for a specific use or to evaluate the utility of particular methods. Thus, there has been virtually no consideration of systems that examine the total job and provide information on which activities should be learned in training and which activities should be learned on the job. Similarly, no established procedures exist that empirically establish the content validity of training programs based upon a match of relevant tasks on the job and in the training program.

An important step forward is the work of Ammerman and his colleagues (Ammerman, Essex, and Pratzner, 1974; Ammerman and Pratzner, 1974, 1975, 1977). They provide a methodology for the development of tasks and for the design of a variety of scaling systems to measure a number of task dimensions. Among these are frequency of task occurrence, importance of tasks, and where and when the task should be learned. Their findings enabled them to decipher clues that indicated the need for training. Their findings could also stimulate some important research questions about the relationship between the various procedures used to scale tasks.

A few interesting procedures have been suggested to measure person characteristics of prospective trainees. In an assessment center study of a group of middle managers, Bray (1976) found that 45 percent were judged not promotable. He noted that the areas in which these managers were deficient are natural topics on which to focus future training programs. In a study designed to resolve a selection problem, Campion (1972) chose tasks for his predictive instrument that were both identified as being important and that applicants were expected to be able to perform at entry. This type of procedure could suggest person characteristics that require training by identifying those tasks that are deemed important to the job but that are not in the repertoire of entering job applicants. Laabs, Panell, and Pickering (1977) developed performance oriented tests to diagnose deficiencies in job performance for United States Navy missile technicians. This study found that performance deficiencies in maintenance skills were apparently related to the fact that the technicians did not get to practice their skills because of the extreme reliability of the missile test and readiness equipment. Also, the instructional programs were not particularly successful because the training was viewed as nonessential to the job, and thus many individuals never completed the instructional packages.

## EVALUATION

Evaluation is the systematic collection of descriptive and judgmental information necessary to make effective training decisions related to the selection, adoption, value, and modification of various instructional activities. The objectives of instructional programs reflect numerous goals ranging from trainee progress to organizational goals. From this perspective, evaluation is an information gathering techinque that can not possibly result in decisions that categorize programs as good or bad. Rather, evaluation should capture the dynamic flavor of the training environments. For example, it may be very beneficial to determine under which conditions and for what kinds of organizations subjects in control groups become upset over being excluded from the treatment.

The present section on evaluation is divided into sections on criterion issues and evaluation methodology issues. Although these two components of evaluation are inextricably tied, a choice was made on the basis of convenience to present them separately.

## Criterion Issues

Appropriately, the main concern in criterion development has been procedures for the establishment of relevant criteria that reflect the dynamic of the training process. In a very important paper, Freeberg (1976) noted that the critical dimensions for criterion development are the need for multiple behavioral indices, the specification of the criteria along the temporal continuum represented by the training process, and the fundamental requirement of relevance. Freeberg developed measures of trainee social, community, and occupational adjustment based upon federal manpower legislation. He used these measures first at program completion and then six months later to show the interrelationships between the various sets of measures.

The application of criterion-referenced testing procedures to training settings is another procedure based upon concern for establishing relevant criteria. As discussed by Glaser and Nitko (1971), criterion-referenced tests are planned to be representative of a specific domain of tasks. Thus, criterion-referenced measures are designed to compare a person's performance to a standard, while norm-referenced measures are designed to compare an individual's test score with the performance of others. Several thoughtful discussions concerning the development and interpretation of criterion-referenced measures have been published (Swezey, Pearlstein, and Ton, 1974). Unfortunately, an inspection of the literature on the use of criterion-referenced measures in training situations indicates that the term is more a philosophy of hope than a reality in the development of relevant criteria. Normative strategies have been criticized because they do not insure that the trainees can perform tasks at a mastery level. However, it is sadly apparent that the problems of translating information from the need assessment into instructional objectives and relevant criteria remain whether or not the measure is called criterion referenced. In a rare exception, Pannel and Laabs (1979) examined a methodology to evaluate a criterion-referenced test. First, they selected test items that both showed a significantly greater proportion of correct responses for a postinstruction group and that were answered correctly by at least 50 percent of the postinstruction group. Then, they used the item on a hold-out sample to see if this would enable them to predict whether the trainees were members of a preinstruction or postinstruction group. After refinement of the items, the investigators predicted, preinstructional and postinstructional members with 68 percent to 92 percent accuracy for the different modules. More research focused on standards for the development of relevant training criteria is badly needed.

Most of the discussion concerning the multiple nature of the criteria necessary to evaluate training still centers on Kirkpatrick's conception of reactions, learning, behavior, and results. His revisions (1976, 1977) included the integration of some of the basic principles of evaluation design with the criterion system. In the best presentation on this topic, Hamblin's test (1974) presented a thorough analysis of each of the four types of criteria, including suggested methodology as well as a review of training studies that have utilized each of the four criteria.

The importance of establishing multiple criteria that reflect the various instructional objectives and organizational goals is reinforced by articles (Foley, 1974) that argue that evaluators can easily be misled by employing a single criterion or criteria that do not reflect the diverse nature of the instructional process. J.P. Campbell (1978) notes that the criteria chosen to evaluate our training programs represent a value judgment on which all concerned parties should agree before the research begins. Otherwise, regardless of the quality of the investigation, the results may be ignored or attacked. It is time for training researchers to consider and examine value judgments as an important factor in their work.

Several recent efforts reflect a trend toward the consideration of cost factors. The importance of these factors was emphasized in a review of military training technology (Alluisi, 1976), which stressed the importance of implementing cost effectiveness research. Levin (1975) provided a thorough discussion of the cost-effectiveness approach emphasizing the comparative effectiveness of various alternatives. Another report (Orlansky and String, 1977; String and Orlansky, 1977) provided a comprehensive illustration of an approach that combined the examination of performance improvement and costs in making recommendations about the justification of motion simulation in aircraft simulator programs. Mirabal (1978) listed a large number of cost analysis variables including cost of facilities, travel, development, per diem adjustments, furniture, and a host of other factors. His list is a good starting point for those persons interested in considering the costs of conducting training.

One of the most important recent developments in criterion development is represented by D.T. Campbell's paper (1974) titled "Qualitative Knowing in Action Research." He notes that our evaluation efforts have emphasized outcome and ignored process measures. Thus, evaluation efforts have missed the richness of detail concerning how events occurred and even what went wrong. Goldstein (1978a, 1978b) discussed studies where data misinterpretations would have occurred if the investigators had been unaware of the events that occurred during training. Hettich (1977) described several different types of evaluators' journals that could be used to collect information related to significant events, extraneous variables, and other factors that could provide important information about empirical investigations. Certainly, these thoughts make the data collected by the consultant who appears only to collect pretest and posttest information very suspect.

## Evaluation Methodology

There are a significant number of articles about evaluation that combine an understanding of evaluation design with an appreciation of the problems of performing research in organizational environments. The most important of these articles is Cook and D.T. Campbell's (1976) article on quasi and true experiments in field settings. They updated D.T. Campbell and Stanley's original classic in this area with some particularly intriguing sections on research in organizations; these sections include material on obstacles to conducting true experiments and situations conducive to field experiments. There are a number of papers that discuss evaluation directly relevant to the analyses of training research. Burgoyne and Cooper (1975) offered some insightful glances at the philosophy of evaluation as practiced in the United States and then examined the usefulness of various methodologies in understanding training in organizational settings. Goldstein (1978a) examined the differences in evaluation approaches depending on whether the evaluator is going to analyze training performance, on-the-job performance of trainees, or the job performance of trainees who come through a program after it has been evaluated. Other authors have begun to discuss the creditability of training and what information has to be available in order to sell the value of the program in an organizational environment (Deterline, 1976, 1977; Kirkpatrick, 1978; Thompson, 1978).

Many of the above articles addressed issues specific to the problems of intervening in organizational environments. Cook and Campbell's (1976) discussion of randomization included discussion of the reactive effects of this procedure. In these instances, the evaluation itself (as well as the training program) effects the organization such that it is difficult to determine the source of any resulting changes. Other writers have focused specifically on the issues involved in the intervention process. Thus Scriven (1975), Weiss (1975), and Sjoberg (1975) discussed the values and politics of evaluation research. Weiss noted that decision maker values often determine how the data from evaluation research will be used. For example, if the decision maker is concerned about trainees holding onto skilled jobs, then negative evaluations about the impact of instruction are treated with alarm. However, if the evaluator is interested in keeping the ghetto quiet, then negative training evaluations might be treated as irrelevant and ignored.

These types of results and thoughts have led some investigators to suggest alternative approaches to the evaluation process. Some of these methods include: a goal-free evaluation where the evaluator is not informed of the intended effects (Scriven, 1975); an adversarial method adopted from the legal model (Levine, 1974); a decision theoretic method, which attempts to quantify the goals and values in the evaluation process (Edwards, Guttentag, and Snapper, 1975); and D.T. Campbell's (1974) process variable approach, which is used to collect qualitative information to help further understand the process of intervention as well as the meaning of quantitative indices.

## A FEW CONCLUDING REMARKS

Research on training processes appears to be approaching an important stage. While the vast majority of writing in this area is neither empirical, theoretical, nor thoughtful, there is a small but increasingly significant literature that focuses on important issues and raises the expectations of this reviewer about the future possibilities. One hopes there will be continual attention given to training issues, which might include some of the following suggestions.

First, it should be possible on the basis of need assessment techniques to determine what tasks are performed, what behaviors are essential to the performance of those tasks, what type of learning is necessary to acquire those behaviors, and what type of instructional content is best suited to accomplish that type of learning. Clearly, psychologists concerned with the instructional activity of children in school systems are moving more swiftly toward these goals. Training researchers should consider all aspects of the instructional process and begin the development of adult instructional theories. As a first step, attention should be given to the development of need assessment techniques that emphasize the type of information needed as input to the training process. J.P. Campbell (1978) has noted that the field has ignored descriptive studies. Thus, he suggests that understanding leadership might be enhanced by actually observing and recording what leaders do when they are leading. It is also likely that this type of information would provide very useful information for training.

Second, in order to gain an appreciation for the degree to which training programs achieve their objectives, it is necessary to consider the creative development of evaluation models. These models should permit the extraction of the greatest amount of information within the constraints of the environment. Thus, it is important to continue to develop information about constraints that threaten the understanding of data collection in organizational environments. However, it's just as necessary to design models (e.g., Komaki, Waddell, Pearce, 1977) that allow the collection of data with maximum confidence. Researchers can not afford to be frozen into inactivity by the spectre of threats to validity. It would be helpful to have further information about alternative evaluation models, including the use of individual difference methodology and content validity strategies. One hopes these models will emphasize the relationship between training and on-the-job performance as well as the examination of selection and training performance. It is also important to recognize that all models are dependent upon the thoughtful collection of relevant criteria that reflect the dynamic processes of training programs. Further attention to the necessary multiple criteria (e.g., Freeberg, 1976) and the possibilities of criterion-referenced testing (e.g., Pannel and Laabs, 1979) might pay dividends.

Third, further understanding and recognition that training is a process within an organization must be reflected within the study of instructional systems. Thus, need assessment should consider the possibility that relevant instructional programs might be consumed by organizational conflicts. Also, evaluation designs must recognize that the training program and the evaluation are interventions within the structure of the organization. Research on topics such as hard core unemployed, the aged, fair employment practices, career development, and realistic expectations continue to identify variables in addition to instructional quality that require examination. Attention must be given to training as a system within work organizations, rather than simply treating instruction as a separate technology. It is also important to enhance knowledge by studying decisions that organizations make, rather than trying to experimentally control all of the variables. Thus, researchers might ask what kinds of individuals in what type of organizations are threatened by being selected as members of a control group. Also, it is possible to explore what can be learned about organizations by the procedures their leaders employ to choose partici- pants. It would also be interesting to examine what types of persons and training programs are selected by different organizations.

Finally, there is a desperate need for high quality empirical investiga- tions that examine the usefulness of training techniques. It is sad that there are so few good illustrations that can be cited. It is important to conclude by noting that the advent of high technology will only intensify many of the problems discussed in this paper. If high technology changes job requirements, it will be necessary to use appropriate need assessment and evaluation techniques in order to effectively design training pro- grams. Otherwise, job relevant training is not likely to occur. Considering the complexity of the high technology tasks to be performed, job relevant training in the future is likely to become a requirement rather than a luxury.

## NOTE

[1]Many of the ideas and words in this article are liberally borrowed from previous work (see Goldstein, 1974, 1978a, 1978b, 1980) by the same author.

## REFERENCES

Allen, R.F. and Silverzweig, S. Group norms: Their influence on training effectiveness. In R.L. Craig (Ed.), *Training & Development Handbook.* New York: McGraw-Hill, 1976.

Alluisi, E.A., Chair. *Summary report of the task force on training technology.* Office of the Director of Defense Research and Engineering, Defense Science Board, Washington, D.C., 1976.

Adams, J.A. On the evaluation of training devices. Presented at the annual meeting of the American Psychological Association, Toronto, 1978.

Ammerman, H.L. and Pratzner, F.C. Occupational survey report on business data programmers: Task data from workers and supervisors indicating job relevance and training criticalness. R&D Series No. 108, Center for Vocational Education, Columbus, Ohio, 1974.

_____. Occupational survey report on automotive mechanics: Task data from workers and supervisors indicating job relevance and training criticalness. R&D Series No. 110, Center for Vocational Education, Columbus, Ohio, 1975.

_____. Performance content for job training. Vols. 1–5. R&D series No. 121–125. Center for Vocational Education, Columbus, Ohio, 1977.

Ammerman, H.L., Essex, D.W., and Pratzner, F.C. Rating the job significance of technical concepts: An application to three occupations. R&D Series No. 105, Center for Vocational Education, Columbus, Ohio, 1974.

Baumgartel, H. and Jeanpierre, F. Applying new knowledge in the backhome setting: A study of Indians managers' adoptive efforts. *Journal of Applied Behavioral Science* 1972, 8(6):674–94.

Bray, D.W. The assessment center method. In R.L. Craig, (Ed.) *Training & Development Handbook.* New York: McGraw-Hill, 1976.

Burgoyne, J.G. and Cooper, C.L. Evaluation methodology. *Journal of Occupational Psychology,* 1975, 48(1):53–62.

Campbell, D.T. Qualitative knowing in action research. Presented at the annual meeting of the American Psychological Association, New Orleans, 1974.

Campbell, J.P. What we are about: An inquiry into the self concept of industrial and organizational psychology. Presidential address to Division of Industrial and Organizational Psychology, at the Annual Meeting of the American Psychological Association, Toronto, 1978.

_____. Personnel training and development. *Annual Review of Psychology* 1971, 22, 565–602.

Campbell, J.P., Dunnette, M.P., Lawler, E.E. III, and Weick, K.E. Jr., *Managerial behavior, performance, and effectiveness.* New York: McGraw-Hill, 1970.

Campion, J.E. Work sampling for personnel selection. *Journal of Applied Psychology*, 1972, *56*(1):40–44.

Catalanello, R.F. and Kirkpatrick, D.L. Evaluating training programs—the state of the art. *Training and Development Journal*, 1968, *22*, 2–9.

Cook, T.D. and Campbell, D.T. The design and conduct of quasi-experiments and true experiments in field settings. In M. Dunnette, (Ed.) *Handbook of industrial and organizational psychology*, pp. 223–326. Chicago: Rand McNally, 1976.

Deterline, W.A. Credibility in training. *Training and Development Journal*, 1976–1977, Parts 1–6, *30*, 12 and *31*, 1–6.

Edwards, W., Guttentag, M., and Snapper, K. 1975. A decision-theoretic approach to evaluation research. In E.L. Struening, and M. Guttentag, *Handbook of evaluation research, Vol. 1*. Beverly Hills, Calif.: Sage, 1975.

Foley, J.P., Jr. Evaluating maintenance performance: An analysis. AFHRL Technical Report 74-57. Wright-Patterson Air Force Base, Ohio. 1974.

Freeberg, N.E. Criterion measures for youth-work training programs: The development of relevant performance dimensions. *Journal of Applied Psychology*, 1976, *61* (5):537–45.

French, S.H. Measuring progress toward industrial relations objectives. *Personnel*, 1953, *30*, 338–47.

Gilbert, T.F. On the relevance of laboratory investigation of learning to self-instructional programming. In A.A. Lumsdaine and R. Glaser (Eds.), *Teaching machines and programmed instruction*. Washington, D.C.: National Education Association, 1960.

Glaser, R. and Nitko, A.J. Measurement in learning and instruction. In R.L. Thorndike, (Ed.) *Educational Measurement*, 2nd ed. Washington, D.C.: American Council on Education, 1971.

Goldstein, I.L. *Training: Program development and evaluation*. Monterrey, Calif.: Brooks/Cole, 1974.

———. The pursuit of validity in the evaluation of training programs. *Human Factors*, 1978a, *20*,131–44.

———. *Understanding research in organizational environments: Can process measures help?* Presented at the annual meeting of the Eastern Psychology Association, Washington, D.C., 1978b.

———. Training in work organizations. In *Annual Review of Psychology*. Palo Alto, Calif. Annual Reviews, 1980.

Hamblin, A.C. *Evaluation and control of training*. London: McGraw-Hill, 1974.

Hand, H.H. and Slocum, J.W., Jr. A longitudinal study of the effects of a human relations training program on managerial effectiveness. *Journal of Applied Psychology*, 1972, *56*:412-17.

Hettich, P. *The evaluator's journal: A qualitative adjunct to program evaluation*. Presented at the annual meeting of the American Psychological Association, San Francisco, 1977.

Kirkpatrick, D.L. Evaluating training programs: Evidence vs. proof. *Training and Development Journal* 1977, *31*,(11):9–12.

———. How to plan and implement a supervisory training program. *Training and Development Journal*, 1978, Parts 1–5 *32*(4–9).

———. Evaluation of training. In R.L. Craig (Ed.) *Training and development handbook* New York: McGraw-Hill, 1976.

Komaki, J., Waddell, W.M., and Pearce, M.G. The applied behavior analysis approach and individual employees: Improving performance in two small businesses. *Organizational Behavior and Human Performance* 1977, *19*,33—52.

Laabs, G.J., Pannel, R.C., and Pickering, E.J. A personnel readiness training program: Maintenance of the missile test and readiness equipment (MTRE MK 7 MOD 2). NPRDC Technical Report No. 77-19, 1977.

Levin, H.M. Cost-effectiveness analysis in evaluation research. In M. Guttentag, and E.L. Streuning (Eds.) *Handbook of evaluation research, Vol. 2.* Beverly Hills, Calif.: Sage. 1975.

Levine, M. 1974. Scientific method and the adversary model: Some preliminary thoughts. *American Psychology, 29,* 666—67.

Miller, R.W., and Zeller, F.H. Social psychological factors associated with responses to retraining. Final Report, Office of Research and Development, Appalachian Center, West Virginia University, U.S. Department of Labor, 1967.

Mindak, W.A. and Anderson, R.E. Can we quantify an act of faith. *Training and Development Journal,* 1971, *25,* 2—10.

Mirabal, T.E. Forecasting future training costs. *Training and Development Journal,* 1978 *32*(7), 78 and 87.

McGehee, W. and Thayer, P.W. *Training in business and industry.* New York: John Wiley & Sons, 1961.

Orlansky, J. and String, J. Cost-effectiveness of flight simulators for military training. Vol. 1: Use and effectiveness of flight simulators. Technical Paper, Institute for Defense Analysis, Arlington, Va. 1977.

Pannel, R.C. and Laabs, G.J. Construction of a criterion-referenced, diagnostic test for an individual instruction program. *Journal of Applied Psychology,* 1979, *64,* 255—62.

Prien, E.P. The function of job analysis in content validation. *Personnel Psychology,* 1977, *30,* 167—74.

Salinger, R.D. Disincentive to effective employee training and development. Washington, D.C.: U.S. Civil Service Commission Bureau of Training, 1973.

Scriven, M. *Evaluation bias and its control.* Paper #4 in Occasional Paper Series. West Michigan University, Kalamazoo, Michigan, 1975.

Sjoberg, G. Politics, ethics, and evaluation research. In M. Guttentag and E.L. Streuning (Eds.) *Handbook of evaluation research, Vol. 2.* Beverly Hills, Calif.: Sage, 1975.

String, J. and Orlansky, J. Cost-effectiveness of flight simulators for military training. Vol. II: Estimating costs of training in sumulators and aircraft. Technical Paper, Institute for Defense Analysis, Arlington, Va. 1977.

Swezey, R.W., Pearlstein, R.B., and Ton, W.H. Criterion-references testing: A discussion of theory and of practice in the army. *ARI Technical Paper 273-A18- (1)-IR-0474-RWSW.* Virginia, 1974.

Thompson, J.T., Jr. How to develop a more systematic evaluation strategy. *Training and Development Journal,* 1978, *32,* 88—93.

U.S. Civil Service Commission. *Catalog of basic education systems.* Washington, D.C.: U.S. Government Printing Office, 1971.

Weiss, C.H. Evaluation research in the political context. In E.L. Struening and M. Guttentag, (Eds.) *Handbook of evaluation ressearch, Vol. 1* Beverly Hills, Calif.: Sage, 1975.

# New Technology for Business Telephone Users: Some Findings from Human Factors Studies

## D. James Dooling and Edmund T. Klemmer

In this paper we would like to share with you some of the conclusions we have drawn from studying the needs of business customers in the area of telecommunications. While our data and experience are substantially limited to the domain of business communications, we believe that most of the conclusions we present will be directly relevant to other human factors issues related to new technology. In generalizing from our results, it is important to consider the particular characteristics of work with business telephone systems and how they relate to the theme of the conference.

## IMPACT ON USER

Six or seven years ago, the technology of business telephones took a giant leap forward. The user of an ordinary TOUCH-TONE® telephone was given access to a wide variety of new features. For example, the user can set up a three-way conference call without operator assistance. Or a user can dial a code and answer a telephone call that is ringing at another person's desk. In addition to the implementation of these features on familiar, simple telephones, users were also offered new electronic telephones that provided buttons for feature activation and light emitting diodes (LED's) for feedback. All things considered, the business world has been experiencing significant changes in the familiar old telephone. As in other areas of technology, the user has had to cope with new ways of performing old functions. Our paper addresses user problems associated with the new technology.

## THE "ORDINARY" USER

For the most part, our work has been directed toward the "common man" referred to in the Chapanis paper. While there are a number of specialized jobs associated with business telephone systems, the work we will be discussing refers to the ordinary user, the person who has a telephone on the desk as an aid to other job responsibilities. We believe that the human factors problems are different for people who have to use a piece of new technology equipment as their main job responsibility. There are, for example, substantial differences between the casual user and the professional user in motivation to participate in training programs. The ordinary business telephone user does not want to invest a great amount of effort in learning how to use the new telephone. We believe that this characteristic is true of many users of new technology.

We would like to emphasize that the work we describe is the result of a collaborative effort with many colleagues in human factors. The names of many individual contributors will be mentioned throughout the paper. Even though the work to be described represents a substantial human factors effort involving many people, the recurring "we" in our paper should not be interpreted as representing all of human factors at Bell Laboratories, let alone the company as a whole. Human factors studies of business telephone users is only a small part of the overall human factors effort in the Bell System.

## A TRUE–FALSE TEST

Our paper is structured around the ten true–false items shown in Table 1. The test contains statements about human factors in high-technology industries and provides a convenient device for discussing a list of otherwise unstructured human factors issues. Before reading further, we recommend that you actually take the test, selecting "true" or "false" for each item. We have attempted to make each statement interesting enough so that the answer would not be obvious to anyone. Your forced-choice selection, therefore, may have to be based on an alternative that applies only 51 percent of the time for some items. The remainder of this paper consists of our answers to the ten items given.

## TECHNOLOGY AND HUMAN FACTORS

### Statement 1: Difficulties with Technology

It is not necessarily true that technology makes our life more difficult. In fact, so much technology is easy to use that we take it for

**TABLE 1**
Psychology, Industry, and New Technology

---

**Indicate "True" or "False" for each statement.**

1. Technology makes it increasingly difficult for people to interact with their environment.  T  F

2. Training sessions for new technology should cover all commonly used system features.  T  F

3. Hands-on training is an important part of initial training for skills related to new technology.  T  F

4. Training by an instructor is superior to self-instruction.  T  F

5. Training should be evaluated on the basis of user performance, not perceptions and attitudes.  T  F

6. More can be accomplished by improved training than by design changes.  T  F

7. A simple, general purpose terminal that accepts sequential codes is better than a specialized interface with many buttons and lights.  T  F

8. Human factors work is really only effective early in the product development cycle.  T  F

9. Human factors recommendations should always be based on adequate data with statistically significant differences.  T  F

10. Psychologists can best contribute to technology by producing good data and theories.  T  F

---

granted and do not see it in terms of human factors problems. The self-starter and automatic transmissions on automobiles come to mind as technical innovations that have made life simpler, not more complicated. It would be radically false to characterize technology as making our lives increasingly more miserable. Would anyone trade in a photocopy machine for a roomful of monks with quill pens?

Still, there is no doubt that technology creates user problems in some instances. We wouldn't be here if it didn't. It is instructive, however, to consider what has happened in the evolution of many technological products and services. In the natural course of things, products that were at one time technological innovations and unfamiliar to users have become familiar and easy to use. Of course, there has been some learning by the populace. But we are impressed by the number of products that have themselves become simpler as they have become more sophisticated. The modern color TV, for example, is technologically more sophisticated than the old models of 20 years ago. When first introduced, however, the user paid a price in having to learn the tuning. Modern sets, however, have introduced features that have used technology to make the tuning itself easier and more automatic. We take this example as an instance of a general principle: Technology should simplify, not make more difficult, the use of complex systems.

The color TV example also tells us something about the role of human factors regarding technological innovation. The market place itself eventually enforces good human factors in products. Automobiles, televisions, and calculators may have started out as unfamiliar and difficult to use. But they have evolved inexorably toward ease of use. The products that are difficult to use simply don't sell if there are comparable capabilities in competing products. What human factors studies can do is to short circuit the processes of the marketplace in the laboratory and thereby increase the chances of the individual product "surviving." Our job as psychologists, therefore, is to accelerate the process of making technology fit the needs of the user.

## TRAINING

Statements 2 through 5 deal with training. When new electronic telephone systems began to be widely sold throughout the country, human factors people were called in to consult on "training problems." Although users were very satisfied with the new systems, they were not as happy with the training they received. Furthermore, their complaints had little to do with the actual content of the training; their main complaint was that they wanted more. Telephone companies, on the other hand, had their own complaints. They were spending much more money on training than they had anticipated. They were providing hands-on training sessions to small groups of users for approximately two hours per group. For a customer with hundreds, perhaps thousands, of telephones, this is a very expensive proposition. In addition, the telephone companies were also responding to customer requests for extra follow-up training weeks after the system had been installed. In this section, we describe how human factors studies were used to deal with the training problems.

**TABLE 2**
A List of Telephone Features for a Typical User

| Feature | Description |
| --- | --- |
| Automatic Callback | You can be called back automatically when a busy telephone becomes free. |
| Call Forwarding (All Calls) | All of your incoming calls will ring at another telephone. |
| Call Forwarding (Busy or No Answer) | Your incoming calls will ring at another phone if you are busy or do not answer. |
| Call Hold | Your call is held while you consult privately or activate other features. |
| Call Park | A call can be held at one telephone and retrieved at a different telephone. |
| Call Pickup | You can answer a ringing call at someone else's phone from your own phone. |
| Call Waiting (To Answer) | While busy on one call, you can hold it to answer a second call. |
| Call Waiting (To Send) | You can signal a busy called party that you are trying to get through. |
| Three-way Conference | You can get up a three-way conversation without operator assistance. |
| Transfer | You can transfer a caller (or called party) from your telephone to someone else's. |
| Trunk Answer (Night Bells) | When no attendant is on duty you can answer general calls at your phone. |
| Trunk Queuing | When a special line (e.g., WATS) is busy the system will keep your place in queue and call you back when a line becomes free. |

## Statement 2: Training All Features

Table 2 provides a list of some of the new features that a user might have available on a modern business telephone system. For purposes of discussion we can assume that this is the feature set that a "typical" user would be expected to learn in a training session. Such a session would consist of an instructor explaining and demonstrating each feature to a group of eight or ten people seated around a conference table. Following the demonstration of each feature, one or two people from the group would be given the opportunity to try out the feature on a working system. This procedure would be employed with different users so that each had an opportunity to practice a few of the features. This training strategy naturally evolved from telephone company trainers and had two properties that we would like to discuss in this section. First, users were trained on all of the features assigned to their telephones. Second, the training for each feature consisted of a detailed step-by-step description of how to operate it.

**All features.** For professional telephone company trainers it was obvious that users had to be trained on all of their features. To experimental psychologists who interviewed customers and attended training sessions it was equally obvious that users could not absorb that much material in a single session. We believe that the "magical number seven" (Miller, 1956), or something very much like it, applies directly to this situation. The users are not given very much practice on any one feature and should not be expected to comprehend all 12 in a single session. The usefulness of novel features is not always obvious until the system is installed, and many users are resistant to serious learning about their telephones. Furthermore, not everyone needs all of the features that are covered in a training session. Of course, customizing training to individual needs could be considered. But it is just not possible to schedule sessions so that all users get instruction on only those features that will be useful to them. For one reason, no one knows for sure just what that feature set would be for each individual, including the individual.

A great deal of the Bell Laboratories human factors effort on training, therefore, has been to streamline it and make it more efficient. In later sections we will describe some of the particular findings that led to specific changes in training strategy. A key element of that strategy has been not to attempt exhaustive coverage of all the features in a group training session. A shorter version of the training was developed in conjunction with AT & T (Ellis and Coskren, 1979). In a field test with 17 large businesses (1,685 users) Susan Nassau[1] demonstrated that the new training package led to feature usage and knowledge that was equivalent to the old training method. In effect, group training sessions were reduced from two hours to one without any measurable loss in performance.

**Performance aids.** The old training methods, while covering all features, also stressed the operational details for each feature. Users were given step-by-step instruction on activating each, and then they

| FEATURES | WHEN YOU WANT | PROCEDURE |
|---|---|---|
| [X] AUTOMATIC CALLBACK | to activate | listen for dial tone·DIAL (#0)—DIAL EXTENSION··· HANG UP IMMEDIATELY· you will be called back |
| ( to be called back when a busy | when you are called back... | listen for 3 short rings·LIFT HANDSET AND HEAR RINGING·WAIT FOR ANSWER |
| extension becomes free) | to cancel | listen for dial tone·DIAL (#0)··· HANG UP |

**Figure 1.** Example of a feature operation description from a performance aid.

tried out each feature on a working system. The great amount of detail on each feature compounded the problem of information overload that was inherent to begin with in the coverage of 12 features. The way out of this problem is to give the users a performance aid that describes the procedure for using each relevant feature. The performance aid that was developed was a one-page card that summarized all feature operations in step-by-step fashion. Stephen Ellis and Heidi Muench tested a number of alternative formats and ended up recommending a left-to-right format with the feature names and descriptions in a column at the left. An example of the recommended format is shown in Figure 1. It is not necessary to get into the specifics of their experiments or the rationale for each section of the card. The important point here is that the training method relied on the card for details of feature operation. The training sessions, therefore, were aimed at a more abstract level of encoding where memory is known to be better (Dooling and Christiaansen, 1977). Users were taught the main ideas of feature operation, and details were left to the card. An important part of the training session became instruction on the use of the performance aid itself. By training to the performance aid, rather than to the details of system operation, users were able to selectively process the information they needed without any undue burden on their memory capacity.

## Statement 3: Hands-on Training

Telephone company training for modern business telephone systems originally included "hands-on" training, as described in the previous sections. It was clear to just about everyone concerned that the operation of a complex set of features required actual practice by the users. As a result, telephone companies went to the considerable expense of providing a working telephone system for training for several weeks before the installation of the new system. It is also true that hands-on practice added to the length of the training sessions and required that training be conducted in small groups. But is hands-on training necessary?

Learning the feature operations of a telephone system is mainly a cognitive skill, not a motor skill. (The same can be said for the operation of computer terminals and electronic calculators.) A careful analysis of the task facing the user reveals that the main problems involve memory, i.e., remembering the purpose and meaning of all the features and remembering the correct sequence of operations for activating them.

Motor skill is a very minor part of the enterprise. Indeed, a seven-year-old child can dial codes into a TOUCH-TONE® pad. The training difficulties revolve around teaching the user the meaning of the features and providing a memory aid for the details. There is much reason, therefore, to question the necessity of hands-on practice.

The effectiveness of hands-on practice was tested in the laboratory by James Harrison. He had Bell System trainers conduct hands-on sessions for 29 subjects and the same training without the practice for 29 others. The subjects were then individually run through 20 problems that required them to use the system features. The result was no significant difference in error rates between hands-on and hands-off training (14 percent vs. 16 percent). But does the result generalize under actual field conditions with customers?

Ellis (1977) investigated the effectiveness of hands-on training with 478 users at eight customer locations. The customers had recently ordered a new business telephone system, and the training was conducted in the normal manner by the usual telephone company instructors. Approximately one-half were trained with hands-on practice, and one-half without. A large sample of the users was tested immediately after training, and the result was no difference in feature knowledge: The hands-on trainees were 66 percent correct; the hands-off, 70 percent. In follow-up interviews conducted six weeks after system installation there was no significant difference in feature usage. The Ellis study conclusively demonstrates that hands-on practice has little or no effect on user performance with business telephone features. In addition, the users showed no difference in rated satisfaction with the system as a function of training type. We believe that this result would generalize to a wide variety of similar training situations where the main component of the learning is cognitive, rather than motor.

The training studies have been able to show concrete payoffs in terms of cost savings to telephone companies. Karlin (1977), for example, pointed out that the Ellis (1977) study of hands-on training ended up cutting training costs by $2.5 million dollars in a single year. So training has been an area of substantial success that has enhanced the visibility and credibility of human factors at Bell Laboratories.

## Statement 4: Self Instruction

Since our objective was to make user training more efficient and cost—effective, the idea of using self-instruction came readily to mind. Is it necessary to send trainers out to customer premises to conduct live classes? The Harrison experiment previously referred to also contained a group of 29 subjects who were given self-instruction training. They spent an hour reading a training manual, while the other subjects received one of the two types of group training given by the instructors. Performance tests on system features yielded no differences between subject groups in error rates. The self-instruction group made 15 percent errors, as compared to the 14 percent and 16 percent error rates of the hands-on and hands-off groups, respectively. In the laboratory, there was no evidence that instructor training was superior.

The viability of self-instruction was tested in the field in two separate studies with two different types of business telephone systems. Stephen Ellis had five large businesses trained in the standard manner in group sessions and five trained by self-instruction. The users were simply given instruction books one week before system installation. In a similar experiment, Dooling had six moderately sized businesses trained in group sessions and six by self-instruction. In both experiments individual users were given questionnaires and interviewed about their feature usage and feature knowledge. The result from both studies was the same: no significant differences as a function of training method. In addition, there were no differences in the users' rated satisfaction with either system as a function of training method. From these studies we conclude that self-instruction is a viable training method for business telephone users. We suspect that this conclusion would apply to many other areas as well.

## Statement 5: Performance vs. Attitudes

In describing human factors studies of training, we have focused on measures of user performance. The less expensive training methods were shown to lead to performance that was essentially equivalent to that from the higher priced versions. We also found that user attitudes toward the new system were not measurably affected by the type of training. Do these results then require that we immediately replace the established training methods with either "hands-off" group sessions or self-instruction? Not necessarily. Attitudes toward a telephone system need not be the same as attitudes toward training.

In all of the various field studies of customer training the users were asked to rate the training itself. The result was invariably significantly lower ratings for "hands-off" training as compared to "hands-on," and significantly lower ratings for self-instruction as compared to group training with an instructor. Ellis' (1977) results are typical. When users were asked if the training session had adequately prepared them to use the new telephone system, 73 percent of the "hands-on" trainees said "yes." In contrast, only 54 percent of the "hands-off" trainees gave an affirmative response.

These results demonstrate the importance in applied work of considering attitudes as well as performance in the evaluative process. If users perceive that their training is inadequate, even if it is demonstrably effective, then a manager in industry has to pause before deciding to implement specific recommendations. It is of overriding importance to ensure that customers are satisfied with our products and services—and that includes training. The challenge for human factors in this arena is to understand and to deal with user attitudes as well as their performance. It certainly should be possible to convince people that a system offering greater performance efficiency is desirable, but we often observe that such insight is not automatic. The user attitude problem presents an unconventional, but real, challenge for the human factors specialist.

## SYSTEM DESIGN

Our summary of human factors work on business telephone systems has so far described only work on training. Experimental psychologists have also done applied research on the design of features and their activation procedures. Statements 6 and 7 address the human factors of system design. In this section, we would like to share with you some of our findings and observations. We begin with the question, "Which is more important, training or design?"

### Statement 6: Training vs. Design

This question may seem to some like comparing apples and oranges. You may feel that we have unfairly forced you to choose between two very important alternatives on our true-false test. Nevertheless, decisions such as these have to be made all the time in a human factors group in industry. With a limited number of people to work on projects, priorities have to be established. In our area of human factors at Bell Laboratories, we have been putting increasing emphasis on the human factors aspects of design in recent years and much less on training. Why?

The studies of training that we reported demonstrated time and again that we could cut back on the time and costs of training while maintaining equivalent performance. Another way of characterizing such results is to acknowledge that training is not a very potent variable with business telephone systems. Substantial manipulations of training in a wide variety of experiments failed to reject the null hypothesis.

The impotence of the training variable is perhaps not surprising when you consider the environment in which telephones are used. Business telephone users are not motivated to invest a great deal of time and energy in training. Many prefer to learn by experimenting with the system or by asking coworkers for assistance. Some companies are reluctant to let their employees attend even one-hour training sessions, and we know that not everyone conscientiously reads the instruction manual. In the grand scheme of things, formal training by the telephone company represents a small part of the learning that takes place. It is not surprising, therefore, that manipulations of formal training account for very small proportions of the variance in user performance. In the real-world environment in which we operate, no kind of training is likely to be effective in influencing performance on a complex system.

Our comments on training apply to the casual user of technology, not to the professional. It is important to distinguish between the person who uses a new telephone system as one of many tools in performing a job and the person who has telephone responsibilities full time. When a person has to use a particular device for her full-time job, training could be expected to be a much more powerful variable. Indeed, PBX attendants ("operators" who run the "switchboard" at a large business) are given individual hands-on training. We would expect manipulations of training to have significant effects on their ability to learn their job. Nevertheless, the "casual" user whom we have described with business telephones is representative of a large population of users of new technology. We believe that our conclusions about training with business telephones generalize to other domains as well.

A fundamental goal of our current human factors efforts on business telephones is to design them so that training is unnecessary. (The paper by Chapanis in this volume reflects a similar philosophy.) We do not view improved training as a realistic solution to problems. Rather, we view training as an expensive problem to be minimized. Training is a problem, not a solution. Human factors work on training comes at the end of the development cycle for a new product. Our recent emphasis has been toward influencing the product as early as possible. Positive benefits at an early stage have ripple-through benefits throughout the development process.

An important part of our current human factors work involves the testing and evaluation of new user procedures for business telephone services. Laboratory subjects are given role-playing problems that force them to activate all of the system features. We measure error rates and user preferences for a wide variety of system designs. For example, Terry Spencer tested 16 different experimental telephone systems in a laboratory study. Each system had function buttons for feature activation and LED's for visual feedback. They differed, however, in the procedures required to hold calls, transfer calls, and set up conference calls. It should be mentioned that these 16 possibilities did not represent a variety of "dummy" conditions. Rather, each had been proposed by somebody as a good method. A summary of the results is shown in Figure 2. The various systems are labeled alphabetically on the abscissa with error rates on the ordinate. As can be readily seen, there is no null hypothesis problem here.

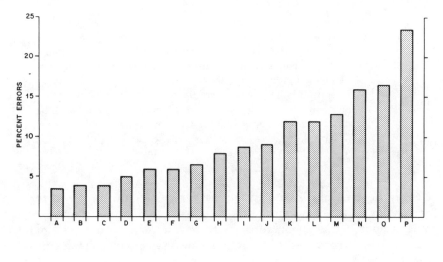

FEATURE ACTIVATION PROCEDURE

**Figure 2.** Error data for 16 different sets of feature activation procedures.

In stark contrast with the usual training results, apparently minor variations in activation procedures led to substantial differences in user performance. Fortunately, this study was completed in time to influence the next generation of business telephone systems. The Spencer study, along with many others like it, has convinced us that better design is more fruitful than improved training.

## Statement 7: Codes vs. Dedicated Buttons

Statement 7 raises a question about the design of terminal equipment for users. The particular terminal could be a computer terminal or a communications terminal such as a telephone. Is it better to design a terminal that is very flexible such that many different services and features can be activated from a single device? Or is it better to design a terminal for a particular application and optimize the user interface with dedicated buttons for the various features to be activated. Here are some examples of the issue:

• A TOUCH-TONE® pad on a telephone is a general purpose device. By dialing different combinations of numbers, the user can be connected to millions of different telephones. On the other hand, it is possible to purchase a telephone that provides dedicated buttons for automatic dialing of telephone numbers. With the TOUCH-A-MATIC® telephone, for example, the user can program various buttons to provide one-touch dialing of different telephone numbers.

- Many fast-food restaurants now have dedicated keys on the cash register for each item to be served. The clerk need not enter the amount of money associated with each item, it is all done automatically. In contrast, an old-fashioned cash register is a general purpose device capable of handling a greater number of items.
- Text-editing systems for "word processing" have followed two different approaches. One approach is to have all editing commands be entered from a general purpose keyboard. For example, to delete a line, you type "d." The alternative approach is to have a dedicated button for each feature. To delete a line, you press the "delete" button.

Clearly, no general answer to this question will be entirely correct for all applications. Our experience, however, leads us to prefer the dedicated button approach as being superior from a human factors standpoint. Data collected from users of modern business telephone systems support this view.

Business customers can presently choose between the two approaches in business telephones with advanced features. In one case, users can be given access to a wide range of features on a simple TOUCH-TONE® telephone. Features are activated by dialing codes on the TOUCH-TONE® pad. For example, to have all of your calls answered by someone else, you can activate "Call Forwarding" by dialing "*3" followed by an extension number. As an alternative, the customer can purchase a more expensive telephone that provides dedicated buttons for features. For example, you might have a telephone with a "Call Forwarding" button. The function-button telephones also provide visual feedback on the status of calls. For example, if your line is in use an LED is illuminated.

Human factors studies of dial codes vs. function buttons have found many cases where the dial-code approach has been successful. Indeed, most users of such systems are very satisfied with their service. There are, however, a few specific areas where users have problems (Dooling, 1980). The most important of these is in the area of holding calls and in returning to held calls. Telephones with dedicated buttons not only provide the convenience of the familiar "hold" button, but also provide visual feedback that is essential to complex call handling. From a human factors point of view, users who have to routinely deal with two calls at once as part of their job responsibility need the visual feedback provided by the more expensive terminals. By dedicating different buttons to different calls, the terminal makes call processing more efficient and less prone to error.

In the domain of business telephones, we would confidently answer "false" to statement 7 in Table 1. That does not mean, however, that specialized terminals can or should always be used. Clearly there is a need for general devices such as typewriters and computer terimnals. Our data would indicate, however, that when specialized devices are possible, they are better from a human factors viewpoint, particularly for occasional users.

## ROLÉ OF HUMAN FACTORS

The final three statements deal with broader issues about the role of human factors in industry. We offer our opinions boldly, being fully cognizant that not even our closest colleagues would agree with everything we say here. (We do, however, agree with each other. Mostly.)

### Statement 8: Effectiveness Early vs. Late

Our discussion of training vs. design included in it the underlying theme that work done early in the development cycle is more valuable than work that comes at the end, e.g., training. We believe that our observation is generally true. In fact, it has become a truism that human factors should be involved at the beginning of every project. As we have already indicated, we believe that human factors can be very effective at the early stages before decisions are made with respect to the design and working of any system. It is not our opinion, however, that early work is the *only* effective work. It would be a gross overgeneralization to hold that human factors specialists cannot make important contributions late in the development cycle. The training work cited earlier in the paper stands on its own as an important contribution. We also agree that many investigators in other industries have had impact at the training end of the development cycle.

Another postproduction area in which significant human factors contributions are both possible and necessary is in choosing and configuring systems for individual users. In an age of technological complexity and diversity specifying individual options for users is a major stumbling block. You may have encountered these problems in choosing and assembling computer systems. We have faced such problems in defining modern communications systems for business customers. The development of methods to determine the exact needs of each user is a human factors opportunity that Duncanson (1980) has tackled with some success. But much more needs to be done. Effective contributions can and must be made here even though it is late in the product development cycle.

### Statement 9: Recommendations and the Data

Most of us working in applied experimental psychology were trained in graduate departments that stressed good experimental designs, including the requirement that conclusions be based on statistically significant data. We would like to carry over those same principles to the real world of products and services. But there is one fact of life that is more important than statistical significance. Data presented before decisions are made can readily influence those decisions. Data presented after decisions are made are usually ineffective regardless of the level of statistical signficance. To have impact, data must be timely.

Of course, it would be wonderful if we could anticipate decision points well enough in advance so that adequate data could be collected and waiting. We should certainly try to do this, but frequently, if not usually, that is not possible. It is difficult to predict what decisions will be made a year ahead, so much work done on that time scale will be irrelevant to questions actually being asked. Moreover, if most of the effort is looking a year ahead, inadequate attention will be given to questions needing answers next week or next month. If we in human factors fail to contribute to current decisions because of a preoccupation with the future we may not be around to see the completion of our work.

Another important factor in applied settings is the requirement that all relevant variables be considered in the decision-making process. If a decision must be made, we do not have the luxury of studying one or two variables in a powerful experiment, while controlling (i.e., ignoring) the effects of others. One example from the past may help illustrate this point. Several years ago there was a proposal by telephone engineering people to change from letter-digit telephone numbers (e.g., GR9-7715) to all-digit numbers (e.g., 479-7715). Some psychologists opposed this decision on the ground that letter-digit numbers were easier to remember. Indeed, long-term memory experiments have shown a small advantage for the letter-digit numbers. But, as Karlin (1963) has pointed out, consideration of other relevant variables clearly favors the all-digit approach. In a short-term memory task, there were no significant differences between letter-digit and all-digit telephone numbers. The all-digit numbers have a slight, but significant, advantage in speed of dialing and also yield slightly fewer errors. All things considered, the all-digit numbers are superior. The failure to consider factors other than long-term memory, however, could have led to the wrong conclusion. When decisions have to be made, they must take all relevant variables into account. As a result, it is often a better strategy to aim for studies that provide unbiased, but perhaps limited data. The alternative of highly reliable data that is too narrow must be rejected.

One final note with regard to statistical significance. The presence or absence of statistical significance says little or nothing about the importance of the findings. This point has been made often enough with respect to the proportion of variance accounted for in psychological experiments (e.g., Vaughan and Corballis, 1969). In human factors work, the issue arises in a somewhat different form. Applied researchers are constantly forced to decide if a statistically significant difference is important enough to warrant a change. The decision on "important enough" cannot be made on the basis of statistical or experimental considerations alone. Cost is one very important factor that has to be considered in applied settings. Something may be better, but not at any price. Indeed, marketing considerations and user preferences must be taken into account. In this environment, statistically significant data is only one element to be considered. Human factors recommendations based on such data alone will often miss the mark.

## Statement 10: Psychologists' Best Contribution

How can psychologists in applied settings best contribute to the human design of advanced technological systems? Academic training would suggest the cycle of hypothesis, data collection, and theory building. But in actual practice, the scientific model is often not a successful model. Good data and theories are not the goal of applied work. In an applied setting, data must be collected, not to test hypotheses, but because relevant data and theory from the literature are almost nonexistent. The choice of what data to collect is a function of which decisions on present projects are most likely to affect the human interfaces adversely. Academic psychologists usually collect good data, but too often the data are not on the right questions. To define the right questions it is essential to understand the system that is the specific focus of the investigation.

Understanding the system and defining the questions requires that the human factors specialist work with the people who are designing the system, typically engineers. Working with the system designers ensures that the important questions are asked and that they are asked in a timely fashion. The psychologist needs to know what decisions are to be made and by whom in order to influence those decisions. Working with system designers also means that the psychologist will be known by them and included in relevant deliberations.

Thus, although data collection is important, psychologists can best contribute to technology by integrating themselves into system design organizations, identifying key human factors questions, and proposing answers to those questions in a timely fashion. The starting point is the applications area, not data collection or theory.

A corollary of our view is that the human factors specialist should become a specialist in one or more application areas rather than a specialist in an academic discipline. The best way to be effective is to be familiar with the history, language, people, and past problems of the systems to be studied. Our experience is that most Ph.D. experimental psychologists have enough background in the methodology and content of experimental psychology to work in a variety of content areas effectively. It is not unusual, for example, for someone trained in learning or memory to work effectively on problems that have major components in the fields of visual or auditory perception. But the psychologist who has not worked on a similar telecommunications system before is likely to have difficulty with the engineering, economic, and marketplace factors that must be considered in defining and executing the human factors study. For example, there is very little in the way of psychological data or theory that is directly relevant to the design of new control procedures for business telephone users. But understanding the functionality of existing systems, as well as the needs of business customers, is essential. This viewpoint is expressed in somewhat different form by Gould (1977) and Klemmer (1977).

## CONCLUSIONS

When this symposium was organized, several key questions were put out for discussion. Among them were "How well prepared is the consumer to master technology?" and "How will this technology be absorbed?" In the brochure announcing the symposium, the user is described as the "bottleneck" retarding the advance of technology. The underlying theme seemed to be that changing the behavior of users should be the goal of experimental psychologists and human factors engineers.

While we agree that training and attitude changes will be needed, we prefer to turn the questions around: How can technology be molded to meet the needs of the consumer? The job of human factors is to ensure that new products and services are designed to accommodate user capabilities. The speed with which new technology is absorbed into our society will be mainly dependent on the behavior of designers and the support they get from experimental psychology. The success of this endeavor depends to a large extent on the effectiveness of human factors specialists. In short, we are the "bottleneck."

## ACKNOWLEDGEMENTS

We are grateful to the many colleagues at Bell Laboratories who contributed to the research summarized in this chapter. The "we" and "our" that occurs so often in the text is meant to include them. Each is mentioned by name at the appropriate place in the text. In addition, we would like to thank Mary Carol Day and Martin H. Singer for their helpful comments on an earlier version of this paper.

## NOTE

[1]When a researcher is cited without a specific reference, we are reporting conclusions from Bell Laboratories memoranda that are not available for public distribution.

## REFERENCES

Dooling, D.J. Station user control procedures for business customers: A review of Bell Laboratories findings. In *Proceedings of the ninth international symposium on human factors in telecommunication.* Holmdel, N.J.: Bell Laboratories, 1980.

Dooling, D.J. and Christiaansen, R.E. Levels of encoding and retention of prose. In G.H. Bower (Ed.) *The psychology of learning and motivation, Volume 11.* New York: Academic Press, 1977.

Duncanson, J.P. Letting users specify their own telephone capabilities in complex systems. In *Proceedings of the ninth international symposium on human factors in telecommunication.* Holmdel, N.J.: Bell Laboratories, 1980.

Ellis, S.H. An investigation of telephone user training methods for a multiservice electronic PBX. In *Proceedings of the eighth international symposium on human factors in telecommunications.* Harlow, Essex, England: Standard Telecommunication Laboratories, 1977.

Ellis, S.H. and Coskren, R.A. New approach to customer training. *Bell Laboratories Record,* 1979, 57, 60–65.

Gould, J.D. Human factors research in industry. In J.P. Duncanson (Ed.) *Getting it together: Research and applications in human factors.* Santa Monica, Calif.: Human Factors Society, 1977.

Karlin, J.E. All number calling (ANC). In *Summary of the Second International Symposium on Human Factors in Telephony.* Copenhagen, Denmark: 1963.

_____. The changing and expanding role of human factors in telecommunication engineering at Bell Laboratories. In *Proceedings of the eighth international symposium on human factors in telecommunications.* Harlow, Essex, England: Standard Telecommunication Laboratories, 1977.

Klemmer, E.T. Human factors and new business telephone systems. In *Proceedings of the eighth international symposium on human factors in telecommunications.* Harlow, Essex, England: Standard Telecommunication Laboratories, 1977.

Miller, G.A. The magical number seven plus or minus two: Some limits on our capacity for processing information. *Psychological Review,* 1956, 69, 344–54.

Vaughan, G.M. and Corballis, M.C. Beyond tests of significance: Estimating strength of effects in selected ANOVA designs. *Psychological Bulletin,* 1969, 72, 204–13.

# Training Technology:
# An Ecological Perspective

## J. Dexter Fletcher

Discussions of training technology often generate more heat than light. Developers and implementers of training technology end up arrayed against those who resist encroachments of technology, in general, and technology applied to instruction, in particular. At root, however, technology means "systematic treatment," and it seems difficult to argue against some systematization of information presentation in instruction. On the other hand, instructional technologists could do much more to fit their developments into full programs of instruction and argue convincingly for the benefits of doing so. There seems to be an area of agreement shared by those on both sides of the technology argument, but at present this common ground is poorly identified and little understood. This situation may be improved by altering the way we view instructional technology.

Toward this end, this paper presents a perspective on training technology. It argues for a point of view that seeks to change modestly the way we now view training technology, what we perceive is important, how we interpret our data, and what priorities we assign to research and development. The emphasis, however, is on training. "Training" and "education" are probably best viewed as opposite ends of a dimension roughly labeled "instruction." Training is driven by the requirements of specific jobs. That is, training objectives are determined by deciding first what specific tasks are required by specific jobs, second what specific skills are needed to accomplish these tasks, and third what levels of mastery must be achieved by students given all the practical constraints of time, resources, and opportunities for skill growth in training and on the job. Education is not keyed to specific jobs, but is probably best viewed as a general means for better preparing people to meet life experiences, one of which may be job-specific training. Notably, education involves some elements of training and training involves some elements of education; distinctions between the two are drawn for convenience of exposition and emphasis.

"Training technology" then concerns systematic procedures undertaken to enable people to perform specific jobs. To be maximally effective these procedures must produce the same results in all hands. That is, they must be relatively independent of the talents and enthusiasm of the people using them. For this reason they are increasingly based on computer technology or other means for instantiating effective procedures.

In the last several years many papers, presentations, and invited addresses have called for research and development on procedures that combine various media and technologies to achieve optimally efficient, cost-effective, and productive training. Appropriate responses to these calls for action have been as rare as the calls themselves have been numerous. Nonetheless, this aspect of an "ecological approach" to training technology is receiving some attention, and the potential thereby built up may sooner or later precipitate appropriate, and needed, activity.

Another aspect of an ecological approach to training technology has been largely ignored. We need to understand better the way training technology and training in general fit into the full spectrum of alternatives that can be used to maximize the productivity of systems. Hardware design, availability of parts and spares, maintenance schedules, personnel selection, personnel classification, training, and other components all contribute in some measure to system productivity. An investment in any one of these affects what resources must be allocated to the others. Interactions among these system components are poorly understood. Typically, those who are responsible for system performance single out one of these components and invest resources in it with little quantitative assurance that the component they have chosen is the best choice or even an appropriate selection.

More remains to be said about these issues. First, however, some background comments may be in order. Training technology is being pursued with a mild sense of urgency by the Department of Defense (hereafter known as DoD). The reasons for this urgency are worth mentioning both because DoD training is a large activity in its own right—approaching $9 billion in fiscal year 1981—and because it presages what may be to come in industrial training, which is an immense activity. Second, some discussion of what has resulted from this pursuit of training technology—the technology "push"—may be in order. Many new technological opportunities relevant to training are now appearing. They are both changing the nature of what we must account for in pursuing an ecological approach to training technology and increasing the need, if not the pressure, for such an approach. Finally, after the requirements "pull" felt in DoD, and elsewhere, and the technology "push" for training technology are described, it seems reasonable to return briefly to a discussion of what an ecological approach to training technology might involve.

## TRAINING IN THE DEPARTMENT OF DEFENSE

A current and doubtless correct assumption behind defense planning is that in any major confrontation, ranging from deterrence to combat, our adversaries will be able to supply greater numbers of people than we can. We have sought to counter this superiority in manpower quantity with quality, partly in manpower but primarily in advanced material. We try to supply the Services with faster tanks, more heavily armed aircraft, more sensitive radar and sonar, more accurate fire control devices, more powerful and complex computers to aid tactical and strategic decision making, etc. However, we must operate, maintain, and deploy this material close to the limit of its intended performance. If we do not, the high cost of the material will be wasted, and the competitive edge it is intended to buy will be lost. Yet when defense planners consider "military systems," they are almost entirely concerned with engineering design and what it will accomplish in terms of enhanced readiness and effectiveness *assuming* it is operated, maintained, and deployed as envisioned. In point of fact, no understanding of military systems is complete without consideration of the human performance they require to function as designed. Put in another way, human performance is an inseparable, essential component of every military system.

Some understanding of this aspect of military system effectiveness seems to exist in the military, and it is not surprising to discover that the DoD investment in training is immense. On an average day in FY 1981 about 204,000 active duty personnel and about 36,000 National Guardsmen and Reservists will undergo some type of formal training. The cost of this effort will exceed $8.77 billion in FY 1981, and the support of about 184,400 mililtary and civilian personnel will be required for formal instruction, instruction support, school administration, and student supervision. More than 1.8 million officer and enlisted personnel will benefit from this effort, and about one-sixth of active duty personnel will be in formal training at any one time (*Military Manpower Training Report for FY 1981*, 1980).

Expenditures of DoD on formal training are categorized and tabulated as shown in Table 1. These data help to identify "high drivers" for allocation of scarce training resources. For instance, it is apparent

**TABLE 1**
Residential Training: Costs and Student Input (FY 1981)

| Type of Training | Number of Students Input (000) | Cost ($ M) |
|---|---|---|
| Recruit | 337 | $ 736 |
| One-station unit | 127 | 291 |
| Officer acquisition | 4 | 275 |
| Specialized skill | 428 | 2,012 |
| Undergraduate flight | 6 | 987 |
| Professional development | 31 | 299 |
| Medical | 17 | 259 |
| Support | — | 3,914 |
| Total | | $8,773 |

*Source: Military Manpower Training Report for FY 1981,* Washington, D.C.: Department of Defense, 1980.

from Table 1 that more leverage may be gained by attending to the problems of specialized skill training (23 percent of total expenditures) than to the problems of professional development (3 percent of total expenditures). However, these data are by themselves insufficient for setting research and development priorities. Information is needed on how successful activity in each of these categories has been in meeting Service requirements and on how much improvement can be expected to accrue from research and development.

It should be noted that the data in Table 1 cover training conducted in formal courses by organizations whose predominant mission is training—in other words, they concern only "institutional" training. They exclude all job-site training, factory and unit training for new systems, organized team training for the performance of specific military missions, and field exercises. The magnitude of resources allocated to these latter activities, which can be called "unit" training, is difficult to determine, but it is doubtless very large. It is possible to find arguments to the effect that everything the military does in peacetime is training, but these do not stand up under analysis. It does seem reasonable to estimate that two to three times the resources expended on residential training are spent on unit training.

In any event, DoD training is a sizable undertaking. Few enterprises of this magnitude function perfectly, and DoD training is no exception. The problems discussed here are to some extent outside the control of DoD manpower, personnel, and training establishments. These problems cluster about three current issues: manpower supply, job complexity, and cost.

## Manpower Supply

Availability of manpower, both in terms of quantity and quality, is increasingly noted as a military problem. We are losing pilots to the airlines, electronics technicians to the computer revolution, heavy equipment mechanics to the construction industry—the litany of lost human capability can go on almost endlessly. Today in the All-Volunteer Force, only about 70 out of 100 military recruits will finish their first tours of duty. Of those remaining, 26 will reenlist for a second tour. Only eight of the original 100 will stay in the military long enough to retire (*Manpower Requirements Report for FY 1981,* 1980). Among Army combat unit officers only 44 percent elected to reenlist for a second time in 1979, and even among West Point graduates 25 percent may leave the Army after their first tour of duty (Fialka, 1980b).

The result of this attrition is predictable. Many stateside Army units have only 70 percent of the noncommissioned officers they need. The Army Independent Ready Reserve is somewhere between 300,000– 700,000 people short of those needed for rapid mobilization. The ratio of officers to total Army strength has dropped from 17 percent to 11 percent over the last eight years (Fialka, 1980b). Presently the Navy is short almost 20,000 petty officers for middle-grade jobs essential for ship operation, and ship and Navy aircraft squadrons are short an average of 15 percent of the people needed for combat readiness (Kempster, 1980).

These problems arise at a time when the military is drawing from the largest pool of manpower in history. About 4,250,000 people now reach the age of 18 each year. This number will be reduced by at least one-fourth over the next several years. In 1990, only 3,150,000 people will be reaching the age of 18 annually. Right now the Army must recruit one out of every four eligible males age 18--21; by 1990, it will have to recruit one out of every two to maintain its congressionally mandated strength.

Quality, in addition to quantity, of manpower available for military service is also a problem. One widely noted occurrence in the pool of available manpower has been the steady decline in college entry Scholastic Aptitude Test (SAT) scores. Over the last 15 years these scores have declined about 7 percent in mathematical achievement and 11 percent in verbal achievement. This decline is uniform across the country; it is unrelated to economic, racial, or geographic background. The scores are now lower than ever before in the 50-year history of the SAT's (*College Bound Seniors,* 1979). Two common hypotheses for explaining this decline are that the tests are more difficult and that larger numbers of less able students have been taking the tests. Both of these hypotheses were found to be unlikely by a "blue ribbon" committee headed by former Secretary of Labor Willard Wirtz (Wirtz, 1977). That the quality of the manpower pool has been declining is corroborated by data from the American College Testing (ACT) program. These scores have also been declining since the middle 1960s ("No final answer," 1979). Some evidence was presented by Munday (1979) to suggest that the sharp declines in scores have leveled off. However, in an era of increasing technological complexity, the proportion of individuals with high proficiency in basic skills needs to rise, not fall or remain level.

Consequences of this decline in quality of people available for military service are showing up in aptitude surveys of military personnel. Fialka's series (1980b) on Army readiness reported that the aptitude of male recruits in the Army has dropped 5 percent since 1976 and that 28 percent of soldiers training at three recruit centers read at or below the seventh-grade level. Duffy (1977) reported from a sample of 24,729 Navy recruits, that 36.4 percent read below the tenth-grade reading level and that 18.1 percent read below the eighth-grade reading level. Duffy and Nugent (1978) reported that the reading grade levels of 20 Navy occupational manuals range from 11.3 to 15.5. Measures of reading grade level for both people and textual materials are imprecise, but it seems clear that some gap exists between the reading ability of military service personnel and the materials they need to read in order to perform their jobs. This gap may widen in the future.

This gap is particularly troublesome in the light of substantial increases in the volume of technical documentation required by newer, complex material. In 1939, the volume of technical documentation for the J-F Goose, "Catalina Flying Boat," was 525 pages of information. In 1962, the volume of technical documentation for the A-6A Intruder was about 150,000 pages of information. In 1975, the volume of technical documentation for the F-14 Tomcat was about 380,000 pages of information. Estimates for the B-1 bomber were in the neighborhood of 1,000,000 pages of information (Kline and Gunning, 1979). The volume of technical information for the new M-1 tank is expected to exceed that of the tank itself.

Taking another standpoint, the Services key heavily on high school graduation as an index of persistence, motivation, general aptitude, and social adaptibility. Maintaining a high percentage of high school graduates is usually given to Service recruiters as a high priority goal. At the least, high school graduation is viewed as an important indicator of the type of people the Services are attracting. In 1965 only 28 percent of Army recruits were high school dropouts, in 1980 the comparable figure has been running at 46 percent. The other Services are doing a little better. Percentages of high school graduates have been running at 75 percent, 78 percent, and 83 percent in the Navy, Marines, and Air Force, respectively (Fialka, 1980b). Still, these numbers are low considering that 96 percent of the full population graduates from high school.

The lack of quality indicated by these data is showing up in measures of job performance. In a recent survey discussed by Fialka (1980a), 98 percent of Army tank turret and 98 percent of Army artillary repairmen failed their skill qualification tests, 9 percent of nuclear maintenance specialists failed their tests, 86 percent of Army artillery crewmen failed their tests, 77 percent of computer programmers failed their tests, 81 percent of ammunition specialists failed their tests—the list goes on. Under more specific scrutiny, a sample of almost 1,300 M-60 tank crewmen showed that about a fourth of them did not know where to aim their battlesights, a sample of 666 tank repairmen showed that correct mechanical diagnoses were reached only 15–33 percent of the time, and the chances that they would correctly repair the tank once the problem was correctly identified were 33–58 percent. The estimated cost of human performance related errors in F-14 aircraft maintenance may exceed $300M a year (Gold, et al., 1980).

The problems of people performance seem quite real both within and without the military. It is worth noting that the general decline in ability has occurred during a time in which the proportion of our Gross National Product allocated to education has more than doubled. This increased investment has been almost entirely in traditional instructional technology. The lack of return may indicate, as Heuston has argued (1980), that traditional instructional technology has matured to a point of diminishing returns. The only way to increase the productivity of current education and training institutions may be to develop new technological tools and have them incorporated in these institutions. That the productivity of these institutions must be increased seems self-evident.

## Job Complexity

The problems of the Services are not limited to declines in quality and quantity within the pool of manpower for recruitment. The number and complexity of military jobs are themselves increasing dramatically. In the Army there are now 0.78 "systems" per person—there is one wheeled vehicle for every four people in the Army, one tracked vehicle for every 20 people, one radio for every six people, one generator for every ten people, etc. This ratio is increasing in the Army and elsewhere. Cook, Kane, and McQuie (1977) noted that the percentage of skilled personnel required by the Navy increased from 23 percent in 1945 to an estimated 42 percent in 1980. A report prepared for Congressman Beard noted that seven out of ten Army jobs require technical training (Beard, 1979).

Additionally, new complex material continues to flow into the Services. There are currently about 17 "major" new systems being introduced into the Army, 25 into the Navy, and 32 into the Air Force. These "major" systems generally represent more than $100 million each in research and development and more than $500 million each in procurement. They are airplanes, ships, tanks, and other systems of this scale. The important thing about major system procurements is that they must go through a DSARC (Defense System Acquisition Review Council) process, which requires analysis and adequate planning for manpower, personnel, training, and logistics. These procurements represent about half in dollar volume of the total number of new systems coming into the Services. The other half, which includes "smaller" but more numerous systems (800–1,000 over the next six years) such as radios, radars, sonars, and equipment modifications, do not come under the DSARC process; these may eat us alive from a manpower, personnel, training, and logistics standpoint. Although considerable effort may be made to see that these smaller systems are "supportable," there are no formally instituted requirements such as DoD level instructions to insure their supportability. As Funaro and Fletcher (1980) point out, no procurement manager wants to field obsolete equipment. What often happens is that resources set aside to provide supportability for both major and smaller military systems are reallocated to engineering changes and design modifications late in the procurement process. The result is a challenge to manpower, personnel, training, and logistics planners to react very quickly to unanticipated changes with less resources than they had originally counted on. Understandably, there are occasions when this challenge is not met.

Clearly, the increase in numbers (or density) of systems has begotten an increase in the number and types of jobs to be done. However, weren't these new systems supposed to simplify—rather than complicate—things? In effect, they have not. It is true that new systems do more complex jobs much more simply from an operator standpoint. Compared to what they do, they are now quite simple. However, the requirements we have put on them for performance have outstripped our current capabilities to make them simple. They do more complex things more simply, but the tasks they perform are now so complex that in an absolute sense, they are more complicated to operate and maintain. To avoid this increasingly critical problem we need to be able to measure the complexity of systems from the standpoint of the people who must operate, maintain, and deploy them. We need to understand the implications of level of repair analyses for manpower, personnel, and training far better than we do. We need a technology of comparability analysis that will enable us to judge the supportability requirements of new systems based on similar and already fielded systems. This is not a paper on front-end analysis, but the challenge this sort of analysis poses for human factors psychology is genuine and important. The absence of an appropriate technology for front-end analysis is an important aspect of the current challenge to those charged with the development of training technology.

It should be noted that maintenance is a particularly troublesome area. New equipment is modular, so that a technician must simply replace components, or modules, rather than try to repair them. This is not a bad idea in a properly ordered world—particularly one in which an integrated logistics system is functioning. In practice, however, what happens is well understood by anyone with a nodding acquaintance with government functioning. The technician, let's say an avionics technician aboard an aircraft carrier repairing the fire control system of an F-14, will remove the offending module—ignoring for the moment the .42 probability that he has removed a module that works perfectly and the .26 probability that he has damaged the equipment further in troubleshooting it—will report to ship's stores for replacement, and he will be told that an ample supply of these modules exists somewhere but not on his ship. If he is lucky, he will be in a unit with one of the legendary wizards that appear in the military—a 12-year veteran who has not yet been lost to industry and who can repair any piece of electronics made—or there will be a spare system to cannibalize. In many cases, the fire control system will be left inoperative. The aircraft will continue to fly, but one of its primary reasons for doing so will no longer exist.

Additionally, there is the problem of test equipment. We have tried with some success to provide powerful automatic test equipment that greatly simplifies the first order maintenance of new military systems. However, this practice merely serves to move the problem back a step. The sophisticated equipment that is required to simplify maintenance of new systems is itself exceedingly complicated to maintain and repair. Generally, it turns out to be no more reliable than the system it supports. One principle appears inescapable—increases in equipment complexity beget concomitant increases in job complexity.

Oddly enough, this issue of complexity is used as an argument against support for research and development in DoD. If research and development produces equipment that cannot be operated and maintained, then, the argument goes, we should stop supporting research and development. At the level that these arguments occur, the notion that some increased investment in people-related research and development —to improve selection, classification, and training; to simplify jobs without compromising performance requirements of systems; to develop an integrated logistics system—is seldom considered and never given credibility as a way to solve the problem. Planners at DoD are in a bind. They cannot stop increasing the sophistication of needed hardware systems, because the numbers of people needed to compensate for gaps in defense readiness are unavailable. As long as the current emphases on sophisticated hardware continue, the capabilities of people to support these new systems will be farther outstripped. The problem for human factors psychology exists both in the technical challenge presented and in its credibility as a problem solving discipline for defense—and industry— planners.

## Costs

A major problem with training is that it removes from mission-related, operational forces two essential resources, money and manpower. A recent approach to this problem has been to reduce by administrative fiat the resources available to residential schools in the military. These removed resources include experienced instructors, student time, and equipment for hands-on practice. The success of this approach is likely to be limited. At best, it shifts the problem from visible, formal settings in schools to hidden, informal settings in operational units. At worst, it erodes readiness and effectiveness in a sufficiently subtle manner that its consequences will only become apparent too late. Standardization of training, student performance recording, and assurance of student achievement at job sites place demands on the Service operational establishments that they cannot easily meet. These demands are exacerbated by the introduction of new systems and by the loss of experienced operators and technicians.

Fuel and ammunition have been the major contributors to DoD training costs. The increased costs of petroleum products are substantial and well known. Ammunition costs have also been increasing both on their own and because of the introduction of new rounds with which military crews must become familiar and proficient. The results of these increased costs are predictable. Planes can fly fewer sorties, ships must spend more time in port, and fewer people can be sent to training ranges and training centers. The task for developers of training technology is clear. We need technology that maximizes job proficiency and minimizes costs. Beyond this, we must consider more carefully the full range of alternatives that can be used to optimize the performance of military systems subject to all the constraints imposed by manpower, maintenance, logistics, and training costs.

Given the magnitude of training problems—or challenges—and the probable payoff for research and development, one might expect substantial funding to be provided for training research and development. This, however, is not true in either relative or absolute terms. About 34 percent of the funds spent by DoD on material is allocated to research and development. However, of the $7.617 billion spent in FY 1980 for training, $120.3 million was set aside for research and development, about 1.6 percent of the total. Of the $77.1 billion to be spent in FY 1981 for all manpower in DoD, $227 million or 0.3 percent will be spent for people-related research and development. Allocating research and development money to equipment-related and people-related effort is more of a subjective, perhaps political, process than a scientific one; but from any standpoint, the figures associated with personnel-related research and development seem disproportionately low.

The reasons for this limited research and development investment are unclear. The requirements "pull," or need, is not merely established, but appears critical. Technological and scientific "push," or opportunity, seems genuine, given recent advances in computer-assisted and computer-managed instruction; knowledge-based systems to support simulation and stimulation for maintenance and operator training; intelligent opposition for practice in tactical decision making and battle management; instructional systems development; domain referenced assessment; psychometrics of simulation; reliable and portable hardware for distributed training; new measures of basic aptitudes and skills; incentive and motivation management; new understanding of learning, memory, and cognitive processes and the methodology for measuring them; and optimization of instruction subject to such constraints as learner ability, subject matter, and resources, media, and time available. Other more technically specific advances could be added to this list.

It might be argued that there is an insufficient match between the scientific and technology base and training requirements—that however many scientific/technological advances have been achieved, their probable impact on the requirement is too small to warrant increased research and development investment. This argument loses credibility in the light of such examples as the following:

- Through the introduction of an appropriately designed simulator, the Coast Goard is now saving $1.45 million per year in helicopter pilot training (Isley, Corley, and Caro, 1974).
- Through the introduction of an appropriately designed simulator, the Navy may now be saving $2.5 million per year in pilot training for the P-3C Orion Aircraft (Browning, et al., 1977).
- Performance in antisubmarine tactics in the Navy was improved after eight hours of training on a standard simulator costing $250 million ($57.00 per student contact hour) were replaced by six hours of individualized training using a $5 million computer system costing $6.00 per student hour (Crawford, et al., 1976).
- In the Army, TRAINFIRE more than doubled the performance of both low and high aptitude squads in attack modes, and it more than tripled the performance of low aptitude squads in defense modes; REALTRAIN doubled both the offensive and defensive capabilities of infantry troops; lowest aptitude squads with innovative training tech-

nology surpassed by 16 percent the performance of high aptitude squads with conventional training (Root, et al., 1979).

 • Through the introduction of currently available low-cost portable simulation that improves tank gunner proficiency by only 10 percent, analysis indicates savings of well over $15 billion in achieving parity in European tank combat with Warsaw Pact nations (Fletcher, 1980).

 • In 48 studies of student training time saved by the introduction of computer-based instruction, the median amount of student time saved was 32 percent, with a range as high as 89 percent (Orlansky and String, 1979).

This list could be considerably extended. The point is that investment in training research and development can produce major returns to the Services. The reasons for currently limited DoD investment in personnel research and development in general and training research and development in specific may be due to sociological forces—DoD personnel are by inclination, interest, and training likely to favor hardware research and development—or simply to bureaucratic inertia.

Whatever the reasons for currently limited DoD investment in personnel research and development, some skepticism concerning the value of this investment could be removed by an approach to training technology that emphasized its impact on the performance of military systems. Too often we report the benefits of improved military and industrial training in terms of more efficient or more productive training and too seldom do we report the impact on improved systems performance. These benefits are probably much greater than defense and industry planners expect, but they will not be made more credible by rhetoric. Data are needed, and they are not easy to come by. Nonetheless more could be said about the impact of maintenance simulation on the replacement of parts that do not need to be replaced, the time spent troubleshooting, the incidence of errors in preventing maintenance, the "readiness" ratings of units, etc. As it turns out, analyses of this sort are surprisingly scarce. It is difficult to say who has been remiss in their production, but both systems performance—military readiness and effectiveness—and the disciplines of training technology and human factors psychology stand to gain substantially from them.

In any event, there is substantial reason for DoD planners to seek new technological answers to the demands and concomitant problems created by current training requirements. Technological opportunities such as computer speech input and output, artificial intelligence, low-cost high-resolution computer-generated imagery, videodiscs, microcomputers, and high-density digital storage abound. These opportunities have yielded a variety of new application possibilities for training, and these are discussed in the next section.

## TECHNOLOGY INITIATIVES

Most of the new training technologies listed in this section are based on systems developments that have occurred independent of training and education requirements. It should be emphasized that the real opportunities for sustaining and improving human performance are the "functionalities" or capabilities that are based on these systems developments, not the developments themselves. The appearance of any new functionality is often unpredictable and dependent on breakthroughs in imagination and technological creativity. This process is neither trivial nor one that follows automatically on the heels of new systems opportunities. These functionalities most directly determine the new training technologies that must find their place within the full suite of opportunities available for improving system performance.

On the basis of the problems listed in the previous section, it is possible to specify at least in part the kind of training technology the future and the present demand. This technology must be accessible, accessed, relevant, and intelligent.

The technology must be delivered to and available at job sites. In DoD training, as in industry and elsewhere, there is a tendency to abrogate responsibility at the schoolhouse door. Stated more directly, there is an assumption that when a student leaves residential training, the job is done. This is not a productive point of view for at least the following reasons: (1) real expertise requires an amount of experience and practice that is completely impracticable in residential training; (2) much skill growth occurs at job sites, not just in residential schools; (3) current problems assure that less training will be accomplished in schools, and less well prepared people will appear at job sites; (4) declines in manpower will mean that fewer people will have to perform a wider variety of jobs; (5) rotation policies will continue to insure that there are always people present at job sites who are insufficiently proficient in performing their current, specific job assignment.

There are at least three characteristics that an appropriately accessible technology must have. First, it must be inexpensive so that we can afford to buy it, use it, break it, and throw it away. Second, it must be portable; it must be relatively small, compact, light, and independent of exotic power and/or environmental requirements. Third, it must be reliable; if it is physically present and not working, it is inaccessible. A caveat concerning this last point may be in order. The technology to be developed must be reliable, but before this it must be inexpensive. A balance needs to be struck between costs and ruggedness. Too often in DoD the emphasis has gone to ruggedness. We need technology that we can afford to break.

In addition to being accessible, the technology must be accessed or, in short, it must be used. Education and training are gradually shifting from a teacher-centered orientation to a student-centered orientation. This trend is particularly important in DoD where manpower shortages will permit less and less use of expert human instructors. Students are increasingly expected to be self-initiating, self-motivating, self-pacing, self-assessing, and generally, self-reliant. The productivity of students, rather than the productivity of instructors, is becoming the focus in evaluating the success and efficiency of instruction (Olsen, Bunderson, and Gibbons, 1980). More coherent patterns of student-centering are evolving. Student productivity goals are slowly finding their way into instruction, and career-long patterns of training are gradually evolving. As a consequence, technology must be adapted and designed to help students meet goals of productivity rather than be grafted on instructor-centered systems poorly prepared and little motivated to use it.

Three characteristics will help assure use of the technology. First, the technology must be inherently motivating, or, to be blunt, it must be fun. From time to time we speculate that all training problems in DoD and industry would be solved if we could just make training sufficiently fun. This may be an exaggeration, but it has some truth. We could certainly do more to overcome the notion that to be done right, learning must be grim and painful. Malone's (1980) thesis work is an important contribution to our understanding of ways to combine entertainment and learning. Second, the technology must be simple to use. If a student cannot immediately and without prior training begin to use new training technology at some modest level of utility, it will most probably never be used. This goal is a challenge to those concerned with human factors or with the user interface in complex systems, but the development of a system such as the MIT Spatial Data Management System (Bolt, 1979) that is both complex and easy to use is an important step in this direction. Third, in addition to such human factors issues as "knobology," query language specifications, and display design, the technology should be acceptable. This characteristic concerns what might be called "man-machine relations." Computer-based technology provides a good example of this issue. The ubiquity of computation has made it critically important that the strengths and limitations of computers be well understood by those who must use their products but who are not, and have no desire to become, active members of a computer user community. The fact is unavoidable; to some people, the electronics revolution is truly revolting. The problem transcends issues of computer literacy; it concerns people's attitudes and visceral reactions to computers and technology as well as their reasoned information-based opinions. The problem will not be solved solely by better computers or better human factoring.

The technology must be relevant. This is certainly an obvious goal, but one difficult to meet in practice. Unlike accessibility (it is either there or absent) and usage (it is either used or not), which are easy to measure, relevance is difficult to establish in practice. If training is to be relevant, it must be like the job. This means that we must either provide practice on doing the job itself under precisely accurate job conditions—i.e., the student is doing the job and *nothing else*—or we must turn to some degree or another of simulation.

As Raser (1969) has pointed out, simulation has the benefits of economy, visibility, reproducibility, and safety. With regard to economy, simulation reduces the costs of training equipment and training materials preparation. To some degree we can provide hands-on practice through simulation and avoid using the complex and expensive equipment required on the job. Further, rather than anticipate all the students' interactions, we can provide them with a simulation that reacts in a veridical fashion to all their decisions and allows them to see their consequences.

Simulation increases the visibility of the phenomena being studied in two ways. The phenomenon can be made physically more accessible, for instance showing the flow of electrons in a circuit is a substantially more realistic goal in a simulated system than in real equipment. We can also increase the visibility of a phenomenon by separating it from a confusing and chaotic background. Naval tactics provide a good illustration of this capability. If it were necessary to deploy a task force at sea every time there was some tactical training to be accomplished, tactical decision makers in the Navy would learn a great deal about combating sea sickness, ascending and descending metal ladders, and finding ward rooms in the dark, but the basic principles of naval tactics would remain obscure.

Simulation allows students to replay chains of events that they could not otherwise observe repeatedly. This replay capability is valuable for at least two reasons. First, it allows the student to build up increasingly accurate subjective assessments of the probabilities governing uncertain outcomes. Subjective assessment of probabilities is particularly important, for instance, in maintenance troubleshooting. Second, replay capability enables the student to "tinker," i.e., to vary different aspects of the system in ways that yield insight into how it operates. In short, replay permits controlled experimentation by students that is otherwise impossible and/or impractical.

Simulation permits more realistic training than that available in the physical systems that are the target of the training. One good example of this feature occurs in training commercial aircraft pilots to fly with one engine out of operation. Typically, this training is accomplished in lightly loaded aircraft with one engine feathered or idled. Realistically, the aircraft is as likely to experience engine failure with a full load as with a light load, and if an engine fails, it will produce a substantial amount of drag, which is absent when it is idled. The realistic conditions needed for this training are never presented because they are too dangerous, and the result is that many commercial pilots are not fully trained to manage aircraft with an engine failure. Both a full load and the drag of a failed engine can be presented under simulation.

The technology must be intelligent. This is a controversial claim. However, if the new training technology is going to be used successfully at job sites, isolated and distant from subject matter experts and qualified instructors, then it must incorporate in itself some of the qualities and capabilities of expert job performers and tutors—an Aristotle for every Alexander, as Suppes (1966) has suggested.

In discussing intelligent training systems, it is usually necessary to point out hastily that no distinction is intended between "intelligently" designed systems and "unintelligently" designed training systems. Intelligent training systems may be as unintelligently designed as any others. Rather, the development of these systems is viewed as a specific effort to apply artificial intelligence techniques to computer-based instruction (CBI) in the sense of information structure oriented (ISO) approaches discussed and advocated by Carbonell (e.g., 1970) who contrasted ISO efforts with ad hoc frame oriented approaches based on techniques of programmed instruction.

Intelligent training systems can be distinguished from more conventional approaches by the automation of instructional interaction and choice of strategy. These systems enable students to (1) test their own hypotheses concerning the subject matter, (2) probe for information at different levels of difficulty and abstraction, (3) acquire wide experience in minimum time, (4) obtain instructional material generated for their unique abilities and needs, (5) receive instructional aids for partially completed solutions, and (6) receive reviews and critiques for completed problem solutions. Current and anticipated developments in intelligent systems can be categorized into three areas: intelligent simulation, modeling human instructors, and modeling the student.

Work on intelligent simulation ranges from the Generalized Maintenance Training Simulator (GMTS) developed by Rigney, Towne, and King (1974) through SOPHIE (Brown, Burton, and Bell, 1974), to GUIDON (Clancey, 1979). GMTS interrogates students working with electronics troubleshooting simulations to determine what faults they have identified as likely and what faults they have eliminated from consideration. SOPHIE is more sophisticated. It creates a reactive environment in which a student actively interacts with a tutorial simulation of an electronic power supply that helps him formulate, investigate, and "debug" his own ideas about the power supply using what the designers call an "articulate expert." GUIDON not only provides students with an articulate expert in its domain of knowledge (infectious diseases), it also allows the student to venture hypotheses about disparate points in the process, and it can "debug" the student's reasoning. GUIDON both "knows" the subject matter and explains how it reasons to reach a diagnosis.

Another aspect of current work concerns modeling human instructors. Brown's work incorporates this aspect to some extent in its capacity for "coaching," and it is the focus of work by Allan Collins and to a lessor extent of work by Donald Norman. Gentner and Norman (1977) use an advanced "Pandemonium" model to infer correct and incorrect actions by students and provide tutorial advice in teaching a simple programming language called FLOW. Collins' work has progressed through several versions of SCHOLAR (e.g., Collins, Warnock, and Passafiume, 1975) to WHY (Stevens and Collins, 1977), and has made extensive use of student-tutor protocols to develop tutorial strategies and goals to be incorporated in these systems.

Some effort has been expended on modeling the student in computer-assisted instruction, as reviews by Self (1974) and Fletcher (1975) have demonstrated. These models range from purely diagnostic systems implied by the branching strategies of instruction based on intrinsic programming notions (Crowder, 1959) through the WEST coaching systems (e.g., Burton and Brown, 1979), which evaluate suboptimal decisions by students, and WUSOR (Carr and Goldstein, 1977), which evaluates decisions by students for optimality but additionally embodies a psychological model that identifies missing cognitive functions, to BIP (Barr, Beard, and Atkinson, 1975), which uses a semantic network to describe relationships between component skills and operations required in BASIC programming and to generate a uniquely appropriate sequence of problems for each student.

In summary, intelligent training technology intended for job site, stand-alone use must have the following three capabilities:

1.   It must represent the relevant knowledge domain. In effect, it must contain the knowledge and understanding of a subject matter expert.

2.   It must represent the learner's or job performer's capabilities and needs. Just as the technology must "understand" the subject matter, so it must also understand and be able to model the learner.

3.   It must represent an expert tutor. It must know what to say to the learner and when to say it; it must know how to take the learner from one stage of skill to another.

In searching for ideas, "technical approaches," to meet these goals of accessibility, use, relevance, and intelligence, we have pursued development of the following new training technologies:

## Interactive Movies

One of the problems with training in which demonstrations of skilled performance play a significant part is that essential components of the demonstrations are, simply, invisible to viewers. This problem is solved to a major extent by interactive movies. These movies, which are based on microprocessor controlled videodisc technology, allow the viewer to control such aspects of viewing as perspective (front, side, above, below, etc.), speed (fast, slow, still frame, reverse), detail (panning and zooming), abstraction (photographs, video sequence, line drawing animations), plot (different actions at different choice points yielding different results), and simultaneous action (gauge readings, actions by other team members).

## Surrogate Travel

Surrogate travel forms a new approach to locale familiarization and low cost trainers. Under microprocessor control, the user accesses different sections of a videodisc, simulating movement over selected paths of travel. Unlike an interactive movie, the user is able both to choose the path and to control the speed of advance through an area using simple controls. When coming to an intersection, the student can turn left, turn right, proceed ahead, or go back, all under joystick control. The user can travel along a path looking either to the left, to the right, or to the rear, as well as straight ahead.

The videodisc frames the viewer sees originate as filmed views of what one would *actually* see in the area. To allow coverage of very large areas, the frames are taken at periodic intervals that may range from every foot inside a building, to every ten feet down a city street, to hundreds of feet in a large open area (e.g., a harbor). The rate of frame playback, which is the number of times each video frame is displayed before the next frame is shown, determines the apparent speed of travel. Free choice in what routes may be taken is obtained by filming all possible paths in the area as well as all possible turns through all intersections.

## Microtravel

One promising aspect of combined surrogate travel and interactive movies is microtravel. This capability provides interactive, surrogate travel in places where people cannot go. One example of this is microtravel throughout a jeep engine while it is running. It is accomplished through the use of new photographic techniques such as snorkel photography in combination with videodisc technology.

## Virtual Team Trainer

Many tasks are performed in teams or crews where communication and timing of events are critical. However, training of this sort is too rarely provided because of difficulties in bringing together all members of a crew at one location to use expensive equipment that is often required elsewhere for more directly missions-oriented activity. This problem is exacerbated by the fact that frequently only one or two members of the crew are the focus of the training, other members are required only as support for the activity. Within the current state-of-the-art it is possible to assemble a computer-based team trainer that is voice interactive for some class of highly stereotyped messages, that requires a vocabulary of not more than 2000 words, and that is capable of assuming the role of any or all but one member of the crew or team being trained. And as the state-of-the-art continues to progress rapidly, less message stereotyping, larger vocabularies, and more complex roles will be possible.

## Automated Authoring

Current estimates of the amount of time required to prepare one hour of computer-based instruction range from 75–650 hours. Virtually unlimited amounts of computer-based instruction can be generated by a computer program that (1) obtains information about a subject area through computer-initiated inquiry of computer-naive subject matter experts and/or printed reference materials, (2) constructs an adequate knowledge representation of the subject area despite contradictory and/or missing information, (3) generate instructional items, sequences, and simulations for individualized training. Such a system can now be built using nonexotic knowledge representation as in TEIRESIAS (Davis, 1976) existing natural language capabilities, and emerging notions of meta-knowledge.

## Optimized Instruction

Much training requires memorization of relatively discrete items of information. Substantial efficiencies in training are achieved when student time devoted to this activity is minimized and gaming aspects are maximized. The combination of quantitative models of learning, optimal control theory, and computer-based instruction has substantially reduced student learning time over all other procedures evaluated. These results have occurred despite incorporation of quite imprecise parameter estimation and memory modeling techniques. Both of these have been dramatically improved in the last several years. Precision of parameter estimation alone has recently been improved substantially through application of different mathematical models (Paulson, 1980).

## Electronic Libraries

Electronic libraries in the form of Spatial Data Management Systems (SDMS) provide students and instructors access to an assortment of multisource and multimedia information (Levin, 1980). Users can "fly over" information and select what they want by simply pointing. Spatiality is used to group materials into lesson plans, so that different information spaces represent course concepts, additional instruction, and assessment procedures. For the instructor, the SDMS provides ready access to material that might otherwise be inaccessible. Instructors can access the SDMS to create their own information spaces (i.e., courses or lectures) and subsequently present such materials to large audiences in single locations via large screen television projection or to multiple locations through cable distribution systems. Students can independently use the SDMS for self-paced instruction by either working through previously designed information spaces or by browsing on their own. When students and instructors are in remote locations, offsite instruction is facilitated by linking two or more SDMS together using regular telephone lines. In this manner, a student or instructor can "fly" the other to a topic of interest, sharing at geographically remote sites a large library of information.

## Low-Cost Portable Simulators

Videodisc technology has been used to produce low-cost visual simulators. An example of this is the development of a tank gunnery trainer (Thomas, Madni, and Weltman, 1980). In this low-cost trainer, a gunner is taught to locate, track, and fire at enemy tanks. Instructional sequences consisting of both the visuals seen by the gunner and the constantly changing problem information needed to provide instructional feedback are accessed from a videodisc. The videodisc provides rapid access to a wide variety of problem sets as well as high fidelity display of what is normally seen by tank gunners. The trainers can be linked together to provide intratank training, for tank crews, or intertank training for tank platoons. Shoot-offs and "quick-fire" exercises are presented to increase motivation. All sighting devices and sight reticles are included in the trainer. Computer graphics overlaid on the video sequences are used to show trajectory and burst-on-target information. Daytime, nighttime, smoke, and dust sequences are all included. The device captures the entertainment of arcade games in job-relevant training activity. A good example of low-cost portable simulation that is not based on videodisc technology is the Navy's STEAMER project, which will provide a graphically interactive intelligent instructional system for training in operation of ships' propulsion steam plants (Williams, Hollan, and Stevens, in press).

These new developments all meet to one degree or another the need for training technology that is accessible, accessed, relevant, and intelligent. The list is necessarily incomplete, and the full set of possibilities should grow substantially over the next several years. As new training media, these developments add power and flexibility to our ability to bring people rapidly up to levels of performance and skill mastery required by jobs in the military and industry. However, the end goal of this activity is only indirectly the improvement of training; the principal benefit is, or should be, enhanced systems performance. Specific training developments and training technology in general must be fitted into the full spectrum of alternatives available for improving system performance. This consideration leads most directly to what might be described as an ecological approach to training technology.

## AN ECOLOGICAL APPROACH

The preceding comments have presented some of the training problems faced by DoD with a smattering of specifics intended to show that the problem is serious and that, in turn, we need to be serious about solving it. As Heuston (1980) pointed out, we need to get more productivity out of instruction, and it appears that after 400 years we have reached the productivity limits of stand-up lectures and printed material. We need something metaphorically distinct from titanium horseshoes for coach horses; we need something new—we must develop the training analog of the horseless carriage. It will be a while before we learn to use this new technology, after all we are still inventing uses for the telephone. As with the horseless carriage, it will be a while before the new technology competes favorably with what already exists. But we must proceed; we have no choice.

Next discussed were some desirable characteristics for the new technology and then some specific examples of what we are trying to develop. However, one problem is that we do not have much time. We need an approach that will short circuit the process of introducing new technologies and getting them accepted and used. In practice, we seem to be shifting somewhat in the way we think about training and training technology. There appear to be four aspects of this approach.

First, people are assumed to be part of the system. Especially in DoD where we discuss systems such as airplanes, ships, jeeps, and radios, it is easy to assume that performance, effectiveness, and "readiness" begin and end with hardware reliability and availability. This assumption is, of course, false. People design these systems, they maintain them, operate them, and deploy them. People are an integral part of every system. People, as well as machines, make errors. Solutions to the problem of increasing performance, effectiveness, and readiness so often sought by DoD in improved hardware may, in many cases, be more appropriately obtained from a cost–effective point of view by improvements in human performance directly sought through training. Training technology should be sought as at least one engineering solution to system performance problems.

Second, coming from the other side of the issue, training technology is developed for a reason. It is properly viewed as a solution to a system problem. The goal of training R & D is not improved training; it is improved system performance. The criteria for effectiveness in training technology should not concern end-of-course performance so much as skilled performance on the job and whether or not it has contributed in a positive fashion to readiness, effectiveness, and system performance. Probably, we have lost sight of this perspective because it is difficult in practice to implement. It has been easier to examine course and end-of-course performance measures, but times are now more difficult, and these measures, which typically yield miniscule correlations with job performance measures, no longer suffice. They are particularly inappropriate when we find ourselves outside of the residential "course" paradigm and must evaluate the efficacy of job-site training.

Third, we need to escape the information theory metaphor for training. Contemporary advances in psychology are reminding us that human cognition is an overwhelmingly active, constructive process. In training, as in all communication, we are not simply shipping chunks of information across a channel to be pasted intact onto a blank slate. Instead, what we seem to do is pass cues for sensory simulation that are built up by the receiver. Memory itself appears to be reconstructive, or re-creative, rather than reproductive. We do not simply dredge up items for recall, we reconstruct them. We do not teach in the sense of dumping whole chunks of information into the students' heads. Rather, we seem to create environments in which, to greater or lesser degrees, students learn. It is far more efficient for people to be doing something in a learning environment than simply receiving information. This is particularly true of the verbally unskilled populations from which we must draw our missile repairmen, sonar operators, and avionics technicians—hence the emphasis on intelligent simulations that are accessible at job sites. The further training is removed from job relevant activity, the less effective it is. This is not to ignore the issue of cost. We need to know what amount of training effectiveness is purchased by a unit of cost in designing training technology.

Finally, we must learn to view training as a subsystem. Interdependency abounds in this business. Manpower, personnel, and training requirements depend on hardware requirements, and vice versa; training simulator requirements depend on the full training systems designed, and vice versa; training depends on selection and classification, selection and classification on training, job design on training, training on job design, job design on supply, supply on job design, etc. An adequate analysis capability demands an integrated approach to all these components. We need a "capping" technology so that we can at least make these tradeoffs explicit if not optimal. It goes almost without saying that such a technology is presently absent.

It can be argued that little in this approach is truly novel. However, the tendency among developers of instructional technology to pursue technological opportunities with little regard for how their products fit within the full spectrum of instructional possibilities has long been noted and frequently lamented. That instructional technologists are not only considering the role their products should play among all instructional possibilities, but also beginning to consider instruction itself as just one of several alternatives for increasing systems productivity, may come as something of a shock to those long used to the foibles of instructional technologists. In retrospect, however, this trend seems less surprising. As mentioned earlier, "technology" in the broadest sense refers to any systematic treatment. It may be that instructional technologists, despite their prior predilections, are among those best equipped to deal with these larger issues of instruction.

## NOTES

[1]The opinions expressed in this document are those of the author and do not represent official views or policies of the Department of Defense.

[2]Secondary reference sources are used in instances where the primary sources have not yet been released for publication (see below).

## REFERENCES[2]

Barr, A., Beard, M. and Atkinson, R.C. A rationale and description of a CAI program to teach the BASIC programming language. *Instructional Science*, 1975, 4, 1–31.

Beard, R. The all-volunteer army: Hard facts and hard choices. *Strategic Review*, 1979, 42–46.

Bolt, R. *Spatial data management system.* Cambridge, Mass.: Machine Architecture Group, Massachusetts Institute of Technology, 1979.

Brown, J.S., Burton, R.R. and Bell, A.B. SOPHIE: A sophisticated instructional environment for teaching electronic troubleshooting (an example of AI in CAI). BBN Report No. 2790. Cambridge, Mass.: Bolt Beranek and Newman, Inc., 1974.

Browning, R.F., Ryan, L.E. Scott, P.G., and Smode, A.F. Training effectiveness evaluation of device 2F87F, P-3C operational flight trainer. TAEG Report No. 42. Orlando, Fla.: Navy Training and Evaluation Group, 1977.

Burton, R.R. and Brown, J.S. An investigation of computer-coaching for informal learning activities. *International Journal of Man-Machine Studies*, 1979, *11*, 5–24.

Carbonell, J.R. AI in CAI: An artificial intelligence approach to computer-assisted instruction. *IEEE Transactions on Man-Machine Systems*, 1970, *11*, 190–202.

Carr, B. and Goldstein, I.P. *Overlays: A theory of modeling for computer aided instruction.* Artificial Intelligence Memo No. 406. Cambridge, Mass.: Massachusetts Institute of Technology, 1977.

Clancey, W.J. Tutoring rules for guiding a case method dialogue. *International Journal of Man Machine Studies*, 1979, *11*, 25–49.

*College bound seniors, 1979.* New York: College Entrance Examination Board, 1979.

Collins, A., Warnock, E.H., and Passafiume, J.J. *Analysis and synthesis of tutorial dialogues.* BBN Report No. 2789. Cambridge, Mass.: Bolt Beranek and Newman, Inc., March 1974.

Cook, P., Kane, T.P., and McQuie. R. *Advanced technology manpower forecasting.* BKD TR-3-235. Rockville, Md.: B-K Dynamics, Inc., 1977.

Crowder, N.A. Automated tutoring by means of intrinsic programming. In E.H. Galanter (Ed.), *Automatic teaching: The state of the art.* New York: John Wiley & Sons, 1959.

Crawford, A.M., Hurlock, R.E., Padilla, R., and Sassano, A. *Low cost part-task training using interactive computer graphics for simulation of operational equipment.* NPRDC TR 76TQ-46. San Diego, Calif.: Navy Personnel Research and Development Center, 1976.

Davis, R. *Applications of meta-knowledge to the construction, maintenance, and use of large knowledge bases.* Memo HPP-76-7. Stanford, Calif.: Stanford Computer Science Department, Stanford University, 1976.

Duffy, T.M. Literacy training in the navy. In J.D. Fletcher, T.M. Duffy, and T.E. Curran (Eds.), *Historical antecedents and contemporary trends in literacy and readability research in the Navy* NPRDC TR 77-15. San Diego, CA: Navy Personnel Research and Development Center, 1977.

Duffy, T.M. and Nugent, W.A. *Reading skill levels in the Navy.* NPRDC TR 78-19. San Diego, Calif.: Navy Personnel Research and Development Center, April 1978.

Fialka, J. Army views manpower situation as a crisis. Washington, D.C.: *Washington Star*, March 1980a.

_____. Can the U.S. Army fight? Washington D.C.: *Washington Star*, December 1980b.

Fletcher, J.D. Models of the learner in computer-assisted instruction. *Journal of Computer-Based Instruction*, 1975, *1*, 118–26.

_____. New directions in training technology. In *Conference proceedings for new directions in training systems and technology.* Los Angeles, Calif.: AIAA Conferences, 1980.

Funaro, J.F. and Fletcher, J.D. Front-end analysis for emerging systems. *Defense Management Journal*, 1980, *16*, 33–37.

Gentner, D.R. and Norman, D.A. *The FLOW tutor: Schemas for tutoring.* La Jolla, Calif.: Center for Human Information Processing, University of California at San Diego, 1977.

Gold, D., Kleine, B., Fuchs, F., Ravo, S., and Inaba, K. *Aircraft maintenance effectiveness simulation (AMES) model: Final report.* TR-NAVTRAEQUIPCEN-77-D-0028-1. Orlando, Fla.: Naval Training Equipment Center, 1980.

Heuston, D.H. Testimony before the subcommittee on science, research, and technology, 2–3 April, 1980. In *Information technology in education.* Washington, D.C.: U.S. Government Printing Office, 1980.

Isley, R.N., Corley, W.E., and Caro, P.W. *The development of U.S. Coast Guard aviation synthetic equipment and training programs.* FR-D6-74-4. Alexandria, Va.: Human Resources Research Organization, 1974.

Kempster, N. Military skills drain. Los Angeles, Calif: *Los Angeles Times,* March 1980.

Kline, J.M. and Gunning, D.R. Human interface—its role in ATE. Washington, D.C.: *ATE Newsletter,* Navy Materiel Command, 1979.

Levin, S. Video disc-based spatial data management. In *Proceedings of the AFIPS 1980 office automation conference.* Washington, D.C.: American Federation of Information Processing Societies, Inc., 1980.

Malone, T.W. *What makes things fun to learn? A study of intrinsically motivating computer games.* CIS-7-SSL-80-11. Palo Alto, Calif.: Xerox Palo Alto Research Center, 1980.

*Manpower requirements report for FY 1981.* Washington, D.C.: Department of Defense, 1980.

*Military manpower training report for FY 1981.* Washington, D.C.: Department of Defense, 1980.

Munday, L.A. Changing test scores, especially since 1970. *Phi Delta Kappan,* 1979, *60*, 496–99.

No final answer yet on questions about test score decline. *ACT Newsletter,* May 1979, 4–5.

Olsen, J.B., Bunderson, C.V., and Gibbons, A. *Learners and learning system productivity* (TR-DIS-3). Orem, UT: Learning Design Laboratories, WICAT Inc., 1980.

Orlansky, J. and String, J. *Cost-effectiveness of computer-based instruction in military training* (Technical paper, Institute for Defense Analyses) Arlington, Va. 1979.

Paulson, J.A. *A transformation yielding an addictive representation of data in two-way array.* TR 80-1. Portland, Oreg.: Department of Psychology, Portland State University, 1980.

Raser, J.R. *Simulation and Society: An Exploration of Scientific Gaming.* Boston: Allyn & Bacon, 1969.

Rigney, J.W., Towne, D.M., and King, C.A. *Interactive computer graphics for performance-structure-oriented CAI.* Technical Report No. 73. Los Angeles, Calif.: Behavior Technology Laboratories, University of Southern California, 1974.

Root, R.T., Knerr, C.M., Severino, A.A., and Word, L.E. *Tactical engagement simulation training: A method for learning the realities of combat.* Technical Paper No.

370. Alexandria, Va.: U.S. Army Research Institute for the Behavioral and Social Sciences, 1979.

Self, J.A. Student models in computer-aided instruction. *International Journal of Man-Machine Studies*, 1974, *6*, 261—76.

Stevens, A.L. and Collins, A. *The goal structure of a Socratic tutor.* BBN Report No. 3518. Cambridge, Mass.: Bolt Beranek and Newman, Inc., 1977.

Suppes, P. The uses of computers in education. *Scientific American,* 1966, *215,* 206—20.

Thomas, J.O., Madni, A., and Weltman, G. *Systems requirements analysis and prototype design of a low-cost portable simulator for performance training.* Annual Technical Report PATR-1085-80-2. Woodland Hills, Calif.: Perceptronics, Inc., 1980.

Williams, M.D., Hollan, J.D., and Stevens, A. STEAMER: A computer-based instructional system for instructing steam propulsion engineering. *Behavior Research Methods and Instrumentation,* in press.

Wirtz, W. *On further examination: Report of the Advisory Panel on the Scholastic Aptitude Test score decline.* New York: College Entrance Examination Board, 1977.

# General Discussion

## Symposium Participants

**Nickerson:** I'm not quite sure what I'm expected to do at this point.

**Laughery:** Say something brilliant! [*Laughter*]

**Nickerson:** That's helpful.

Maybe we could get the participants up here—those of you who are still here—and have whatever a "debate" is supposed to be.

**Laughery:** Can I make a couple of comments?

**Nickerson:** Sure.

**Laughery:** I didn't have any planned remarks, but something Bill (Howell) said prompted me to make a few remarks here. Bill, if I understood you correctly, it was your observation that most of the things you've heard raised don't substantially differ—"in kind," I think was your word. You pointed out that acceptance, design, and training are issues that people in human factors have been worrying about for a very long time and that you didn't see or hear things happening here, yesterday, or today that were substantially different from the problems we've faced for 15 or more years.

It's been my perception that there are some very substantial changes that have been going on in this area, in this discipline, particularly in the last decade or so. As I thought about it, I'm inclined to agree with you that there may be some discontinuities, there may be some differences

*Editors note: After the presentation of papers, a general discussion by the symposium participants was led by Raymond Nickerson. Dr. Nickerson's analysis of the symposium, which preceded the general discussion, is contained within the Conclusion section of this volume.*

in kind, but I guess the sort of difference that is really in my head is differences in context. A couple of "for examples":

One that's not so related to the theme of this symposium—but has clearly had a big impact in the general field of human factors—is what's been going on in this country in ergonomics, in work physiology, in the last ten or 15 years. That's clearly been a big development in the field of human factors. There are probably a couple of reasons for that. One is the fact that human factors was partially taken over by the field of industrial engineering, which for a long time had been worried about problems in job design. And the importation of that stuff from Europe— where it was always big—I think has had a big impact in this country.

But the other reason is the advancing technology, and what I see.... Let me say it this way: As you look around today, you see human factors groups—people doing work on products, on training, and so forth—at Xerox, at Texas Instruments, at Kodak, at Bell, at IBM, and in a lot of places in the country where you didn't see it ten years ago—quite outside the military-aerospace industry, where it had so much of its earlier impact. In some sense, this is a difference in context. Maybe we're already getting tired of the Three Mile Island example, but it is certainly giving us a lot of visibility as a discipline, and I suspect we ought to milk it for all it's worth.

I have the feeling that while in some sense I agree with you, that there's not a difference in kind, there may be some significant differences in context: in settings, in problems and in the receptivity of industry, for inputs from human factors people.

The Bell Lab group is discovering that, and they may be starting to get in further up front in the process of designing systems. As long as I can remember, human factors people were always complaining about the fact that when it came to hardware design they always got in on the tail end of it. Engineers designed it, and by the time human factors people come in, the best you could hope to do is jiggle it around a little and then, through training programs, worry as to how somebody was going to use it. Well, we're seeing more and more examples of where it might be coming in on the front end. I find that encouraging.

**Howell:**  I didn't really want to suggest that nothing had changed, particularly. I think a lot of emphases have changed, and I think, in particular, that we have a lot more tools than we used to to work with. I think one of the things I was trying to suggest was that perhaps we need to go outside of our typical sphere where we typically look for the tools, in order to seek answers to these things. For example, the industrial-organizational field, I have found, has been dealing with some of the things, some of the measurement issues, some of the problems that I feel have been raised here. I suspect that others, with which I am not as familiar, such as social psychology, from what I hear of what they do occasionally, are addressing some of these. So I guess what I'm saying is that perhaps, concerning the problems that we are addressing, the emphases may have changed to some extent; but I think we do have more options, and perhaps we ought to even try and broaden them.

**Nickerson:** Dexter.

**Fletcher:** I'd like to add to that, particularly with regard to schools, because both issues of fidelity and motivation that have been raised are relevant to it. For a long time in devising, say, simulators, we had to include motion or not. And that was a simulator for that specific training program. Or we would include a front panel or not. Now with computer-based displays and some of the rich capabilities that we have, we have more of a capability, more nearly a capability, of continuous simulation. So this business of actually changing the simulation without having to buy a multi-million dollar device, but, in fact, changing it as the student learns in accordance with these capabilities, is kind of a new thing. It's the old issue of fidelity; but we've got a new tool, and the rules of the game have changed.

The same thing applies to motivation. A long time ago we could have brought up our cave games, of course, and put them into our beer halls, and perhaps made them job relevant. but today we can make them much cheaper. Anybody can play one of these little basketball games or something like that. We can put these things into people's hands, and—again, because of this kind of simulation capability that we have from the displays and the market processes and the kinds of intelligence you put into it—we have much greater possibility of making—in effect, what are toys—job relevant again. So, again, this issue of motivation comes up. You've got some new capabilities or a new range of capabilities over which to explore the possibilities of having this impact.

**Howell:** I'd like to just—this is off the topic altogether, but I think this occurred to me when you [*gesturing to Nickerson*] were speaking—again a heretical position. I just wonder if there is the possibility that in worrying too much about the problems, and so forth, that you may encounter in the future, if we may not wind up wasting a lot of time. That is, is there the possibility that we might run into the limits-of-growth kind of problem where we wind up dealing with issues, dealing with some problems that may not ever arise. I saw in Al's [Chapanis] approach, for example, that there we're dealing with something we know is there. We're dealing with a strictly empirical fashion, and we're getting something that's serviceable. Do you see that as a possible problem?

**Nickerson:** Well, I don't know if this is going to be the answer to your question. I think that thinking about the potential negative effects of a technology is not a waste of time. Quite the contrary, I think it would be crazy not to do that. I think that we have been surprised many times: accumulation of carbon-14 in the stratosphere, the pollution of waters from such a benign invention as nonbiodegradable detergents, and there are certain areas of the country where pollution reached very severe proportions before we thought about it. The problems of acid rain that we have today might have been avoided if we'd thought about it some time ago. The way we solved the problem was to use taller smokestacks to distribute the pollutants more widely to the neighbors. I think we could go on and on and on, and I don't think that's being negative, excessively negative, to recognize the fact that any technology can have both good and bad effects, and one should do some planning to minimize the bad effects. I am trying to make a different point of the issue. It's not my point; I'm really tired of people who wholeheartedly endorse it, because this is a different kind of technology. I believe that it's a point of view—that I personally adopted—that it's the quality of different kind of technology, because I think the computers are qualitatively different kinds of machines than any we have dealt with before. I don't know if that was the answer to your question.

**Howell:** Well, it was just because of the fact that things are somewhat more complex that there are so many future possibilities that it would be stupid to say we shouldn't think about them. We try to do what planning we can, but I guess it's a question of investment. How much do we want to invest in researching "what ifs"?

**Nickerson:** Well, for example, a topical question at the moment is the question of information, privacy, and data banks. I'm sure you're all aware of the fact that the National Science Foundation commissioned a fairly large study to look into that issue, and I think that's a very reasonable thing to do, rather than to let data facts grow without limits. Clearly large centralized data banks can be tremendously beneficial things. They also can be badly abused. It's just as well to recognize that fact and consider what to do about it.

**Klemmer:**    I'd like to change the level of discussion for a moment and take advantage of being in the university and talking with university people, which I don't always get a chance to do—well, at least not very often. Dexter Fletcher, I think, said correctly that all problems are ultimately people problems. The only question is what class of people are being considered. I suggest that maybe we can start with ourselves. I have a four-minute statement here, if you'll bear with me, because I think it's relevant.

This year Bell Laboratories will hire about 30 Ph.D. psychologists, almost all of whom will go to work in applied human factors. I submit that such employment of competent applied experimental psychologists into industry is a basic and necessary first step in beginning to apply the skills of behavioral science to the problems of modern technology. We cannot hope that the research of experimental psychologists in universities will lead to friendly human interfaces for the next generation of information handling systems. That research is generally not relevant to decisions that are now being made in system design, and not even the relevant work, such as Al Chapanis', will be used unless there are practitioners in industry to use these results.

For many years there has, in my mind, been a gross imbalance between basic theoretical and applied work in experimental psychology, both in number and quality. Not enough good psychologists have gone into applied work. As a result, psychology and human factors now endure a poor reputation in many parts of industry as disciplines that have little to offer in solution of real problems. Reputation is a function of the quality of people and their work. Perhaps the greatest disservice that academic experimental psychologists have done to their own field is to spread the myth that applied work requires less intellectual skill than pure research. And so they can safely send their less competent students to industry. This negative attitude and lack of understanding of applied work greatly slowed the growth of human factor jobs in industry. The fruits of this attitude is a paucity of jobs for current graduates of experimental psychology programs.

Fortunately, the situation is not stable in this unhappy condition. Good people are now taking applied jobs. Some of these people will demonstrate what human factors can do. This will lead to more jobs, which will attract more good people. I remain optimistic about the future.

**Nickerson:** It sounded like you were trying to scrounge a date there. I don't know.... [*Laughter*]

**Laughery:** I think you're right about everything up to the last two sentences, and I hope you're right about that!

**Klemmer:** I did want to say that, while I have a chance, I'd like to get anyone to straighten me out, if I said something that's not correct.

**Nickerson:** Al.

**Chapanis:** I agree with everything you say except the last thing. I'm pessimistic. I guess I'm pessimistic because I've been in this business for pretty near 35 years now. And I guess I'm pessimistic because psychologists at universities don't really see the problem, and they don't intend to do anything about it. Frankly, I think people in experimental psychology and basic psychology do the things they do because they're easy. What you want to do is to take a nice simple little problem, and get your Ph.D. thesis, or get an article in the *Journal of Experimental Psychology*. And it is an awfully easy thing to do a trivial experiment by manipulating nonsense syllables out here and measuring what kind of effects occur over there. These are things you can roll off in one week in the laboratory. They're divorced from any practical problem.

The kinds of things that you're [*gesturing to Klemmer*] doing, the kinds of things I'm trying to do, are damned hard. They take a lot of work, they take a long time to study, and they don't turn out a lot of papers. And I don't think most people in psychology are willing to put that effort into it. The thing that I've seen that I find very distressing is a much greater trend towards this abstract kind of basic psychology that's off here in the stratosphere and has nothing to do with reality.

Well, I'm too old now; it's no longer my problem, but it's a problem for you younger folks over here.

**Klemmer:** No, I don't agree with Al. I think that education does not change as fast as some other institutions, perhaps, but I see very strong signs of change in attitude. I see very significant change in attitudes in people we've been interviewing this year and last year for jobs at Bell Laboratories.

**Chapanis:** A few years ago I was on the Board of Scientific Affairs for the American Psychological Association. Eventually I resigned because I just got nauseated by the kind of attitude I found in it. The Board of Scientific Affairs, at that time, was greatly concerned about the lack of job opportunities for psychologists. What they were saying was: "We've got to expand opportunities for Ph.D.s in psychology. What we've got to do is push all these people from experimental psychology into applied areas because that's where the jobs are." My feeling was, "Well, what are you going to do about changing your basic education? All you're saying is we'll just train the same kind of psychologists we used to train and just shove them off into industry." But my feeling is that what they needed to do was go back into the universities and say: "You're going to have to change. You've got to train a different kind of psychologist." They weren't willing to face that issue. So eventually I resigned from the board; I couldn't stand it.

My own university, when I retire, is going to literally stop all human factors work. There will be no more human factors work at Johns Hopkins because they are determined to deal with the basic kinds of psychology. I am not sure what you're facing here in Houston.

**Klemmer:** Is somebody going to come to the defense of recent research?

**Nickerson:** I wasn't going to go into this.

**R. Lachman:** I'll take issue with one thing: Trivial studies take a year to do, not a week. [*Laughter*]

**Laughery:** It doesn't make a difference. [*Laughter*]

**Chapanis:** My colleagues are grinding out cognitive papers at the rate of one every two or three weeks, because they're easy to do. They have a computer which generates all of the stimuli, and you get your students to assist in the analyses.

**Audience:** Do they get published?

**Chapanis:** They get published all of the time.

**R. Lachman:** Just prior to the International Congress in Moscow over ten years ago Eleanor Gibson gave a colloquium at SUNY—Buffalo about the work that she was doing on reading. During the period of behaviorist domination of psychology, she took Hull's theory and mapped it onto verbal learning. And now she was shifting over to the study of reading research and processing of symbolic materials. She apologized for perhaps the first 15 minutes for doing something

that may have some social relevance. These attitudes are
ingrained.

**Chapanis:** The kinds of things that Dexter talked about, the kinds of
things that you talked about are damn hard problems. They
are tough problems. But they are not going to be solved by
going into the laboratory and doing simple experiments.
You've got to get out into the field to do research. They are
hard. They're a really hard thing to do. I don't think this
realization has gone back to the professors of psychology in
the major universities.

**Laughery:** I guess I'm more optimistic than you are.

Somebody recently in print referred to you as the Dean
of American Human Engineering. I've been known to
disagree with deans before. [*Laughter*] I don't know if you
like that title.

I think if we expect some radical changes overnight,
we're not going to see that, but I think that there are a
number of signs which make me optimistic. If we weren't
feeling this way, I wouldn't be doing a lot of things that are
happening here right now, but I have picked up signs in
other places. Part of what I said earlier is a basis for my
optimism about where I see psychologists and human
factors people, not in that field, but out in organizations,
trying to wrestle with the problem. I don't know how well
they're wrestling with those, whether they've taken that
bag of academic research experimental tools. It might not
fit very well to those, but I think that's a hopeful sign. The
other thing is that I've been picking up only recently
indications of serious interest along these lines in some
academic sectors.

We've had a couple of people here at this meeting—
John Mueller came from Missouri, Don Foss came down
from the University of Texas at Austin—because they're
concerned about this problem and what we can do in
academia.

**Foss:** That's right.

**Laughery:** I noticed recently that Don Norman had a letter to the
editor in the *Bulletin of the Human Factors Society* that we join the
Human Factor Society because he thought it was time. One
of the things that he said, was that cognitive psychology
had some things to offer to applied programs, and it was
about time to get on with it.

I don't know how much hope that legitimately generates, but I see some things happening in this direction. Of
course, behind us pushing is that tightening academic

marketplace. Now that's a set of forces at work here that we're all familiar with. So I'm increasingly optimistic, but I don't expect it to happen overnight.

**Chapanis:** To the things that I've said, I'd like to make just one more brief comment. In my rather long career I've seen a lot of very bad mistakes made by improperly trained people who got into the human factors area. Some of these are people who have applied for a job and were not properly trained to do it, who have botched it, or done a terrible job, and made some terrible mistakes. In some caes the industries where these people worked said they would never hire a psychologist again. And I think this is a very serious problem.

**Klemmer:** I'm sure Al and I agree in having a somewhat different impression from most people about the relative importance of training versus intellectual ability. At Bell Laboratories, and at IBM—considering that they hire from the top 10 percent of the best engineering schools in the country to staff their facilities—we cannot send a mediocre psychologist with a Ph.D. in there and have him gain the respect of these really bright engineers.

**Chapanis:** Industry deserves the best we got, not mediocrity.

**R. Lachman:** And they're starting to get it. There are no academic jobs. In fact, without naming who or what, we invited somebody from an industrial research setting in Palo Alto, and he said, "I cannot come. I'm teaching a human factors course at Stanford." So there are forces at work for change. It's not the 1960s, when you could train anybody, give them a Ph.D., and place them in a university without any problem. Times have changed.

**Nickerson:** I'd like to react to the polarization of thinking, which may be a misinterpretation, that puts basic research on one end of the continuum at easy and poor and applied research on the other end at difficult and good. It seems to me the quality of research can be drawn from that dimension which would confirm many examples of good research on the basic end and on the applied end. And the same is true for poor research. The company for which I work has a number of people who do applied research in part because it's a very easy process that is possible to support. But in many cases they work on what they think, at least there, would seem to be quite basic problems because we believe that that's the way to solve the end problem in the long run.

I guess the case in point that I would cite as an example is the work on natural language processing. We've adopted an approach to that which I think, personally, was very appropriate, if you've got a well defined fairly tightly constrained problem, where you can identify the various utterances that a person is likely to make and analyze them exhaustively, both in terms of their deep structure as well as their surface structure. I would submit that that would not be the good general top solution to the problem of how to get a computer to be able to carry on a conversation with a person in an unconstrained situation. That approach is a very effective approach for certain types of problems, but it will run into a subtle limit. People who I'm familiar with who are attempting to solve that problem will be quite free to admit to you, or anyone, that they will not come up with a solution to the specific, highly contextually constrained problem. That's not the one they're working on, but the approach they're taking is to address some very basic and fundamental issues; they're taking it not because it's easy, but because they think that problem is manageable.

**Chapanis:** I will turn around something you said and change just a few words. We will learn more about natural language processing from trying to build an artificial machine to do that. Those are the words you said.

**Nickerson:** Well, I believe that. Did you misunderstand? I'm talking about people who are trying to....

**Chapanis:** I think what I'm saying is I'm trying to build an artificial machine to do this, and I think I will learn more about natural language than your people will on the basis of basic studies.

**Nickerson:** I'm sorry. I didn't express that right. I'm talking about people who are trying to design languages and build the capabilities of the computer to understand natural language. You're familiar with that work?

He's not studying. He's not doing experiments. He's trying to build. He's trying to do the same things you are, but I'm saying that he is looking at it as a basic problem, and I'm reacting to your sweeping assertion that people who work on basic problems, or what they see as basic problems, do it because it's easy. For one, I want to go on record as saying I don't believe that that's true, in general.

**Chapanis:** I understand that. Of course, I wouldn't call that very basic. I would call that very applied. [*Laughter*]

**Nickerson:** Maybe it's a good time to quit. Rick?

**Kasschau:** Thank you. There are a number of people here whom I would like to thank. Personally, would like to thank very much the members of the Houston Symposium Committee, including Jim Campion, Dale Johnson (who isn't here today), Frank Kessel, Roy Lachman, and Ken Laughery.

And both personally and on behalf of both the committee and the department of psychology, I would like to extend my hearty thanks to all the participants—both those who have remained throughout the three days of the symposium and those who were called away for various reasons.

In addition, there are a number of less obvious people who are equally vital to the success of the symposium. These include, first, the members of the faculty of our department, who submitted the various ideas to the committee, from which we ultimately selected the topic that was originally suggested by Ken and Roy. Second, our department chair, Roger Maley, who has been the interface between our committee—with its various needs—and the upper administration. Third, a number of graduate students who helped us with transportation: Rich Fowler, Mike Rudd, and Dan Taylor. Finally, I would like to thank Mike Lum, who is behind the wall here. He has been responsible for a vast array of invaluable services involving recording, projectors, and all the technical assistance that we have needed.

To each of these individuals and groups I would like to extend my sincere thanks and to each of you, good evening!

**Laughery:**  I think a note of thanks is in order to Rick—who did more than anybody.

# Conclusion: Information Technology and Psychology: A Retrospective Look at Some Views of the Future

## Raymond S. Nickerson

The papers presented at the third Houston Symposium touched on many subjects. This is not surprising. Information is a broad concept, and information technology, including as it does both computer and communication technologies, subsumes a wide variety of topics. The fact that participants in the symposium included people from industry, government, and academia and represented several different disciplines also contributed to the diversity of subjects discussed.

For a discussant such diversity is a bit intimidating. One cannot hope to do justice to the many ideas that emerged. In selecting specific topics on which to comment, I have tried to identify those that are particularly important vis-à-vis what I understood the objectives of the symposium to be. That my choices were influenced by my own interests and biases, however, is undoubtedly true.

The substance of the symposium papers, which constitute the preceding chapters, can be classified roughly under four topics:

    1.   What has happened in information technology in the recent past?

    2.   What is likely to happen in the near future?

    3.   What are some of the implications of these developments for society, for the quality of our lives, for our perception of ourselves as workers and as human beings, for our relationships with others, and so on?

    4.   What role can or should psychologists play in making this technology more useful and usable, especially to people not trained in computer technology, and in assuring that its impact on the quality of life will be a positive one?

This chapter is organized around these four general topics.

## WHAT HAS HAPPENED IN INFORMATION TECHNOLOGY OVER THE PAST FEW DECADES?

I believe that most people believe that ours is an era of unprecedented rate of change. (Dr. Sheil challenged the tenability of this belief, and I will comment on his thought-provoking argument later.) Nowhere is the evidence for this notion more apparent than in information technology. Major trends are easily identified: decreasing component costs, decreasing size and increasing packing density of components, decreasing power requirements, increasing speed, increasing reliability, increasing size of market, increasing distribution of and accessibility to computing power. The following observations, some of which were made by Mr. Case and Mr. Phipps, provide a sense of the speed with which the technology is moving.

- The cost of production of a logic gate has gone from about ten dollars in 1960 to about ten cents in 1970 to less than one cent in 1980.
- The cost of dynamic random-access memory (RAM) has gone from about one cent per bit in 1970 to about .05 cent per bit in 1980.
- The size of the smallest feature on an integrated circuit has gone from about ten microns in 1970 to about three microns in 1980.
- The number of active element groups that can be placed on a single semiconductor chip has gone from less than ten in 1960 to a few thousand in 1970 to approximately 70,000 in 1980.[1] The rate of increase has been roughly an order of magnitude every five years since 1960.
- Random-access memory power dissipation has gone from about 500 microwatts per bit in 1970 to about four microwatts per bit in 1980.
- Access time for dynamic RAM has gone from about 400 nanoseconds in 1970 to about 150 nanoseconds in 1980.
- The reliability of logic gates has increased by about five orders of magnitude in two decades.
- In 1979 microprocessor sales increased by more than 35 percent over 1978. At about the same time the cost of a microprocessor dropped from about $65 to about $5 over a period of 18 months.
- In spite of enormous efforts to expand production capacity— $800 million for new plant and equipment by the semiconductor industry in 1979—the demand appears to be growing faster than the supply.
- Lead times for many semiconductor components are now six months to one year.
- The estimated number of active element groups in the average U.S. home has gone from about ten in 1940 to about 100 in 1960 to a few thousand in 1980.

Toynbee (1946) has suggested that the history of the development of technique reveals a principle of "progressive etherialization" that seems to govern technological progress. That which is ponderous and bulky gives way to that which is fast and light. The general trend is in the direction of increasingly greater freedom from space-time constraints. This principle is seen quite clearly in the history of communication and information processing technology. Miller (1965) has pointed out how the matter-energy costs of storing the markers of information have decreased over the centuries: "Cuneiform tablets carried approximately of the order of $10^{-2}$ bits of information per gram; paper with typewritten messages carries approximately of the order of $10^3$ bits of information per gram; and electronic magnetic tape storage carries approximately of the order of $10^6$ bits of information per gram" (p. 195). As is clear from the trends noted above, the 15 years since Miller made these observations have carried the etherialization process to extremes that could hardly have been imagined even in 1965. And the end of the process is not yet in sight.

Perhaps a more meaningful characterization of recent trends for our present purposes is to say that collectively they represent an enormous increase in our ability to manipulate, store, and transmit very large amounts of information very rapidly and at steadily decreasing cost. If one wants to capture in a single term what has really increased, one could do worse than the term "access bandwidth." Thanks to Gutenberg and the later discovery of how to make paper from linen rags it has been possible for some time to store large amounts of information in certain locations, such as the major libraries of the world. In our own century, the development of electronic means of storing and accessing information has increased the ease of both storage and retrieval. What current developments in information technology are doing is making it increasingly feasible to store truly huge amounts of information very economically, to make this information far more immediately accessible to people who want to use it, and not only to deliver to the users the information in prepackaged form but to provide them with processes and procedures for manipulating it in useful ways.

## HOW WILL THIS TECHNOLOGY CONTINUE TO DEVELOP DURING THE NEXT DECADE?

Predicting the future is a fool's game. There is only one way to be right, but an infinity of ways to be wrong. We must try, but having tried, we must expect to be surprised. Hopefully, if our predictions have been carefully made, the degree of surprise and the extent to which we find ourselves unprepared to cope with the future that actually occurs will be less than they otherwise might have been.

Among the things that we can be sure will occur are continuations of most, if not all, of the trends that were noted as characterizing the last few decades. The costs of computer components will continue to decrease, as will their size and power requirements. Speed will increase as will reliability. The demand for components and systems will continue to grow. Applications will continue to proliferate.

These predictions all seem reasonably safe. Of course, they amount to nothing more than a timidly qualitative projection of the past. When one attempts to quantify what will happen one begins to run the risk of almost certainly being wrong. Nevertheless, one can find some guesses of a quantitative sort regarding what will happen during the next few years. Bylinsky (1981), for example, has reported a prediction that the production cost of IC (integrated circuit) memory will drop to less than .005 cent per bit by middle of the decade. The size of the smallest feature on an integrated circuit is expected to decrease to less than one micron by the mid-1980s (Kahn, 1978). Young (1981) anticipates several million components on a VLSI chip by the end of the decade. Leonard (1980) has predicted that the worldwide demand for semiconductor random-access memory will be about 20 trillion bits by 1982 (up from about 1.5 trillion in 1980). The number of active element groups in the average U.S. home is expected to be close to .5 million by the end of the decade, up from a few thousand in 1980 (Robinson, 1980b).

Among the dazzling assortment of numbers Mr. Phipps presented to illustrate how rapidly the semiconductor industry is moving, one that I find particularly fascinating is the per capita consumption of electronic circuits in the United States. Phipps pointed out that 15 years ago this was approximately three, whereas today it is roughly 10,000, and by 1990 it is expected to be about 2 million. The term "mind boggling" is overworked these days, but I must confess that, to me, the expectation that by the end of this decade the number of electronic circuits available for use in the United States will be roughly 2 million times the size of the population is a mind-boggling thought. I find the prediction quite believable; in fact, I will not be surprised if it turns out to be conservative, but I cannot begin to imagine what its realization will mean.

Some of the expected advances can occur as the result of further refinement of existing techniques. Others will require the development of qualitatively different ways of doing things. Production of integrated circuits with submicron feature sizes, to illustrate the latter case, will require the use of X-rays, electron beams, or some other form of relatively short wavelength radiation inasmuch as the current feature size is close to the limit imposed by the resolving power of visible light.

Two developments that are currently causing considerable excitement in the computer industry, and that are likely to play a significant role in continuing the "progressive etherialization" of information technology in the 1980s and beyond, are the magnetic-bubble memory and the Josephson junction. In a magnetic-bubble memory one bit of information is represented by the presence or absence of a tiny area (magnetic bubble) that has a direction of polarization opposite to that of bulk of the material in which it is embedded. The most common material for bubble memories at the present is synthetic garnet, which permits the use of bubbles about .5 micrometers in diameter. Bubble memories built with thin films of metallic glasses may make feasible the use of bubbles of about .1 micrometer in diameter, thus allowing a 25-fold increase in packing density over the current state of the art. Normally-conducting vortexes in superconducting metallic glasses offer the possibility of another two-orders-of-magnitude increase in storage density over the .1 micrometer bubble memories, inasmuch as the vortexes measure only .005 to .01 micrometer (Chaudhari, Giessen, and Turnbull, 1980).

The Josephson junction, a device invented by Brian Josephson in 1962, could replace the transistor as the fundamental element of computer technology just as the transistor replaced the vacuum tube. The Josephson junction works on principles different from those of either the vacuum tube or the transistor, but like both of them it can act as a switch for an electronic signal. Among the advantages of the junction are the speed with which it can switch from one state to another (about six picoseconds) and its relatively small power requirements (because it is a superconducting device). It also can store information as well as function as a switch. The expectation is that when Josephson junction technology is further developed it will be possible to construct computers from these devices that will consume a fraction of the power of today's microcomputers and will have memory cycle time of less than one nanosecond (Matiso, 1980).

Thus even with techniques that are already known, albeit in some cases still at an experimental stage, one can see a continuation at least for the near future of the recent trends in size, speed, power requirements, and so on. That is not to say that these trends can continue indefinitely. Although the most exciting developments are likely to come from the least predictable quarters, there are—the physicists tell us—some fundamental limits that some of these trends will sooner or later encounter. Size can be reduced only so far, for example, until it runs into the limits of atomic structure. Indeed, the .01 micrometer mentioned in connection with bubble memories is within two orders of magnitude of the diameter of a hydrogen atom. Moreover, problems arise long before such fundamental limits are approached.

There is, for example, a mode of computer failure that is similar to genetic mutation in two respects: it occurs at random, and it is induced by radiation. This mode is referred to as soft failure, and the probability of its occurrence increases with the density of packing of memory elements.

On a semiconductor memory chip one bit of information is represented by an electric charge on an area about 100 square micrometers in size. The charge consists of about 1.5 million free electrons and an equal number of "holes" (places that could be occupied by electrons but are not) in the silicon lattice. When a fast-moving electrically charged particle, such as an alpha particle or helium nucleus, passes through a memory cell in a chip, it can ionize (creating an electron and a hole) as many as three million atoms. Thus it can change the status of a memory cell, creating a charge where there was none to begin with. A charge-coupled device, in which a bit is represented by only 50,000 electrons and holes, is more vulnerable to such failures than is a conventional chip because of its greater packing density. Ziegler and Lanford (1979) have estimated that the soft failure rate for a charge-coupled memory device capable of storing about 256,000 bits is about three per thousand hours.

Such radiation-induced memory failures are a source of some concern in spite of their relatively low frequency of occurrence. They are unpredictable both with respect to time and location: any cell in the memory is susceptible to such a soft failure, and inasmuch as the source of the ionizing radiation may be either decaying atoms of radioactive substances found in trace amounts in the materials of which semiconductors are made, or high energy particles in the atmosphere, it can happen at any time. The effects, moreover, are completely unpredictable. The approach that is taken to combat this problem is that of representing information within the memory with error-detecting and error-correcting codes. The price of this is the need to assign extra (redundant) bits to the representation of the coded elements.

While the question of how far current trends can continue before encountering fundamental limitations is an open one, it is not clear that it has any very significant immediate practical implications. Moreover, it is likely that before current trends are pressed to their limits, fundamentally new computing architectures and approaches will be developed that will make these limits irrelevant. What is clear is that the computing resources that will be available in the foreseeable future will be enormous and widely available. Long before progress in information technology is halted because of fundamental physical limitations, we are likely to encounter obstacles of a quite different kind, namely, our limited ability to exploit effectively the potential that the technology represents, and to do so for the good of humankind.

What kinds of *applications* of information technology can we anticipate in the foreseeable future? If we assume that computer resources are going to be increasingly widely distributed, readily accessible, and inexpensive, then efforts to predict how they will be used are probably doomed to failure, or at least to gross understatement. Imagine the challenge of predicting the future uses of electricity just before it began to be commercially available toward the end of the nineteenth century. One could hardly be expected to have been able to anticipate the countless uses that have been made of this resource or the plethora of inventions that its availability has made possible.

One can list a number of ways in which it *now* seems likely that information technology will be developed and used in the next few years. Undoubtedly many of these expectations will be realized, and some will not. Undoubtedly too, many developments will occur—perhaps those with the greatest and longest lasting effects—that would not appear on anyone's list. The following list includes some of the things that are mentioned in the other chapters in this book, and a few others as well.

- Development of new architectures for processors and memory utilizing new materials and techniques including gallium arsenide logic, superconducting devices such as the Josephson junction, charge-coupled devices, magnetic bubbles, optical communication and storage, and three-dimensional integrated circuits.

- Increasing use of fiber optics, microwave, and satellite technologies in communication systems with the effect of broadening bandwidth greatly and providing increased accessibility to information of almost every sort.

- Satellite transmission directly to homes, increasing enormously the amount of information that can be delivered and thus the range of options among which consumers can choose.

- Development and refinement of software tools to help designers and programmers cope with the increasing complexity of their tasks.

- Increasing emphasis on distributed computing systems and parallel processing approaches to the solution of complex problems.

- Much greater attention to practical applications of artificial intelligence, made feasible by the availability of sufficient computing speed and memory capacity provided by very-large-scale integration.

- Increasing use of speech as a means of communication between people and computers, and between people and people via computer networks.

- An increasingly important role of information technology in military systems: guidance systems for individual missiles, air surveillance and attack warning systems, tactical fire control systems, submarine tracking systems, and so on.

- Widespread use of electronic mail, electronic funds transfer, and computer-mediated communication more generally.

- Increasingly powerful word-processing, document-preparation, and information-management tools in the office.

- Increasing use of electronic means of composing, proofing, editing, and disseminating "publications."

- Computer-based job hunting and recruiting, classified advertising, and shopping—and proliferation of computer-mediated information services generally.

- Increasing involvement of computers in monitoring and control processes across a wide range of activities of systems: from the computerized fuel injection system in automobiles that optimizes energy usage by adapting the fuel mix to match the conditions of the moment to the operation of a complete economy.
- Increasing use of automation and robotics in industry.
- Concentration of very large amounts of information of various types, increasing the possibility of information monopolies or the control of access to various collections of information for the benefit of groups with special interests.
- Increasing use of smart (and instructable) devices in homes, offices, and personal vehicles.
- Inexpensive ways of storing large amounts of information electronically for business or personal use in the office or the home.
- Two-way, real-time communication between broadcasting facilities and the home, permitting greater participation in decision making (instant polls and referenda) and greater variety and selectivity in home entertainment (dial-up movies, interactive games).
- Electronic accessibility from the home of information stored in libraries, museums, and other major repositories.

Another change that we are beginning to see, and that will become increasingly apparent, is a change in the predominant mode of computer use. The technique of time-sharing was developed in the early 1960s and has served us well through the last two decades. I believe there will continue to be a demand for time-sharing services throughout the 1980s and perhaps indefinitely. The primary motivation for developing time-sharing, however, is no longer as compelling as it once was. When time-sharing was developed, economic considerations dictated that the only way that many people who had a need for a significant amount of interactive computing power could get it was by sharing very costly resources with many other users.

In the future we will see the rapidly increasing availability and use of "personal" computers that are as powerful as the most powerful machines of a decade ago and that will sell for a small fraction of their cost. They will be usable in a stand-alone mode, but they will also communicate with other computer resources via networks and thus will provide users with facilities that are beyond the capabilities of their personal machines. A common use of personal computers in scientific environments will be to support complex displays and word-processing applications locally while depending on remotely located and shared facilities for long-term storage of programs, large number-crunching applications, and so on.

Mr. Phipps spoke of the abundance of low-cost logic and memory that we can expect in the future. This is a common theme among people who are close enough to the computer industry to be most aware of the rapidly falling unit cost of computing power and storage. There seems to be a growing belief that in the foreseeable future it will be possible for anyone to have all of the information processing capacity that he can effectively use. The challenge, if that is the case, is to find ways to use this abundant resource effectively and for worthwhile ends.

## WHAT ARE SOME OF THE SOCIAL IMPLICATIONS OF INFORMATION TECHNOLOGY?

Almost every participant in this symposium demonstrated an interest in the question of the social implications of recent and anticipated developments in information technology. Not a few expressed concern for the possibility of negative or undesirable effects and uneasiness about where the technology might take us. Some even wondered aloud whether, on balance, the overall impact might be bad. No one argued that it will be, and on the whole both the substance of the papers and the general tone of the meeting seemed consistent with the assumption that the developments we are witnessing are perceived not only as exciting but as more promising than threatening. But the cautionary note was there: this technology will bear not only watching, but steering.

The papers that focused most directly on social issues were those of Professor Holton and Congressman Brown. (The term social is used here in a sufficiently broad sense to include philosophical, political, and ethical.) Professor Holton began by reminding us of several ways in which science has bruised our collective egos in the past by forcing us to modify our beliefs about our position or status as human beings in the grand scheme of things. I want to return to this point at the end of these comments, so will say no more about it here.

The main message in Professor Holton's remarks, as I understand it, is that the old way of viewing science, technology and society as being motivated by independent imperatives will no longer do. He contrasted the conventional scientific goal of increasingly inclusive and parsimonious explanations (the Faustian dream of omniscience) with a growing emphasis on the impact of scientific research and technological innovation on the quality of life. He played a provocative variation on the familiar theme of the responsibility of scientists and technologists to consider the social consequences of their work. Implicit in this theme is a rejection of the notion that the proper role of science is the development of knowledge for its own sake and that the uses of the knowledge that is developed are someone else's concern. Implicit also is the assumption that unless the goals of science, technology, and society are coordinated, at least to some degree, there is a real likelihood that they will conflict, perhaps catastrophically. To demonstrate the reality of this likelihood Holton noted the difficulty one has of determining whether the obvious social benefits of the past accomplishments of science and technology (e.g., increased availability of energy, food, information, and medicine) outweigh the attendant liabilities (e.g., depletion of limited resources, environmental pollution, the threat of nuclear destruction).

In expressing this type of concern Holton is in good company. The fear has been voiced by more than one scientist of note (Barry Commoner, Rene Dubos, Alduous Huxley, and Bertrand Russell, to name a few) that we have gotten smarter faster than we have gotten better and that our technological capabilities have gotten dangerously far ahead of our ability to use them wisely and humanely. Much in the same vein, Botkin, Elmandjra, and Malitza (1979) began their recent report to the Club of Rome with a reference to the emergence of a "world problematique," a complex tangle of problems—often fostered or complicated by technology—relating to energy, population, and food, and accompanied by an air of concern and apprehension:

> Only ten years ago, the mood was one of great expectations. Now, after a decade of global issues, it appears not only that the world situation has substantially deteriorated but also that adverse trends are steadily strengthening. Even though the techno-scientific enterprise has progressed on many fronts, its achievements are neither systematically nor globally coordinated, all too often engendering more serious problems than the ones they solve. Meanwhile, still other problems of a political, social, and psychological character keep emerging. All of these intertwine, so that the predicament of humanity becomes ever more difficult and the overall condition continues to deteriorate (p. 1).

Happily, there are signs, Holton claims, of an increased interest on the part of scientists in addressing basic research to areas of ignorance that seem to lie at the heart of social problems. Also there is increased involvement of national policymakers in the identification and prioritization of research problems. "Combined-mode research" is the term he uses to denote basic research motivated by social concerns. As an example of a socially relevant research problem that relates directly to information technology, Holton cites the question of the impact of this technology on individual privacy. He notes also the growing belief that computers represent a threat to that privacy. The concern, I believe, is well founded; the threat need not be realized, but to ignore it would probably assure that it will be.

Holton's parting observation that "any professional activity has a just claim to moral authority when, and only when, it is widely seen to honor both truth and the public interest" returns to the theme of the untenability of the old view of science, technology, and society as independent entities. One gathers from this observation that he hopes the trend toward combined-mode research will continue for a long time to come. This hope is, I suspect, one that the participants in this symposium generally share.

Congressman Brown touched on many subjects of unquestioned importance to anyone concerned about the impact of technology on their lives:

- The appropriateness of the application of the overworked word "revolution" to characterize what has happened in information technology over the last few years, the notion that every revolution has its victims, and the need to strive for equity and humaneness as well as efficiency in the use of this technology.
- The problem of evaluating a technology in terms of its potential contribution to productivity goals and improvement in the quality of life.
- The need for research on how people organize and access knowledge, on the interaction between people and machines, and on how people will relate to each other in highly automated environments.
- The potential that satellite communication holds for moving large amounts of information quickly over long distances and, consequently, for providing cost-effective means of communication for small groups in relatively isolated environments.
- The merging of communications and computer technology and the resulting emergence of new modes of communication that threaten old monopolies, such as the postal and telephone services, and impose new problems relating to government regulatory policies.
- The emergence and proliferation of computerized data bases and the numerous issues relating to their future development, use, and control: centralization, interdatabase communication, information sharing, control of access and dissemination, and protection of privacy.
- The need for standards for internetwork communication protocols, and data bank access, and the need for a coherent national policy for the management of information resources.
- The idea that access to information has social as well as economic implications and that changes in information flow may alter traditional relationships among individuals, organizations, and nations in as yet unknown ways.
- The international problem of "information inequity" and in particular the need for the developed countries of the world to help ensure that Third World countries benefit from information technology in ways that meet their own needs.
- The need to attend to implications of the new technology in the workplace for issues relating to the dignity of the workers and the humanness of work situations.
- The potential educational benefits of information technology: the possibility that delivery of educational services to the home may

change dramatically the role of schools and the educational process, and the possibility of information technology (and in particular satellite transmission, cable, and interactive TV, computer networks linking many information and educational resources) turning the whole community into a learning environment.

•  The need to try to understand the implications of information technology for equity and personal liberty.

All of these topics are worthy subjects of thought and discussion. I will comment briefly only on the last two. Congressman Brown's vision of the whole community becoming a learning environment—because of such aspects of information technology as satellite transmission; interactive TV; the interconnection via computer networks of schools, museums, libraries, and government entities; microcomputers in the home providing access to networks and thereby to numerous information sources—is an exciting vision indeed. The question is how to assure that these new technological possibilities become realities and that the new systems will, in Brown's words, "be used in socially constructive and equitable ways." As he points out, television also has, and for several decades has had, enormous educational potential, but it is a potential that with some notable exceptions has remained largely unrealized.

The implications of information technology for equity and personal liberty? One indeed would like to understand what they are. One can only speculate, but two possibilities suggest themselves. First, it seems likely that information technology will continue to increase the freedom of choice of many of us by extending our range of possible actions and giving us more alternatives from which to choose. Technology, in general, has certainly done this in the past. On the average, people in technologically developed countries today travel much greater distances and more often than did their grandparents or probably even their parents. Higher education, which used to be the prerogative of a privileged few, is now a possibility for a large fraction of the population. The range of job opportunities is immensely greater than it was only a few decades ago. Books are readily available, and entertainment opportunities have multiplied. (Consider the difference between the average music lover of today in the United States and his counterpart of 100 years ago with respect to the availability to them of the various kinds of music the world has to offer.)

This trend toward increasing the average person's options is very likely to increase, perhaps to accelerate, as a result of the truly remarkable developments in information technology that we are currently witnessing. Many of these increased options are appropriately characterized as providing greater freedom from space-time constraints. The availability of large-capacity storage devices in the home, (video cassettes now, video discs and semiconductor memories soon) and the resulting possibility of storing TV programs frees one, at least potentially, from braodcast schedules: One can record one's favorite programs automatically and view them at one's convenience. Similarly, the prospect of inexpensive dial-up movies piped into the home over cable or beamed by satellite transmission will free one from the necessity of going to a theatre at a particular place and time in order to see a film of one's choice. Electronic mail will eliminate some of the constraints that characterize the telephone and conventional mail: One does not have to make connection with the recipient of a message (no busy-signal or unanswered-phone problems) so one can send a message at one's convenience; one need not know where the recipient is, inasmuch as his mailbox is accessible wherever he may happen to be. Teleconferencing presumably will reduce the need for travel by providing another means of eliminating a space constraint. Computer networks linking homes and offices will make it possible for many jobs to be performed, at least in part, in the home; more generally, networks with broadband communication capabilities providing remote access to widely distributed information resources will mean for many people that their ability to do their jobs will be much less dependent on where they happen to be located at any particular time—or on the constancy of that location. Examples of how space-time constraints will be decreased by further developments in information technology can easily be multiplied. That this is one of the effects the technology will have seems certain, and unless one believes with Fromm that freedom is a heavy burden, one cannot help but see this as a major plus. But this is not to say that accommodating to these developments will not require solving some problems. Moreover it is undoubtedly much easier to anticipate the positive effects of these developments than the negative ones.

Another possible implication of information technology for individual liberty is more worrisome. Although information may not imply control, no control system can operate effectively without information, and the more complete the information it has, the more control it can exercise. Wiener understood this principle very well, and he worried about it. He was undoubtedly bothered, as are many technologists, by the inefficiencies that are apparent in the way our society is organized and governed. He wondered, however, whether perhaps these inefficiencies had been our salvation.

> As engineering technique becomes more and more able to achieve human purposes, it must become more and more accustomed to formulate human purposes. In the past, a partial and inadequate view of human purpose has been relatively innocuous only because it has been accompanied by technical limitations that made it difficult for us to

perform operations involving a careful evaluation of human purpose. This is only one of the many places where human impotence has hitherto shielded us from the full destructive impact of human folly (1964, p. 64).

To paraphrase Wiener only slightly: the need to be explicit and precise about human purposes becomes acute only when one has the means of carrying out those purposes. As long as our technology is impotent relative to the other forces that shape our destinies, whether or not we worry about purpose may make little difference; but once our technical capabilities are sufficiently powerful to play a significant role in shaping our future, best we think about what kind of future we want it to be. Congressman Brown touched on this theme in speaking of the need for the definition of goals and, in particular, the definition of goals on which government, industry, and academia can agree. This is, I believe, a point the importance that is difficult to overstate.

I want now to return to a question addressed by Dr. Sheil, namely, that of whether we are in fact living in an age of unusually rapid change. It is an important question, because if the answer is yes, the rate of change itself is an important social as well as technological phenomenon, and the problem of coping with it is not a trivial one. Sheil contends that our perception of unusually rapid change is an *illusion* that stems from the fact that we are more keenly attuned to events that are close to the present than to those that are more remote from us in time. The perceived extraordinariness of the rate of change in our own era is a most ordinary consequence of our egocentrism, he suggests, and we may assume that our predecessors perceived their eras to be quite as unusual as we perceive ours to be.

I find this suggestion truly thought provoking and in some respects compelling, but I must admit that having been stimulated to think about it, I find the illusion, if it be that, to be an extremely persistent one. Might it be that the perceived increased rate of change is partly illusory and partly real? The fact, if it is a fact, that people in previous times believed themselves to be living in an era of accelerating change does not carry the logical implication that that belief when applied to the present is necessarily false. Whether it is true or false of the present is independent of how often it has been held, truly or falsely, in the past. Sheil has suggested a plausible explanation for the belief that does not depend on its empirical truth, but in doing so he has not ruled out the possibility that it is in fact true.

There is another point to make about the conjecture that people in previous eras have, like we, believed themselves to be living in times of accelerating change. Egocentrism notwithstanding, they may have been quite right. It may be that the rate of change *has* been increasing not only recently but for a very long time. I believe one could make a strong case for this position. Accepting this notion need not, however, provide one with great comfort for the indefinite future. There are many processes that can be accelerated safely for a limited time but not indefinitely. Moreover, any process that grows by doubling periodically can be deceptively benign until the moment that it becomes catastrophically destructive.

The important question that must be asked about the current rate of change, not only of change that is technologically based but of other types as well, is not whether it is greater than in the past but whether we are maximizing our chances of coping with it effectively. I do not believe it is wise to assume that the mechanisms that have worked in the past will continue to do so in the future. Indeed, what is the evidence that they *have* worked in the past? As mentioned above, at least one noted technologist has suggested that the fact that we have survived as long as we have as a species may owe less to our genius for adapting to change than our good fortune in remaining so impotent so long.

My excuse for this lengthy comment on the question of whether or not we really are living in an era of unusually rapid change is that I think it is a particularly important question, especially from the point of view of the potential impact of technology on society. If the change really is as rapid as it appears to be, and if it really is accelerating, the ability to accommodate gracefully to it will become an increasing challenge in the future. That is not to suggest we cannot learn to do it; but only that the problem may be worth more thought than we have been prepared to give it in the past.

Before leaving the topic of the social implications of information technology, I would like to mention one subject that, unfortunately, does not receive much attention in this book: that is, the potential that information technology holds of providing new educational, vocational, social, and recreational opportunities for disabled people. There are many possibilities:

- Jobs brought to the home-bound through computer networks and computer-mediated message technology.
- Portable computer-based reading machines for the blind.
- The possibility of dynamic computer-driven full-page braille displays.
- The possibility of computer-mediated teaching of reading to illiterate adults.
- Speech production and speech recognition devices for persons with communication disorders.
- The possibility of smart devices to give paralyzed people greater control over their immediate environments.

A conscious effort to find ways to apply information technology to the amelioration of problems that people with various types of disabilities have is clearly in the interest of striving for the equity to which Congressman Brown refers. Moreover, it is not safe to assume that equity issues will take care of themselves. It has not been true in the past that technological developments have benefited all people, even within a given society, equally. In particular, it is not difficult to find instances in which products of technology have served to widen the opportunity gap between people with certain types of disabilities and people without them. How well information technology will serve the needs of disabled people will depend very directly, I believe, on the amount of effort that is devoted explicitly to this objective by people who understand both the technological possibilities and the needs that should be addressed.

## WHAT ROLE(S) CAN PSYCHOLOGISTS
## PLAY IN SHAPING
## THIS TECHNOLOGY?

What if all the engineering psychologists and human factors specialists in the world suddenly disappeared from the scene? How might the absence of this influence be expected to impact the development of information technology in the 1980s? How would information technology be different in 1990 than it will be given that the profession is around and doing its thing during those ten years? One could make a plausible case that engineering psychology, as a discipline, has not had a great impact on the development of information technology to date. Will it in the future?

Drs. Dooling and Klemmer made the point that, at least insofar as consumer products are concerned, the marketplace acts to promote good designs from a human factors point of view. Products that require too much of their users are driven out of the market by competing products of superior design. As a result of marketplace pressures, one sees a trend toward greater ease of use in many products of technology. Dooling and Klemmer cited the automobile and the color TV set as two examples. So why the need for human factors input to the design process? What one can hope to accomplish, they point out, is to anticipate the demands of the marketplace by laboratory studies, thereby accelerating the process of getting technological products to meet well their users' needs.

I believe there is another answer to the question as well. Information technology in the future will present to applied psychology some old problems in new guises, but it will present some new problems as well. Some of these problems will have to do with designing technological tools so as to assure their usefulness and their useability. Others will have to do with understanding and influencing the impact of the introduction of these tools on society in general and on the quality of the lives of the individuals who use or are affected by them in particular. The latter type of problem will, I believe, grow in importance as the tools of information technology increase in complexity and power. Professor Holton's call for more emphasis on basic research motivated by social concerns is an eminently timely one, and it should find a sympathetic audience among psychologists. Who should be more sensitive to the importance of assuring that technology serves human needs? And who should be more aware of the danger of assuming that it will do so automatically in the absence of energetic efforts directed consciously toward that end?

What are the specific challenges that information technology will provide to psychologists in the near-term future? The following list, while certainly not exhaustive, includes I believe, many of the most important ones:

- Design of person-computer interfaces, with particular attention to the intellective or cognitive aspects of computer uses.
- Studies of person-computer interaction, and especially of the effects of new developments such as speech I/O.
- The development of more effective information-handling procedures.
- Facilitation of accommodation to change.
- The study, and development, of user models of information systems.
- Studies of the cognition of programming.
- Involvement in the introduction of "intelligent" devices and programs in the workplace.
- Attempts to understand and, when possible, to anticipate social implications of information technology.
- Work on the problem of dealing with complexity, as, for example, the problem of designing VLSI circuits with a million or more components.
- Participation in the development of user-oriented languages.
- Participation in the preparation of training material, user aids, and other documentation.
- Participation in the development of effective ways of interacting with very large data bases.
- Studies of potential misuses of information technology and development of effective methods for precluding them.
- Development of effective methods for measuring workload in person-machine system contexts in which the demands on the person are largely cognitive.
- Studies aimed at improving the allocation of function between people and computers in interactive systems.
- Development of methods for maintaining the skill and motiva-

tion of people who act primarily as monitors of automated systems but have to be ready to take over in case of system failure.

- Studies of effects of new (or anticipated) developments in information technology on people's perceptions of themselves, attitudes toward jobs, and so on.

- Studies of how such developments as electronic mail, computer-based office systems, and teleconferencing systems change the ways in which people communicate with each other.

- Projections of how the introduction of new technology-based methods in a workplace are likely to change productivity and attitudes and studies of changes the actual introduction of new methods have caused.

- Studies of new intellectual tools and approaches to problem solving that may be identified in information technology.

- Studies of goals and the explication of purpose.

Many of these topics were touched upon by the participants in this symposium. Professor Chapanis identified what he considers to be a variety of ways in which current computer systems fail to meet acceptable human factors standards. Drs. Dooling and Klemmer described some human factors work that is being done at Bell Laboratories in connection with the design of computer-based business telephone systems and the introduction of these systems to users. Dr. Sheil touched on the question of the role that psychologists might play in the design of information systems and had some harsh words for the approach that has sometimes been taken of criticizing specific features of existing systems without considering the constraints and tradeoffs that may have necessitated those features. Dr. Goldstein reviewed some work on needs assessment and training and pointed out the importance of these functions for the users of information technology in the coming decade. Dr. Fletcher documented the fact that technical training has become an increasingly troublesome problem in the military and emphasized the importance not only of better training methods but of minimizing the need for training insofar as possible by improvements in design. In what follows, I will comment on just a few of the many ideas that caught my attention in these papers.

## What Is Wrong with Current Systems?

I find myself in agreement with much of what Chapanis had to say about what is wrong with computer software. However, I confess to feeling that his general assessment of computer software usability is unduly critical of computer scientists and engineers who have developed that software. In my view, interface problems and human factors problems notwithstanding, computer scientists have been impressively productive over the past two or three decades and have given us some tools, the power of which we are only beginning to appreciate. The fact that all of these tools are not yet readily available to the untrained user is not necessarily an indictment of the work that has been done. The fact that they exist at all is a spectacular accomplishment. Moreover, some system developers have been quite sensitive to user needs and preferences and have done remarkably good jobs of being responsive to them, given the constraints under which they have had to work. To be sure, functionality has been of greater concern than the interface but understandably so. Unless one has a system that is capable of doing something of interest, there is little point in worrying about how to make it easy for someone to use.

With respect to the unnaturalness of programming languages, I agree that there is much room for improvement. It is well to acknowledge, however, that very significant advances have been made. The language of a computer, after all, is binary logic. Programs are represented by patterns of bits stored in collections of bistable devices. The program is interpreted and executed when these bit patterns are fed, usually one constant-length string at a time, into logic circuitry that can decode them (interpret them as instructions) and execute them. When computers first appeared on the scene, it was necessary to program them at the level of these bit strings. The programming languages that are available today are very much closer to "natural" language than were those original codes. If one traces the evolution of programming languages one sees a number of developments, each of which was a step in the direciton of naturalizing the representation and making it easier to use.

Perhaps the first small step in this direction was that of representing bit strings as octal rather than binary numbers. A second step was to represent operation codes with simple mnemonic labels such as "lac" (for load accumulator), "dac" (deposit accumulator), "add," "sub," and so on, and to represent memory addresses with symbolic names. Thus one could produce a sequence of instructions such as lac A, add B, dac C, which meant "load the accumulator with the contents of memory location A, add the contents of memory location B, and deposit the result in memory location C." It was a small step conceptually, but a large one technically, to go to a symbology more similar to ordinary algebraic notation and to permit a representation such as $C = A + B$, which meant replace the contents of memory location C with the sum of the contents of memory locations A and B. Numerous developments in computer language design have followed these early steps. A fair way to characterize them is as efforts to make the languages more nearly like the languages that people ordinarily use and to put an increasingly large percentage of the burden onto the computer of translating from the language in which a program is written into a bit string representation that the computer can execute. While I doubt that anyone would argue that the languages that now exist are really "natural" languages, major steps in that direction clearly have been made and are continuing to be made.

Whether the ultimate objective should be to permit users to interact with computers in a fully natural language, if "natural" is taken to mean "ordinary," is a debatable question (Hill, 1972; Nickerson, 1976). Clearly, computer languages can and should be improved in many ways so as to be more understandable and convenient to use. Ordinary conversational language lacks precision, however, and whether what would be gained by way of naturalness would be worth the cost in terms of vagueness and ambiguity remains to be seen.

## Ease of Use

A theme that emerged many times at this symposium is the importance of making information technology in general, and computers in particular, easy to use. I suspect it would be hard to find anyone who would quarrel with that theme. Certainly I do not intend to do so. One can not dutifully fulfill the role of discussant without saying something contentious, however, so I will argue that, like most good things, this theme can be carried too far. While ease of use is a worthy goal for a system developer to strive for, by itself it is neither a necessary nor a sufficient condition for user acceptability. The objective of ease of use must be viewed in the context of what it is one wants the system to be able to do and the constraints within which the system developer has to work. When simplicity is bought at the expense of functionality, or at the cost of a large fraction of limited resources, whether it is a good trade depends on who the buyer is.

We have already noted the trend toward simplification and naturalization of computer languages. However, at the same time one sees another phenomenon. As some languages, particularly those in the tradition of algebraic compilers, have become simpler and closer in form to more familiar representational schemes, qualitatively different languages have been developed in response to what some computer scientists have seen as severe limitations of these algebraically oriented languages. Notable examples are the list processing languages and in particular the several variants of LISP that are widely used by people working in the area of machine intelligence, knowledge-based systems, and the like. It is not clear that such languages will ever become trivially easy to use. They are proving, however, to be extremely powerful, especially for dealing with certain types of highly complex operations and organizations. It may well be that in some cases simplicity can be gained only at some significant cost in terms of power.

It seems at least a plausible hypothesis that it is not complexity per se that people dislike, but senseless, unnecessary complexity. One does not want to have to cope with a complex machine when a simple one would do just as well, or to perform a complex task when a simple one would accomplish the same purpose. But some things are inherently complex, and it may be that one can simplify them only by making them into qualitatively different things. In such cases the price of simplicity may be too great. At least certain types of programming may require inherently complex activity, and efforts to simplify it to the point that anyone can do it may be bound to fail.

One can make an argument that the major factor in determining whether products of technology have been used in the past is not how easy they are to use but whether or not they provide the users with capabilities that they really want. The telephone and the automobile permit an interesting comparison in this regard. Both address basic human needs, or at least deep desires, the one to communicate with people at a distance and the other to facilitate getting oneself from one place to another. Both help us to overcome some of the constraints of space and time, and both are extensively used. The telephone and the automobile differ considerably, however, with respect to the ease with which one can learn to use them, the complexity of the user-machine interface, the continuing demands they place on the user for attentiveness to the task, and the potential consequence of failing to perform the task adequately. The fact that automobiles are driven makes the point that it is not ease of use that determines the acceptability of a product of technology but the extent to which the product provides one with something one really wants.

A particular danger relating to ease of use as a design criterion is that of focusing on what is easy for the novice user to the extent of forgetting the expert. The strategy of evaluating a system's design features by doing short-term experiments with novice users involves the assumption that what is good for the novice is good for the expert. That may be a safe assumption in some cases but not in others. Given two designs, A and B, it does not follow from the fact that novices find A easier to learn to use than B, that A will prove to be the superior system (more efficient, better liked) by expert users. A tricycle is certainly easier to learn to ride than is a bicycle. But most cyclists apparently feel that the advantages the latter offers over the former to a skilled cyclist justifies the greater learning effort.

I realize that these comments might appear to challenge the inviolability of what may be the most widely espoused human factors objective for system design. My purpose is not to question the appropriateness of the ease-of-use principle as a design goal, but simply to argue that the principle itself may not always be as easy to use as we sometimes assume. It must be interpreted and applied in the context of the other objectives that the designer is trying to realize, and especially those objectives that relate to functionality—what it is one wants a competent user of the system to be able to do.

## Training

Training is often viewed as what one resorts to in order to accommodate the complexities of system operation that one has not been able to eliminate by clever engineering design. Dooling, Klemmer, Fletcher, and Chapanis emphasized the importance of designing systems in such a way that training requirements are minimized. The issue, Dooling and Klemmer assert, is not whether consumers are prepared to master the new technology, but whether human factors specialists are up to making sure the new products and services are designed to be compatible with human capabilities and limitations. But even given the minimization of training requirements as a goal, one can seldom hope to do away with them completely. And as long as we are stuck with them, the question is how to meet them effectively.

Dooling and Klemmer touched on three aspects of training that seem to me to deserve emphasis: (1) the importance of selecting the right amount of material to be covered in a given time, (2) the importance (or lack thereof) of hands-on experience with a system and live tutorial instruction during training, and (3) the merits of the strategy of training around performance aids. It is important to note that they restricted their comments about the effectiveness of training to *casual* users of a computer-based phone system (or other comparable systems). They do not intend for them to be applied to situations in which the device or system is a primary tool that one is obliged to use in order to discharge one's job responsibilities.

The importance of selecting the right amount of information to present in a given time is obvious, but how much is enough is not. Providing too much information at once runs the risk of overload and a consequent failure to absorb what is being taught. But failure to provide training with respect to all system features may have the result that an individual uses a system for a long time in a less-than-optimal fashion. One may learn to do things in an inefficient way and never discover that there are more efficient alternatives. One may fail to discover certain powerful features that the system has.

With respect to hands-on training, Dooling and Klemmer questioned the need for it for users of such things as business telephone systems, computer terminals and electronic calculators. Learning the operations of such systems is primarily a cognitive skill, they claim, not a motor skill. The main problems encountered by the learner involve memory:

"remembering the purpose and meaning of all the features and remembering the correct sequence of operations for activating them." They cited the results of two studies that showed hands-off and self-instructional training for operation of a business phone system to be as effective as hands-on training. Such a finding has considerable practical significance because hands-on training tends to be relatively expensive.

I find these results to be surprising but can offer nothing but intuition to make a case as to why they should be. While it is easy to agree with the assertion that the cognitive demands of learning how to operate a business phone system are much greater than the motor demands, I would have guessed that taking the trainee through the steps of performing the operations that are to be learned would be a relatively effective way of assuring that his cognitive apparatus is engaged. The result that Dooling and Klemmer obtained deserves to be followed up in contexts other than that of the business phone system and in particular with computer terminals and electronic calculators, as they suggested. If it holds it will be a very significant finding indeed.

There is a fair amount of evidence to suggest that how well people learn some new skill depends strongly on how much "engaged time" they spend on the learning task. One may speculate that hands-on training situations and other approaches that force the trainees to attend to the task may have their major effect in assuring that the trainees are in fact "engaged" during the learning session. If one begins with individuals who are highly motivated to acquire the skills that are being taught, such motivational aids may be unnecessary. Thus highly motivated learners may acquire as much from a well written manual as from a formal training session structured so as to force attention to the task. Whether the same will be true for less highly motivated trainees is another question.

Dooling and Klemmer's observation that trainees were less satisfied with hands-off and self instructional techniques than with hands-on and teacher instruction approaches invites speculation. Is it that trainees simply *like* the experience of hands-on practice? Is it that they enjoy the social aspects of the class situation? Do they feel that the company's interest in saving money by not providing hands-on training is an indication that it does not attach as much value to their training as it should? Might they feel that skills that can be acquired without hands-on experience or the use of an instructor are somehow less estimable than those that cannot? Clearly there are some questions here for research.

The last aspect of training on which Dooling and Klemmer touched has to do with the strategy of getting leverage from a training program by focusing it on the use of performance aids. One role performance aids can play for the experienced user of a system as well as for the novice is that of serving as an extension of one's memory. Aids are useful, however, only to the extent that one understands *how* to use them effectively. The acquisition of this understanding, Dooling and Klemmer suggested, should be one of the goals of a training program. The purpose of the aids they used was to provide users with details of the operation of a business phone system. On the assumption that these aids would be available to the user at all times, the goals of the training session were to give the user a general understanding of the operation of the system and some experience in consulting the performance aids for details. This seems to me to be an eminently reasonable approach and one that may be effective in a wide variety of situations.

The problem of designing effective user aids is an important one in its own right, but it relates to the problem of training rather directly. This is especially apparent in the case of on-line aids for users of complex computer systems. One difficulty is that of designing aids that satisfy the needs of users with different degrees of general expertise and experience with that particular system. Another is that of providing the kinds of aids that will facilitate the process by which the novice becomes an expert (Nickerson and Pew, 1977).

Another problem relating to training of users of computer systems involves the question of the conceptual models that people have of such systems. Many of the people who use computers now, and many more who will do so in the future, have no training in computer technology. What kinds of conceptual models of the systems with which they interact do these users develop spontaneously? What kinds should they be given as part of their training in system use?

Most people, whether trained in computer technology or not, probably view the computer as a qualitatively different kind of machine than others with which we have become familiar, and consequently their models of other machines and how they work are not helpful in understanding computers. Unfortunately, although computers resemble people in some ways more than they do other machines, our general knowledge about human beings that helps us understand the behavior of a particular person in a particular situation is not very effective when we use it to help us understand the behavior of a computer. On the contrary, it gets us into trouble because many of the capabilities we take for granted in human beings are lacking in these machines, and when we forget that fact our expectations for the machines will be unrealistic and will eventuate in confusion and frustration.

Paradoxically, some of the efforts to "humanize" computers, to make user-computer interactions more "natural" and interfaces more "friend-ly," have probably contributed to the confusion and amplified the frustration. Having the computer refer to the user by name, intersperse its output with folksy prattle and emotive or humorous expressions, make extensive use of synonyms to avoid repetitiveness, and so on, may create the impression of a machine that is far more flexible and intelligent than it really is. Then users, having been led to believe they are dealing with something like a human being, are likely to interpret the many manifestations of extreme rigidity that they will encounter as obstinacy, or worse, and to respond in emotional and nonproductive ways. If not done with great care, the addition of speech I/O capabilities to existing systems could exacerbate this problem.

The topic of user models prompts the following general question: what degree of understanding of a system should be attained by its various users? Or, more basically, how does one determine what that degree of understanding should be? A particularly interesting variant of this question relates to managers. Especially since the introduction of information technology into many work situations, managers often find themselves responsible for the operation of equipment and processes that they understand only very superficially if at all. It probably is unrealistic to expect every manager to understand in detail the operation of all the machines for which he is responsible; but can one expect a person to make rational decisions and fair judgments about the performance of the machines and the people who operate them unless he has some level of understanding of how they (the machines and the people) do what they do? But how much is enough?

## Programmer Training

The type of computer user that received the greatest amount of attention at this symposium is the user who is not knowledgeable with respect to computers. While it seems clear that the number of users fitting this descripton will increase greatly in the future, it is also well to remember that users who do have some knowledge of computers, or who want to use one in a more than casual way—including ways requiring that they program it themselves—will also increase greatly in numbers, as they have been doing for some time. This being the case, a far better understanding of what programming is all about—understanding what constitutes skill in programming and how it is acquired—is a worthy subject for psychological research.

Dr. Sheil suggested that programming is a knowledge-based skill in much the same way that chess playing is a knowledge-based skill. That is to say, the expertise of the skilled programmer is attributable in some measure to a very large amount of knowledge he has stored about specific programming tasks and situations and about tools and procedures that are applicable to them. We know from the work of DeGroot (1965) and of Simon and his colleagues (Chase and Simon, 1973; Simon and Gilmartin, 1973) that one of the major differences between an expert chess player and a novice is the fact that the expert can recognize a very large number of board configurations, whereas the novice cannot. Moreover, the knowledge that permits the kind of pattern recognition that underlies expert chess playing is typically acquired over a period of many years (Simon, 1980). Recently Hayes (1980) has argued that many, if not most, of the types of activities that are usually considered to be creative are in large part knowledge-based skills. Data that he has gathered suggest that the more famous composers, painters, and other artists typically have not produced master works during the first ten years of their active careers.

To the extent that programming, at least the kind of programming that we would consider highly creative programming, is a knowledge-based skill, designers of formal training programs for such programmers must give some thought to the nature of the knowledge that skilled programming requires and to the question of how to facilitate the acquisition of that knowledge. Perhaps one should not think about how to train a person to be a skillful programmer, but about how to teach one *how to become* a skillful programmer. Perhaps what one needs to do is get the novice started—pointed in the right direction—and give him the tools to acquire the information that he will need if he is to develop his potential.

The training of programmers is a special problem for the immediate future for at least three reasons. First, software is widely acknowledged to be the major limitation to more effective uses of information technology as hardware advances continue to outdistance advances in software development. Second, the demand for programmers and systems analysts already exceeds the supply, and the gap is expected to widen in the next few years. Third, programming is still more of an art than a science, and therefore the teaching of it is especially challenging. Pannenborg (1981) put it this way: "There is no equivalent to Maxwell's laws in software. I still have no method to prove whether a program is correct or not, whether it is consistent or not. I don't even have a yardstick for gauging the efficiency of a certain program. So what I do, in effect, is write poetry. Other 'poets' look at it and say, 'Well, that sounds very beautiful, or it's just rubbish'" (p. 149).

## General Training and Education

In keeping with the emphasis of this symposium, the above comments relating to training have been focused on the problem of training people as users of information technology. But the rapidity of change, and particularly of technological change, represents a serious challenge to general training and education to provide people with the skills and attitudes that will be required for them to cope with a future that will probably change even more rapidly than has the recent past.

Dr. Fletcher reminded us of the immense investment the Department of Defense has made in training. He also provided some sobering statistics to make the point that the quality and effectiveness of this training must be dramatically improved if the military is to assure the ability to operate and maintain its increasingly sophisticated systems successfully.

In discussing the demands that will be placed on training technology in military contexts in the future, Fletcher identified four criteria that the technology must satisfy: (1) it must be accessible at job sites, (2) it must be used, (3) it must be relevant to the job for which the training is intended (it must provide practice on the job itself or on an adequate simulation of it), and (4) it must be intelligent in the sense of being tutorial and adaptable to the individual student's needs. Probably few people would argue with the second and third of these criteria; indeed, they may seem sufficiently obvious that mentioning them is unnecessary. Obvious or not, the fact is that they often are not observed, and Fletcher suggested some reasons why this is the case. The first and fourth criteria may be more controversial, but Fletcher's arguments in their support are quite persuasive. Although Fletcher's discussion relates specifically to the training needs of the military, his observations regarding how instructional technology must develop if its potential is to be realized apply to nonmilitary contexts as well; and his suggestion that the full exploitation of information technology for training purposes will require some radically new perspectives is a compelling one.

With respect to general education, the need for new perspectives may be particularly acute. If enrollment continues to decline as it is expected to do during the coming decade, the number of openings for new faculty will continue to decrease as well. Consequently, the people who will be delivering educational services to the youth of this country ten years from now will, for the most part, be the same people who are doing it today, except that they will be ten years older. This is not a particularly cheery thought, especially if one subscribes to the notion that there is an increasing need to prepare students to deal effectively with rapid change.

Information technology, which is part of the problem by virtue of its contribution to the rapidity of the rate of change, also may provide the prospect of at least a partial solution. The educational possibilities for this technology are, without question, very great. Particularly exciting is the potential for the development and widespread use of truly individualized and adaptive instructional procedures. The extent to which that potential will be realized remains to be seen. It is a worthy challenge for psychologists, educators, and information technologists alike.

### Procedural Reasoning

For me, a particularly interesting point that was made at this symposium was Dr. Sheil's assertion that the most important technical characteristic of information technology is its introduction of the notion of *procedural reasoning*. This "fundamentally new idea," he suggested, introduces a different type of logic, requires the development of a new set of skills, and will change fundamentally the way we think about many problems. What exactly is meant by procedural reasoning is not entirely clear. Two possibilities are: (1) thinking *about* procedures and (2) thinking *in terms of* procedures. Perhaps Sheil had both possibilities in mind. One cannot understand the behavior of computers wihtout knowing about procedures; one cannot use them effectively without being able to think procedurally.

Sheil is not alone in his assessment of the importance of "procedural literacy." Minsky (1967), for example, has referred to the idea of an effective procedure, or algorithm, as

> a technical idea that has crystallized only fairly recently but already promises to be as important to the practical culture of modern scientific life as were the ideas of geometry, calculus, or atoms. It is a vital intellectual tool for working with or trying to build models of intricate, complicated systems—be they minds or engineering systems. Its most obvious application is to computation and computers, but I believe it is equally valuable for clear thinking about biological, psychological, mathematical, and (especially) philosophical questions (p. 8).

These are large claims, and claims that should be of particular interest to psychologists.

The suggestion that the idea of procedural reasoning owes its existence to information technology and, in particular, to the digital computer may well be challenged; however, the activity of programming computers undoubtedly has given it a prominence it otherwise would not have. A closely related idea, and one that also owes its prominence, at least in large measure, to the computer, is the idea that one way to acquire an understanding of a process (or to determine the extent to which the process is or is not understood) is to attempt to simulate it—which is to say to procedurize it.

Sheil noted that one contribution that psychologists could make to the effective utilization of information technology is that of studying "naive procedural semantics" for the purpose of understanding better how people not trained in computer science use procedures or quasi-procedures in their everyday lives, e.g., for giving instructions, specifying recipes, and giving directions regarding how to go from place to place. Unfortunately, although people do reason procedurally to some extent, independently of their involvement with computers, their reasoning tends to be highly anthropomorphic. Instructions written for another human being, for example, typically rely very heavily on knowledge that the recipient of those instructions brings to the situation. In writing instructions for computers, people not trained in computer science often appear to make the same (tacit) assumptions about the computer that they make about other people. A better understanding of how people naturally think about procedures is an important step, Sheil contends, in the direction of better equipping us to exploit effectively the potential that information technology represents.

The notion that procedural literacy is essential to the understanding of computers and their capabilities in anything but the most superficial way, I find quite compelling. Procedural literacy, with the implied understanding of such concepts and principles as parameterized procedures, hierarchical program organizations with nested subroutines, the importance of precision and completeness in procedure specification, clearly is important, if not essential, for anyone who wants to understand computers or to use them effectively. Would that we had some proven effective procedures for developing procedural literacy. But such procedures as we have are not demonstrably effective, and until we have some that are, this is another challenge that psychologists, educators, and information technologists can share.

## The Management of Complexity

A theme that was touched upon by several of the symposium participants is that of the problem of dealing with or managing complexity. The problem of software complexity has been a concern for some time because of the rapidly increasing disparity between the cost of hardware and the cost of the software that is needed to make it run. It is well known, for example, that the cost of the development of the software to operate complex systems now typically exceeds the cost of the hardware in those systems and sometimes by very considerable margins.

There now exist many programs that are far too complex to be understood in detail by a single individual. When the operation of a system depends upon the running of such a program, one has an interesting situation. Who is to verify that the program, both as a whole and with respect to all its parts, is working properly? And who is to guarantee that the system will do what it is intended to do in every contingency? (A related problem is that of assuring that complex software can be understood by people other than those who developed it. This is often the practical problem faced by people who have to operate and maintian systems when the people who originally programmed them are no longer available to debug the "crashes" that inevitably occur.)

The fact that programs can be developed that are sufficiently complex that no single person understands all the details of their operation raises an interesting notion, namely, that of corporate intelligence. It seems reasonable to assume that, at least potentially, the intelligence that is possessed by a group of individuals exceeds in some meaningful sense the intelligence of any member of the group. How to realize that potential and to combine the intelligence of the members of the group so the result is, in fact, better than the best of the parts is not clear. A form of this problem that is particularly relevant to the focus of this book is how to insure that computer programs that are produced by collaborative efforts of groups of skilled programmers represent the corporate intelligence of those groups.

The problem of complexity is also encountered in microelectronics. It is already possible to fabricate VLSI circuits that are almost too complex for people to design. With submicron technology becoming a reality within the next few years, we have the prospects of circuits containing a million or more gates. The design of such circuits will probably be impossible, and certainly impractical, without the help of computer-based aids.

Given currently available design tools, the cost of designing an integrated circuit has been estimated as approximately $100 per gate (Robinson, 1980a). If the cost per gate stayed constant as the number of gates per chip increased, the cost to develop a million-gate chip would be prohibitive. Moreover, the complexity of the design process undoubtedly increases more than linearly with the number of gates per chip, inasmuch as the organization of the gates represents a key component of the problem. Decreasing the cost of the gate by small amounts does not really constitute a solution. Even if the per gate cost could be reduced by a factor of ten, it would still cost $10 million to develop a million-gate chip. Very substantial improvements must be made in the design process, and this probably can only be done with the use of computer-based aids.

Some impressive beginnings have been made in the direction of giving the computer the ability to perform the more tedious low-level aspects of the design task, thereby freeing the designer to function at a relatively high conceptual level. What is happening now in the area of microcircuit design is analogous in many respects to what happened in programming two decades ago. Design "languages" are being developed that will "compile" high-level specifications of circuits into detailed layouts. The designer is able to think in terms of such things as programmed logic arrays, shift registers, and input pads and leave it to the computer to translate the designer's description into an appropriate arrangement of logic gates. Of course, producing the software that can translate high-level descriptions into detailed circuit layouts is no trivial task. The further development of such software and, more generally, the production of better tools to facilitate the design of integrated circuits promise to be among the most exciting activities of computer scientists in the years just ahead.

Some of the social, political, and economic problems that are encountered in today's world are also sufficiently complex that no single person understands them in their entirety. The question arises as to whether information technology provides a means, or at least the potential for developing the means, of representing those problems in such a way as to make them amenable to solution through the combined efforts of many individuals.

## CONCLUDING REMARKS

In the concluding section of this chapter, I want to return to the theme with which Professor Holton began this symposium: the fourth discontinuity. Recall that Holton mentioned three conceptual discontinuities that Sigmund Freud had claimed, early in this century, had been eliminated by the work of Copernicus, Darwin, and himself. Copernicus' insistence that the sun does not revolve about the earth removed us from the center of the cosmic stage and prepared the way for a cosmology that views our planet as an insignificant speck in an unimaginably complex universe and as very probably not unique in any respect. Darwin's unsettling claims regarding our aboreal ancestry appeared to eliminate our status as creatures physically distinct from and superior to the animal kingdom. Freud's speculations about the role of primitive and unconscious needs and impulses as determinants of personality and behavior blurred several distinctions that had been easily maintained before and, in particular, challenged the psychological distinction between humankind and the animal kingdom much as Darwin's work had challenged the physical distinction.

Each of these changes—each "giving way" of a perceived discontinuity to a perceived continuum—represented a radical adjustment in the way we view ourselves, an adjustment that, Professor Holton suggested, has not yet been made completely in any of these cases, in part because of the offensiveness of the changed views to our sensibilities. (As an aside, I do not believe that any of these changes need be viewed as a threat to human dignity, but I will not pursue that point here.)

Holton referred to a discussion by Bruce Mazlish of the elimination of the three discontinuities, a discussion in which Mazlish introduced the question of whether a fourth discontinuity—that between people and machines—may go the way of the other three. If I understand Professor Holton's comments on this point, he takes the view that this question has already been settled, and the discontinuity discarded; the discontinuity

that is currently being eliminated is the distinction between the imperatives that motivate science, technology, and society. I have already
commented on some of Professor Holton's thought-provoking observations in support of this thesis. Here I want to come back to the fourth
discontinuity mentioned by Mazlish, namely, the discontinuity between
human beings and machines.

The question takes on special significance, I believe, when we
consider the kinds of machines that have begun to be developed during
the last 30 years. Computers are quite unlike other machines with which
we are familiar. We usually think of machines as devices for changing
energy from one form to another and for accomplishing work in the
process. In the case of computing machines, energy transformation and
physical work are only incidental. The computer is designed to transform
information structures—not energy. It manipulates symbols—not forces.
In its behavior, it is more analogous to a person thinking than to a person
doing physical work.

This being the case, it is perhaps not surprising that descriptions of
what computers are and what they can do are often couched in
anthropomorphic terms. Thus, we sometimes see them referred to as
"electronic brains" and encounter claims that they "see," "read," "interpret," "decide," "understand," and so on. Some of this choice of
terminology is perhaps attributable to deliberate attempts to sensational-
ize. More often, one suspects, writers simply assume that readers will
understand that such terms are being used in a metaphorical way. One
also suspects that this is not a safe assumption and that readers may
sometimes infer more from these words than the writer intends (or
should intend) to imply by their use. In any case, computers do not, yet at
least, see or read or understand in the sense in which people see and read
and understand; whether they can be made to do so in time is a subject of
some debate.

On the other hand, while many of the claims of what computers can
do today are grossly exaggerated, one cannot deny that they can be made
to perform some impressive feats indeed. Already, they can do many
things that a very few years ago were considered uniquely human
capabilities. Moreover, as we have already noted, computer technology is
in its infancy and the rate at which this field is being developed is nothing
short of phenomenal. If we cannot say with confidence what machines
will be able to do several decades hence, neither can we say with certainty
what it is that they will not be able to do.

Even in the face of the ego-bruising reorientations forced on us by
the work of people like Copernicus, Darwin, and Freud, we still could
take some small comfort in the fact that at least on our own planet we had
no rivals in the domain of thought. Our intellectual superiority was
unquestioned. Indeed, the same scientists who had challenged our status

as the raison d'être of the universe were producing an impressive succession of evidences of our remarkable intellectual capacity and inventiveness. If we were not the center of the universe, it was beginning to appear that we had the wherewithal to become the masters of at least our corner of it. But now it would seem that science is about to deprive us of even that last shred of dignity and self-esteem and to expose us for the dunces that we really are. We are warned that the day is in sight when machines built with our own hands will find us too stupid even to make good opponents for games of our own invention.

Is there, in fact, not a discontinuity between human beings and machines? I believe strongly that there *is* a discontinuity and that that belief has implications not only for the way we view ourselves and each other but for the ways in which we treat ourselves and each other. My belief in the discontinuity is not based on the assumption of either physical or intellectual superiority. It is clear that machines can do many things in the nature of physical work that people cannot do. It is equally clear that they have some capabilities in the intellectual realm that also extend beyond those of human beings. Moreover, it is less clear that there are things that people can do, either physical or intellectual, that are, in principle, beyond the capabilities of a machine. My reasons, which are two, for wanting to maintain the qualitative distinction between people and machine are not based, therefore, on the assumption that people can do things that machines cannot do. My first reason is a philosophical bias that relates to the concept of consciousness, which I will not attempt to defend here. My second reason for maintaining this distinction, however, is germane to the focus of this symposium because it has to do with the way we relate to information technology and the goals we set with respect to that relationship.

Holton's reference to several philosopher-scientists and some of their views prompts me to cast my argument in the form of a variation on Pascal's wager. Consider the assertion that there is no qualitative difference between human beings and machines. The assertion may be true or it may be false. Moreover, there are two ways in which one can err with respect to one's belief regarding its truth or falsity. One may believe it to be true when it is really false, or one may believe it to be false when it is true. Assuming that one cannot find compelling evidence for its truth or falsity (an assumption that I make for purposes of this argument), one is left with a choice of the way in which one would least like to be wrong.

For me the choice is easy. I prefer to think of the machine as existing for the benefit of the human being and not the other way around. I want the person to occupy center stage as far as his relationship to machines is concerned. I prefer to think of him as the user and controller of the machine rather than as its partner. I want him to be the beneficiary of technology and not just a component in the technological mill. I want technology to be designed to meet human needs rather than to exploit human capabilities.

One philosopher-psychologist of some repute put forth the idea that there are meaningful questions that cannot be answered empirically, or what amounts to the same thing, questions for which each of two or more contradictory answers is equally defensible (James, 1897/1979). In such cases, he argues, one should select the answer one prefers. I think the question of whether there is a qualitative difference between human beings and machines may be such a question, at least given our current limited understanding of human beings. My preference, I am sure, is clear. My computer, of course, may see things quite differently. But we have been asked only to look into the future, not beyond it, and I feel reasonably comfortable in assuming that it will be at least a decade before my computer can express an opinion of its own.

## NOTE

[1]Since this chapter was written, Bell Laboratories has developed a microprocessor (the MAC-32) that has over 100,000 components on a single chip, and Hewlett-Packard has developed one with over 450,000 (Johnson, 1981).

## ACKNOWLEDGEMENTS

I am grateful to Theodore Baker, James Dooling, Edmund Klemmer, John Makhoul, Theodore Myer, Richard Pew, Joseph Psotka, and Albert Stevens for helpful comments on a draft of this chapter and of the Foreword to this volume. I also thank Anne Kerwin for her patient retyping of the manuscripts several times and her help in locating some obscure references that I had failed to capture when reading them.

## REFERENCES

Botkin, J.W., Elmandjra, M., and Malitza, M. No limits to learning: Bridging the human gap. Oxford, England: Pergamon Press, 1979.
Bylinsky, G. The Japanese chip challenge. Fortune, March 23, 1981, 115–22.
Chase, W.G. and Simon, H.A. Perception in chess. Cognitive Psychology, 1973, 4, 55–81.
Chaudhari, P., Giessen, B.C., and Turnbull, D. Metallic glasses, Scientific American, 1980, 242(4), 98–117.
DeGroot, A.D. Thought and choice in chess. The Hague: Mouton, 1965.
Hayes, J.R. Three problems in teaching general skills. Paper presented at NIE-LRDC conference on thinking and learning skills, Pittsburgh, Pa., October 8–12, 1980.

Hill, I.D. Wouldn't it be nice if we could write programs in ordinary English—or would it? *Computer Bulletin*, 1972, *16*, 306—12.

James, W. *The will to believe and other essays in popular philosophy*. Cambridge, Mass.: Harvard University Press, 1979. (Originally published, 1897).

Johnson, R.C. Thirty-two bit microprocessors inherit mainframe features. *Electronics*, February 24, 1981, 138-41.

Kahn, R.E. Submicron digital technology. Unpublished memorandum, Defense Advanced Research Projects Agency, Arlington, Va. 22209, June 6, 1978.

Leonard, M.G. Promise of RAM market pushes chip technology frontiers. *High Technology*, June 1980, *1*(5), 57—63.

Matiso, J. The superconducting computer. *Scientific American*, 1980, *242*(5), 50—65.

Miller, J.G. Living systems: Basic concepts. *Behavioral Science*, 1965, *10*, 193—237.

Minsky, M. *Computation: Finite and infinite machines*. Englewood Cliffs, N.J.: Prentice-Hall, 1967.

Nickerson, R.S. On conversational interaction with computers. In S. Treu (Ed.), *User-oriented design of interactive graphics systems, Proceedings of ACM/SIGGRAPH workshop*, October 1976, Pittsburgh, Pa., 101—13.

Nickerson, R.S., and Pew, R.W. Person-computer Interaction. In *The C³ system user, Vol. I: A review of research on human performance as it relates to the design and operation of command, control and communication systems*. BBN Report No. 3459. Cambridge, Mass.: Bolt Beranek and Newman, Inc., 1977.

Pannenborg, A.E. The future of electronics: Nine views from the top. *Electronic Design*, 1981, *29*(1), 148, 149.

Robinson, A.L. Are VLSI microcircuits too hard to design? *Science*, 1980a, *109*, 258—62.

———. Perilous times for U.S. microcircuit makers. *Science*, 1980b, *208*, 582—86.

Simon, H.A. Problem solving and education. In D.T. Tuma and F. Reif (Eds.), *Problem solving and education: Issues in teaching and research*. Hillsdale, N.J.: Lawrence Erlbaum Associates, 1980, 81—96.

Simon, H.A. and Gilmartin, K. A simulation of memory for chess positions. *Cognitive Psychology*, 1973, *5*, 29—46.

Toynbee, A.J. *A study of history*, (abridged by D.C. Somerrell). New York: Oxford University Press, 1946.

Wiener, N. *God & Golem, Inc.* Cambridge, Mass.: M.I.T. Press, 1964.

Young, J.A. The future of electronics: Nine views from the top. *Electronic Design*, 1981, *29*(1), 142, 143.

Ziegler, J.F. and Lanford, W.A. Effect of cosmic rays on computer memories. *Science*, 1979, *206*, 776—88.

# Appendix: Man – Computer Research at Johns Hopkins

## Alphonse Chapanis

*Editors' Note:*

   *At the time Professor Chapanis delivered his paper at the symposium he did not yet have authorization to reveal some aspects of the research he had been conducting that was funded by International Business Machines. As a result, this paper is included now to provide additional details regarding the research he discussed.*

Our current research at Johns Hopkins is directed toward the solution of some of the problems I have described in my paper in the main body of the book. Specifically, our goal is to design an interactive language so that a first-time user can learn how to use a powerful computer and engage in productive work easily, quickly, and with a minimum of frustration.

### OUR STARTING ASSUMPTIONS

Our research is based on these assumptions:

- The user will be a first-time user and, after that, only an occasional user.
- The user should learn how to use a computer with no written instructions except for what appears on the display screen.
- The user should learn how to use a computer without any outside help.
- The user does not necessarily know how to type initially.
- The user has the equivalent of a high school education.
- The user speaks, reads, and writes English.

238

Further, we are not dedicated to any particular computer, system, or programming language. Rather, our research is aimed at the discovery of general principles of design for interactive languages and computer terminals that can be applied to any of a large number of systems. In particular, we are not developing programs as such. We demonstrate only that our products are programmable, that is, that they can be programmed. We leave the precise details of programming to people who are much more competent than we are in these skills and who are capable of writing much more efficient programs than we can.

## ORGANIZATION OF THE PROJECT

Our project is organized as shown in Figure 1. As you see, I have made a distinction between two broad classes of studies: basic and applied. I have already referred to one of the basic studies, that by Miss Zoltan, in my earlier paper. The basic question that Miss Zoltan addressed was: "What attitudes do users have about the computer today?" The results of that study are still being analyzed.

### Language Levels for Computer Users

The second basic study, under the general supervision of Miss Joan Roemer, is directed toward a better understanding of the language levels that are most appropriate for various kinds of users. Specifically, she is using a computer display screen to test instructions and languages at three different reading levels, grades five, ten, and 15. These different language levels will be used by persons who themselves have different levels of reading skills. The subjects will be persons selected from the general population; they will not be college students. Performance will be assessed on a number of measures, among them, how quickly the subjects learn to use the computer and to complete a task. Although this study is well underway, I have no data to report at this time.

### An Introductory Tutorial

The first of the applied studies has to do with the preparation of an introductory tutorial under the supervision of Miss Janan Al-Awar. It's difficult to say whether this is complete or not. Nor can I really say what version we have at the moment. The reason for my uncertainty is that our methodology for preparing the introductory tutorial is a succession of trials and modifications. We write a section, try it out on some naive subjects, discover unforeseen difficulties, and modify the tutorial to

## The Johns Hopkins
## Real Hal
## Project

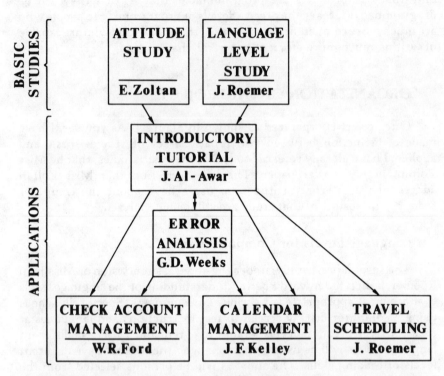

**Figure 1.** Organization of our research program.

obviate those difficulties. This sequence of test and modification has gone through so many cycles that it's difficult to pin down exactly where we are. My general impression is that the tutorial is in very good condition now. Our last few subjects went through the entire tutorial with essentially no problems.

The tutorial takes about one-half hour to complete. Although it is at the fifth-grade reading level, our subjects do not find it offensive or patronizing. Indeed, many subjects have found it fun. It takes the first-time user gently and easily through the operation of the computer terminal, teaching him the operation of essential keys: the alphanumeric, shift, enter, delete, erase input, erase end of field, insert mode, and marker control keys. At the end of the tutorial, there is a short review, which the user may or may not take, at his option. Among the special features that have been designed into the tutorial are these:

- The user is given a practical problem to work within the first five minutes. The purpose of the problem is to excite the user's interest and to show him that he can do something productive early in his training.

- Early in the tutorial the user is assured that he can do nothing to break the system. This is something that we have found many people apprehensive about.

- Early in the tutorial the user is assured that he can take all the time he wants. We found early in our work that some subjects thought they had to respond quickly or computer messages would go away.

- Default and error correcting routines are liberally interspersed throughout the whole tutorial to catch, anticipate, correct, or accept many common kinds of errors or difficulties that first-time users make or get into. On the terminal we're using, for example, users frequently hit the ENTER key when they intend to hit the SHIFT key. When an empty vector is sent to the computer for this reason, the computer comes back with a gentle message suggesting that the user may have made that kind of mistake. The error message then tells him what to do.

- The user is told several times how far he has gone in the tutorial and how much further he has to go.

- In teaching each key, the user is given a carefully graded set of examples to test his understanding and skill.

This tutorial is now being tested once more with a completely new set of first-time users. Our aim is to end up with a tutorial that can be completed successfully by 99 percent of first-time users with no outside help. I think we may be close to that goal.

## Error Analyses

The next applied project is concerned with error analyses. This is under the supervision of my colleague, Dr. Gerald D. Weeks. Since our goal is to have an interactive language that forgives simple human errors, we need to know the kinds of errors that people typically make. For this purpose, we have a device that captures every key stroke a subject makes, records it, and time stamps it. The records can then be played back for analysis. As you may infer from Figure 1, the error analysis uses inputs from all of the applied studies in our project. The importance and relevance of such an error analysis is so obvious that I don't think I need to elaborate on it any further at this time.

## A Travel Scheduling Program

Miss Al-Awar's tutorial is used as an introduction to three practical exercises, shown at the bottom of Figure 1, in which our concepts and our languages are being tested. The travel scheduling program will be used by Miss Roemer to evaluate the several language levels that she will be testing. This program is modeled after a genuine computerized system for making travel arrangements by air.

## Calendar and Checkbook Programs

The remaining two programs are also highly realistic and practical tasks. I emphasize the realism of our tasks because so many so-called natural language programs have been done with artificial puzzles or games. One of our programs, the calendar problem, is being done by Mr. John Kelley. The other, the checkbook management program, by Mr. W. Randolph Ford. As you may perhaps infer from its name, the calendar program asks the user to enter his appointments, routine and non-routine, into the computer. These appointments are then sorted and arranged by the computer. Conflicts in schedule or appointments are noted and called to the attention of the user. The user can also ask for a display of all his appointments for any particular day, or ask for information about a particular appointment, for example, "When do I meet with the treasurer to discuss budgets?" Or, "When am I supposed to meet my wife at the airport?"

The checkbook management program also does what its name suggests. The user can enter into the computer information about deposits to his checking account, checks he has written, and cash withdrawals. He can interrogate the computer about the balance in his account, about checks that have been written to, say, physicians during the past year, or about all checks that he has written in the past month. Two significant features of both the calendar and checkbook management program are that:

1.   The user creates his own data base. In the calendar program the user creates his own calendar; in the checkbook management program, the user supplies all the information about his own account.
2.   The user makes his inputs in his own natural language. No restraints whatsoever are imposed on the way a user phrases his statements or questions.

An additional feature of the checkbook program, and a goal of the calendar program, is that it is technically and operationally acceptable. By this I mean that the program:

1.   Responds to at least 95 percent of the user's natural language inputs.
2.   Is efficient enough so that the computer can respond within two seconds. And
3.   Is efficient enough so that the program takes up less than 70 K of operating space.

## On the Naturalness of the Language Accepted

I want to comment in somewhat greater detail about the natural language inputs. When I say that no restraints are placed on the user's inputs, I mean that. Here, for example, are some kinds of input statements that users can make when they want to enter checks into the computer:

- "I need to enter checks."
- "I have some checks to record."
- "Enter checks."
- "I want you to enter a check for me."
- "Put in checks."
- "I need to have you record some checks for me."

Ungrammatical inputs are accepted. For example, the user may enter a check as:

302 $18.12 4/9/80 to GIANT FOOD

The computer program correctly sorts this out, classifying the 302 as the check number, the $18.12 as the amount of the check, the 4/9/80 as the date on which the check was written, and GIANT FOOD as the payee. The four items of information—check number, date, amount, and payee—may be given in any order. If the user forgets to type in any of the four pieces of information, the computer reminds the user to supply the missing item(s).

Dates may be expressed in every conceivable way that we have observed:

4/9/80
4-9-80
4 9 1980
April 9, 1980
Apr. 9, 1980
Apr. 9, '80
apr. 9, 1980
apr 9 1980
9 April 80
the 9th of April, 1980
April ninth, 1980

I'd like to describe just one more small feature of the language. Although you may, at first hearing, think it is a small matter, I can assure you that it is a common source of difficulty and annoyance to many users.

I feel particularly proud of Mr. Ford's solution to the problem because I had been assured not very long ago by an expert programmer at IBM's Research Laboratory that an error-correcting routine could not be written to correct such errors. The error simply is the use of a lowercase twelfth letter of the alphabet, *l*, for the numeral one, *1*. Users who are familiar with the operation of many typewriters almost invariably type a lowercase letter *l* instead of the numeral, even though both keys may be present on the keyboard. A related kind of error is the use of an uppercase fifteenth letter of the alphabet, *o*, for the numeral zero, *0*. This was an error that used to vex both our users and us. Mr. Ford's program cleverly examines the context in which the 1 or the 0 appears and makes a decision about whether the suspect symbol is a letter or a numeral. His program makes correct decisions almost without exception. I mention this as just one example of the level of detail and care to which we have gone to anticipate and to correct for common human errors.

Mr. Ford has had a set of users working with his checkbook management program, actually keeping their accounts on the computer, for about a month now. Users come to our laboratory once or twice a week as they choose, make appropriate entries into the computer, and ask whatever questions they have at the moment. One user observed that this was the first time she has ever been able to make her account balance.

## OUR STRATEGY

Let me say a few words about our technique and our methodology. First, how do we do what we have set out to do? Our strategy rests on some laboratory work that we did a few years ago in our studies of person-to-person communication (Kelly and Chapanis, 1977; Michaelis, et al., 1977). That study was concerned with the use of restricted vocabularies in person-to-person communication. The technique we had used was to construct a general core vocabulary and a problem-specific vocabulary. With such vocabularies we found that subjects were able to solve very complicated problems with surprisingly few words. Another finding of that study was that 12 subjects used only a total of 1,200 different words, even though there were no restraints on their word usage and even though all misspelled variants of words were counted as unique words. Those basic findings gave us an important clue, which we have adopted into our present strategy.

### Providing Context

Basic to our technique is that we partition the total world of work into manageable units, for example, managing a checking account, maintaining a calendar, or making travel arrangements. Our reason for doing that is to provide a context for the vocabularies that our subjects use. In other words, we do not try to make our natural-language programs do all things for all people. That we feel is an impossible task at the present time. By providing a context at any particular moment, we make the task much easier. For example, when a subject is working with his checkbook we can reasonably infer that the word "balance" refers to a financial account and not to a device for measuring weights in a chemical laboratory or the performance of a tightrope walker in a circus.

## An Empirical Base

A second important aspect of our strategy is that we design our languages for all the things people actually say, not for all the things they might say. In short, we depend on empirical observations to tell us what kinds of inputs we have to anticipate and design for. Let me elaborate on that. If you sit around a table and think up all the possible ways in which people might say something, you can end up with so many different alternatives that you might think it impossible ever to devise a program capable of handling them. When you look at what people actually do type into a computer, however, what you find is that there is a finite and rather small number of ways that people express themselves. So a key to our method is that we depend on empirical observations of what people *do* say, not on what they *could* say.

## Words Versus Meanings

Another essential aspect of our technique is that we analyze human communications into two categories: what the words actually are and what the words really mean. Following Chomsky's ideas we refer to the former as "surface-structure words," and the latter as "deep-structure words." The deep-structure words are what you really mean. That turns out to be a rather small number of things. For example, in managing your checking account, there is a rather small list of things you really mean to do or say. You want to, or mean to:

- Enter checks.
- Record deposits.
- Ask about certain checks you've written.
- Ask about your balance.
- Express affirmation.
- Express negation.
- And so on.

In the case of checking accounts, we've identified only 17 different kinds of things you really want to do.

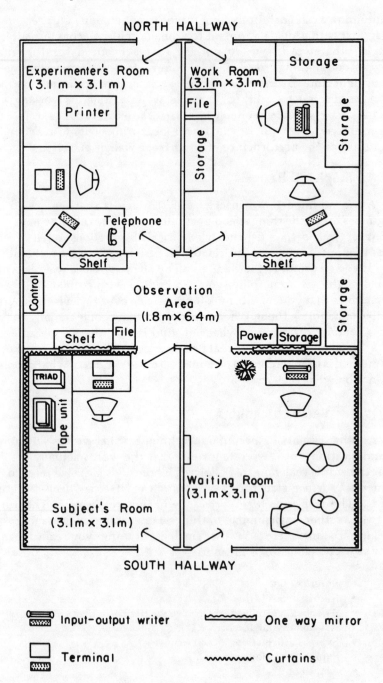

**Figure 2.** Our communication research laboratory.

Now for each of the deep structures there are many different surface words people could, and do, use. For example, in expressing affirmation, they may use the words *yes, yeah, yep, agreed, sure, all right*, and so on.

What we do is to map all equivalent surface-structure words or phrases onto a restricted number of deep-structure words and assign to each deep-structure word or concept a simple number. The latter, of course, is easy for a computer to handle.

## OUR METHODOLOGY

I shall use our calendar program to illustrate one of our methodologies. Users come into an attractively-furnished laboratory and are confronted with only a computer terminal, that is, a keyboard and display unit, a box that records and captures their keystrokes, and a tape recorder (Figure 2). The laboratory is otherwise pleasant and uncrowded. Once the terminal is turned on, a first-time user goes through the introductory tutorial and then, when he's ready, into the program for setting up his calendar. No one else is in the room with the user.

The user thinks he is interacting with a computer. In actual fact, however, our users interact with an experimenter sitting in front of an identical terminal in another room. The experimenter examines the user's input and, if the experimenter thinks our program capable of analyzing the input, he transmits it directly to the computer. The computer responds with a preprogrammed message, which the experimenter again examines. If the response is appropriate, the experimenter relays the response to the subject without change.

If either the input from the user or the response from the computer require modification, the experimenter makes the appropriate changes before the messages are transmitted in either direction.

As our programs become more and more sophisticated, that is, as we refine our analysis programs and error correcting routines, the experimenter has to intervene less and less until finally the experimenter will be completely removed from the loop. The computer alone will be interacting with the user.

As should be clear from this description, our methodology is empirical. It consists of a repetitive process of test, modification, retest, and remodification. When unanticipated problems are discovered during any test session, they are corrected in the program. This continues until we reach a level of performance that we consider acceptable. As I said earlier, our goal is to have a program that will accept 95 percent of all user inputs. For the 5 percent of inputs that cannot be accepted, the computer says:

"I'M SORRY. I DIDN'T UNDERSTAND THAT. COULD YOU PLEASE
SAY IT ANOTHER WAY?"

As you might suppose, this process of test and modification takes
time. Is it too slow to be a viable method? I think not. I have been told that
it took about five years to develop BASIC and about seven years to
develop the APL programming language. We have worked on our
programs for less than a year. Moreover, the strategies we have
developed are sufficiently general so that we can see how they can be
applied to almost any problem you might ask us to handle. In other words
we have developed a general methodology and we know how to apply it
to a wide variety of applications. That is no small achievement. Finally,
we are compiling a set of deep structures, and surface word equivalents,
that can be used in new applications.

## A LOOK INTO THE FUTURE

Let me conclude with a few words about a couple of things that
might be possible in the future. When we run a subject and when that
subject uses some surface words that have not previously been used by
any subject, we, the experimenters, have to map those words onto the
appropriate deep structures. That is typically done after an experimental
session is over. Thereafter, if any other subject should happen to use
those surface structure words again, the computer program will recognize and accept them. We think we see how our methods could be
extended so that the computer would modify its own program to accept
novel combinations of surface words, mapping them instantaneously
onto their appropriate deep-structure equivalents. In other words, the
computer could become a personalized device, accepting and adapting
itself to idiosyncratic expressions that may be characteristic of a
particular user. This would be a powerful extension of our present
methods.

A second extension of our work concerns foreign languages. This
has always been a difficult matter for all computer programs to handle.
Our separation of communications into surface and deep structures
would, I think, allow us to handle foreign languages with a facility that
has not been possible to this time. After all, the things you want to do in
dealing with your checking account, or in making travel arrangements,
or in planning a menu—that is, the deep structures—are small in
number, and I suspect that they are the same for English, French,
German, or Arabic speaking persons. The things that differ are the
surface structures, the particular words that a person uses. Those
particular words, as I see it, could be mapped onto basic deep structures,

enabling us at last to achieve the kind of facility of communication that will bring the computer to everybody, everybody in the world.

## REFERENCES

Kelly, M.J., and Chapanis, A. Limited vocabulary natural language dialogue. *International Journal of Man-Machine Studies,* 1977, *9,* 479–501.

Michaelis, P.R., Chapanis, A., Weeks, G.D. and Kelly, M.J. Word usage in interactive dialog with restricted and unrestricted vocabularies. *IEEE Transactions on Professional Communication,* 1977, *PC-20,* 214–21.

# Authors' Biographies

**The Honorable GEORGE E. BROWN, JR., Representative, U.S. Congress.**

Congressman Brown was a graduate in physics from the University of California. He began public service in the Monterey Park City Council in 1954, serving as mayor during 1955–1956. He was elected to the California State Legislature in 1958 and four years later to the U.S. House of Representatives. In 1970, rather than seeking reelection, he ran for the U.S. Senate, losing by a narrow margin. During 1970–1972 he worked in sourthern California as a teacher and management consultant, being elected once again to Congress in 1972, where he represents a district centered around the cities of Riverside and San Bernardino. His House committee assignments include membership on the Congressional Technology Assessment Board. In addition to other subcommittee assignments on the Agriculture Committee, Congressman Brown belongs to the Science and Technology Committee, on which he chairs the Subcommittee on Science, Research, and Technology.

**RICHARD P. CASE, Vice-President for Development Operations— GTD HQ, IBM Corporation.**

Mr. Case received a bachelor's degree in electrical engineering from Case Institute of Technology in 1956. Since that time his entire professional career has been with IBM. For the first six years his responsibilities were in the engineering design of computers and computing equipment. The next four years were in the Systems Programming Area, followed by five years as Director of Architecture for the Systems Development Division. From 1971–1975 Mr. Case was Director of Advanced Systems, and then for two years he was Consultant to the Director of Research, IBM Thomas J. Watson Research Center, Yorktown Heights, New York. From 1977–1978 he was Director of Advanced Systems Development for the Data Processing Product Group, assuming the Division Directorship of Technical Operations for the System Products Division in December 1979. Mr. Case is now Vice-President for Development Operations—GTD HQ, a Fellow of the IEEE, and a member of a wide variety of honorary societies.

## ALPHONSE CHAPANIS, Professor of Psychology, The Johns Hopkins University.

Dr. Chapanis was granted his M.A. (1942) and Ph.D. (1943) in experimental psychology by Yale University. From 1942–1946 he worked in the Aero Medical Laboratory at the Wright Air Development Center (Ohio). In 1946 he joined the staff of the Systems Research project at Johns Hopkins University and he has continued his association with that university ever since, being promoted to Professor of Psychology in 1956. He has taken leave two times, once in 1953–1954 to work as a member of the technical staff of the Bell Telephone Laboratories, and again in 1960–1961 to serve as liaison scientist in the Office of Naval Research Branch Office of the embassy of the United States in London. A prolific publisher, he is past president of both the Human Factors Society and the Society of Engineering Psychologists—from whom he won the Franklin V. Taylor Award in 1963 "for outstanding contributions to the field of engineering psychology."

## D. JAMES DOOLING, Member, Research Staff, Bell Telephone Laboratories.

After studying philosophy, theology, and psychology as an undergraduate, Dr. Dooling moved to the State University of New York at Buffalo, from which he received his M.A. (1969) and Ph.D. (1970) in cognitive studies. From 1969 to 1976 he was an Assistant and Associate Professor of Psychology at Kent State University. In 1976 he joined the technical staff of the Bell Telephone Laboratories in Holmdel, New Jersey, where he remains a member. He has published a number of articles in both human memory and psycholinguistics, as well as serving as a reviewer for a variety of journals in psychology and education. His current work addresses problems of training and the design of new features for customers of new communications services.

## J. DEXTER FLETCHER, Program Manager, Defense Advanced Research Projects Agency.

After graduating with high distinction in English at the University of Arizona, Dr. Fletcher was awarded both an M.S. in computer science and a Ph.D. in educational psychology from Stanford University in 1963.

Through 1973 he held appointments at the Institute for Mathematical Studies in the Social Sciences (IMSS) at Stanford, where he worked on three IMSS projects concerning computer-assisted instruction and instructional strategies. After a year at the University of Illinois at Chicago Circle, Dr. Fletcher joined the Navy Personnel Research and Development Center at San Diego, where he continued his work on automated instruction and the use of computers in teaching and testing. Following a year at Xerox Corporation, Dr. Fletcher assumed a position as Program Manager of the Cybernetics Technology Office at ARPA where he was responsible for the design, introduction, and management of research and development programs in advanced training and human performance technology. In 1981 he became Executive Director of the WICAT Institute in Provo, Utah. He has authored numerous technical reports, teacher's manuals, and articles in a wide variety of psychology, education, and computer science journals.

**IRWIN L. GOLDSTEIN, Professor of Psychology, University of Maryland.**
Dr. Goldstein was granted his Ph.D. in experimental psychology by the University of Maryland in 1964. After teaching at Ohio State University from 1963–1966, Dr. Goldstein returned to the University of Maryland where he remains now as Professor of Psychology and Director of Graduate Studies for the Department of Psychology. His early research interests were in information processing, man-machine systems, and complex vigilance. More recently, his interests have been in the design and evaluation of training and instructional systems, with a special concern for identifying organizational conflicts that prevent effective use of training programs. Dr. Goldstein is author or coauthor of two books in engineering psychology and training program development and evaluation. A Fellow of the American Psychological Association, Dr. Goldstein also serves on several journal editorial boards.

**GERALD HOLTON, Mallinckrodt Professor of Physics and Professor of the History of Science, Harvard University.**
Professor Holton received his Ph.D. in physics from Harvard University in 1948, having previously attended both the School of Technology at Oxford and Wesleyan University. After early appointments at Wesleyan and Brown University, Dr. Holton joined the faculty at Harvard in 1947, where he remains today. He is now also (concurrently) a Visiting Professor at Massachusetts Institute of Technology. Dr. Holton's research interests are primarily the physics of matter at high pressure and the history of physical science. He is a Fellow of the American Academy of Arts and Sciences, was the Academy's editor from 1957 to 1963, and the founding editor of its quarterly journal, *Daedalus.*

Dr. Holton is the originator and codirector of the Project Physics Course, which developed a new national physical science course for colleges and schools—materials now being used by some 200,000 students in the United States and abroad. In addition to being author of several major texts, Dr. Holton serves on the editorial board of a variety of journals, has received a number of professional awards, and has held several distinguished visiting appointments.

### EDMUND T. KLEMMER, Member, Research Staff, Bell Telephone Laboratories.

Dr. Klemmer started his professional career as a naval architect and marine engineer. Following this he enrolled in Columbia University, from which he earned an M.A. (1949) and a Ph.D. (1952) in experimental psychology. Following six years doing research in human information processing for the Air Force, he then managed the IBM Research Psychology Group from 1957–1962. For the past 18 years he has been at the Bell Telephone Laboratories in Holmdel, where he is now Supervisor for the Human Factors Engineering Group on Customer Services. Dr. Klemmer was a founding member and early president of the Human Factors Society Metropolitan Chapter and is a former president of the Society of Engineering Psychologists. He presently chairs the Steering Committee for the International Symposium on Human Factors in Telecommunications. He has also served for many years on the editorial boards for *Human Factors* and the *Journal of Experimental Psychology*. His present work addresses the design of new communication services for business customers.

### RAYMOND S. NICKERSON, Senior Vice-President, Bolt Beranek and Newman.

Dr. Nickerson received his Ph.D. in experimental psychology from Tufts University in 1965. From 1959–1966 he was a research scientist in the Decision Science Laboratory of the Air Force. In 1966 he joined Bolt, Beranek and Newman as a Senior Scientist, becoming Vice-President and Director of their Behavioral Science Division in 1969. He remains at BB&N now as Senior Vice-President. Dr. Nickerson has also served as editor of various technical volumes and on the editorial board of *Acta Psychologica* and the *Journal of Experimental Psychology*. His most recent published work has concerned conversational interactions with computers.

### CHARLES R. PHIPPS, Assistant Vice-President and Manager, Strategic Development, Texas Instruments, Inc.

Charles Phipps earned his B.S. in electrical engineering from Case Institute of Technology in 1949 and his MBA from Harvard University in

1952. Prior to joining Texas Instruments in 1960, he worked for Motorola and General Electric. During his first seven years, Mr. Phipps was responsible for marketing of integrated circuits, including program management of the early research and development contracts at TI. From 1967–1970 he was Manager of the Logic and Memory Functions Department, after which he managed the Semiconductor Group, Worldwide Strategic Analysis and Planning. Since 1973 he has been Manager of Corporate Development in the Office of Strategic Development, where he is now Assistant Vice-President. Especially during the 1970s he has been a member of numerous task forces and advisory boards for the Department of Defense and various other governmental and educational institutions.

### B.A. SHEIL, Member, Research Staff, Palo Alto Research Center, Xerox Corporation.

Dr. Sheil earned his bachelor's degree with "first class honours in psychology" from the University of Sydney. After brief periods of employment at the University of Melbourne and as an Assistant Scientific Systems Analyst for IBM in Australia, Dr. Sheil moved to the United States, earning his S.M. (1972) and Ph.D. (1976) in applied mathematics from Harvard University while he held various research and teaching positions at both Harvard and MIT. In 1976 he joined the Research Staff of the Systems Science Laboratory at the Xerox Palo Alto Research Center, where he remains a member. He has published a variety of papers on the psychology of programming, nonexpert user models, and programming languages and systems.

# Index

Al-Awar, Janan, 239, 241
American Telegraph & Telephone Co.,
153
APL programming, 127, 248
Armed Services, *See* Defense, Department
of
Atkinson, Richard C., 15
Automated authoring, 184
Automated programming, 91

Bacon, Francis, 3-4
Baker, Theodore, 236
BASIC programming, 129-130, 182, 248
Bay Area Rapid Transit (BART), 58-59
Bell, Daniel, 54
Bell Laboratories, 149, 153, 157, 164-165,
193, 196, 198, 220, 236
BIP training technology, 182
Boulding, Kenneth, 44
Brooks, Harvey, 7
Brown, Rep. George E., 214, 216, 218,
biographical sketch of, 250
Bush, Vannevar, 3, 13, 15

Campbell, D.T., 141-142
Campion, James, 202
Case, Richard P., 204; biographical sketch
of, 250-251
Chapanis, Dr. Alphonse, 220, 224;
biographical sketch of, 251
Clarke, Francis W., 10
Clerical work, 29-32, 81
Club of Rome, 212

COBOL programming, 127
Collins, Alan, 182
Combinatoric specification, 87
Combined mode research, 8-17, 212-213
Commoner, Barry, 212
Communications Act (1934), 47
Complexity, technological, 39, 231-233;
and computer usage, 77-104, 222-
223; and impact upon job training,
173-175, 226-227
Computers, potential uses of: in
communications, 28, 209; for
disabled persons, 217-218; in
education, 34-35, 39, 43, 53, 214,
229; in employment, 215; in health
care, 52, 59; in the home, 21, 34-36,
210, 214; in industry, 32-34, 39, 53-
54; non-technical barriers to, 37-39;
in the office, 29-32; in personal life,
242-245, 248, 249; unpredictability
of, 208-209
Computer technology: characteristics of
nonprofessional users of, 115;
consumer resistance to terminology
of, 32, 39; declining hardware costs
of, 108-111, 204; differences
between, and other technologies,
234; and ease of use, 86-104, 112-
131, 222-227, 238-249; economics
of, 38, 63-65, 108-112, 210-211,
232; an an energy and land
detensive industry, 60; and
engineering simulation, 58;

255